Skid Row 1983
A Photographic Exploration

Scott Shaw

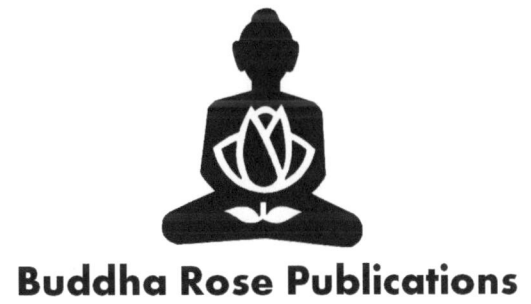

Buddha Rose Publications

Skid Row 1983: A Photographic Exploration
Copyright © 1984 & 2012 by Scott Shaw
All Rights Reserved
www.scottshaw.com

No part of this book may be reproduced
in any manner without the expressed
written permission of the author or the
publishing company.

ISBN 10: 1-877792-62-4
ISBN 13: 978-1-877792-62-5

SKID ROW 1983

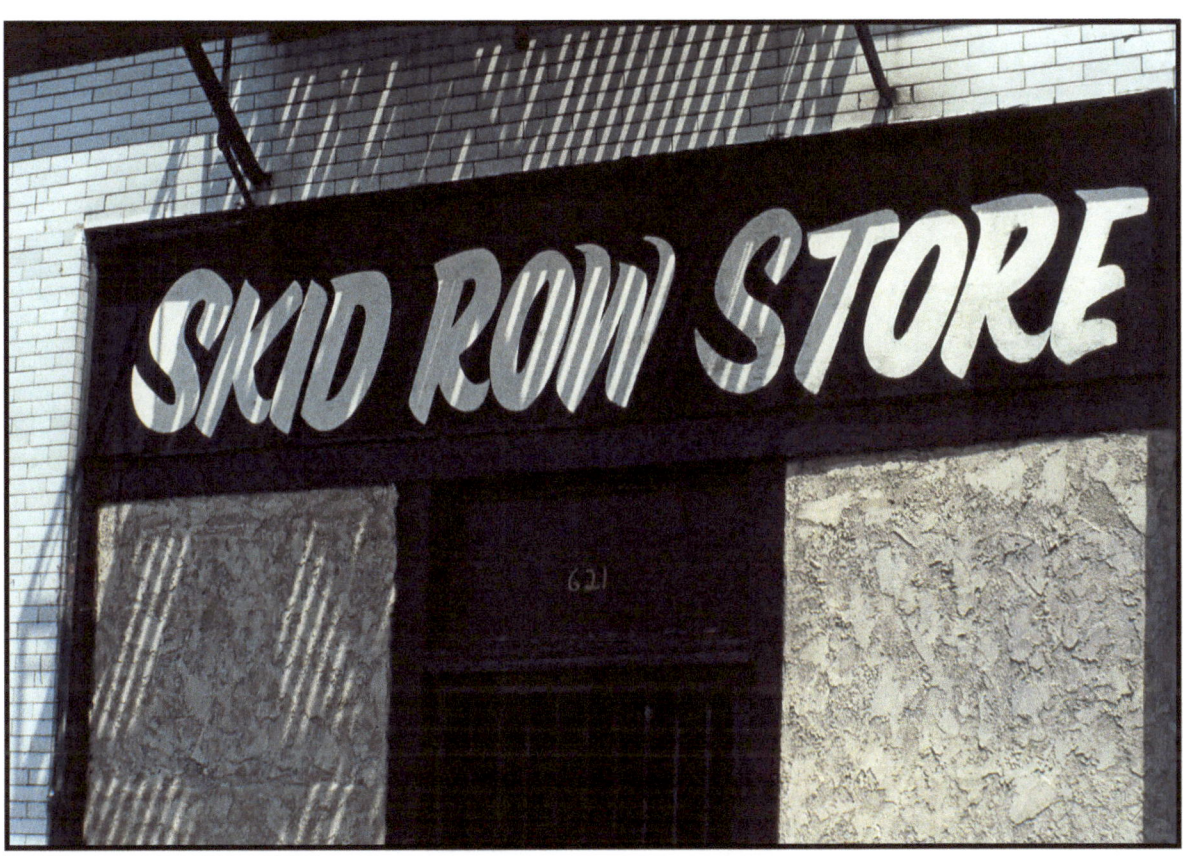

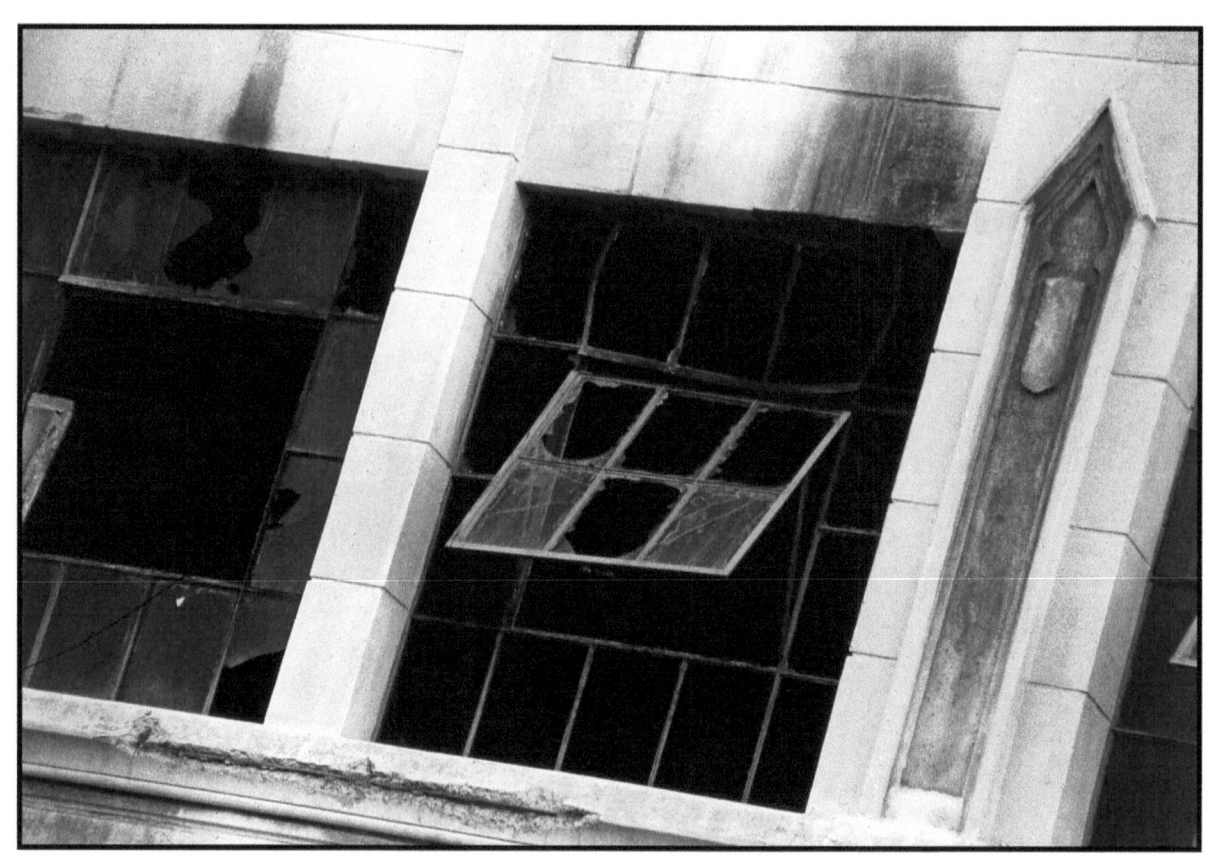

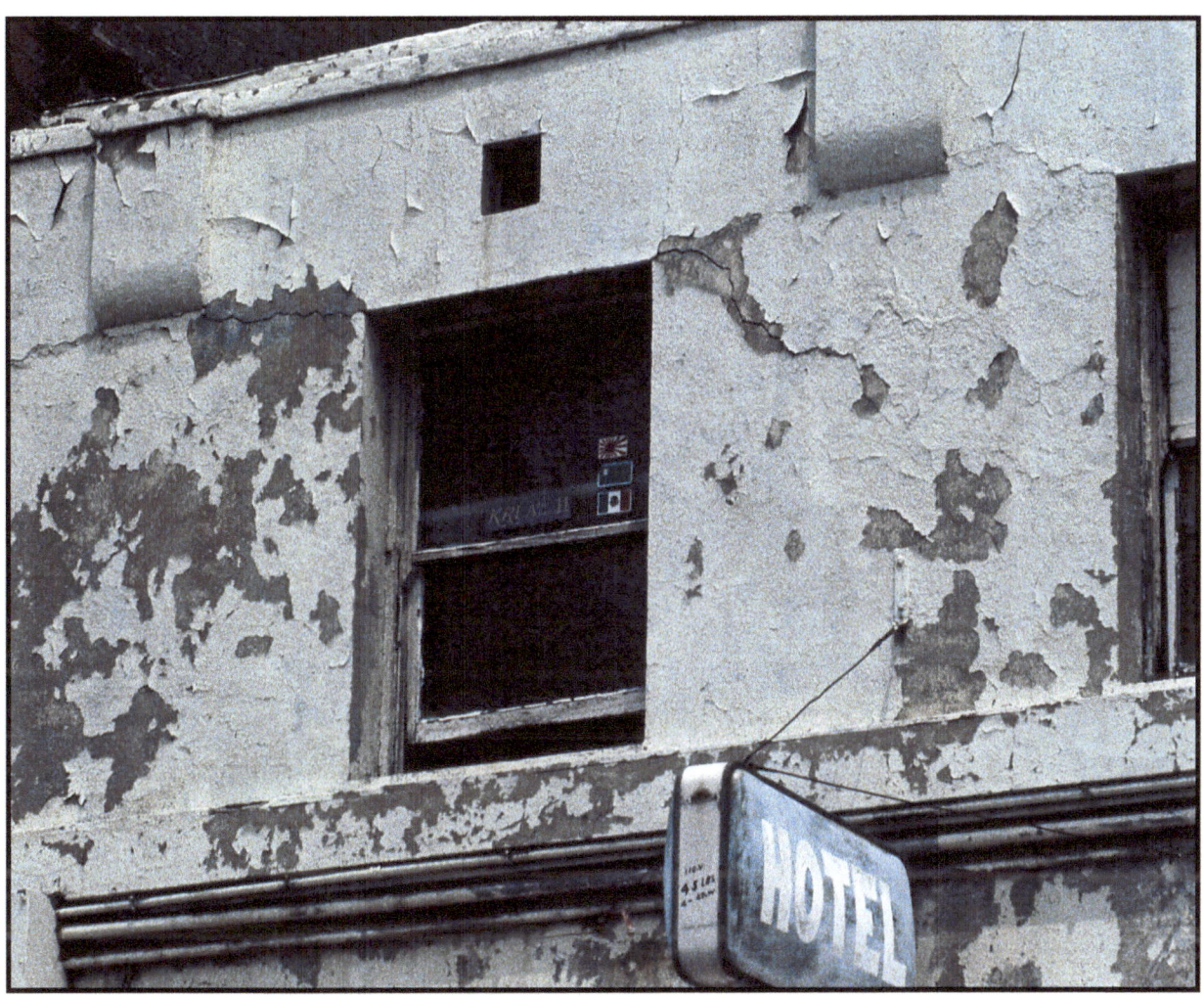

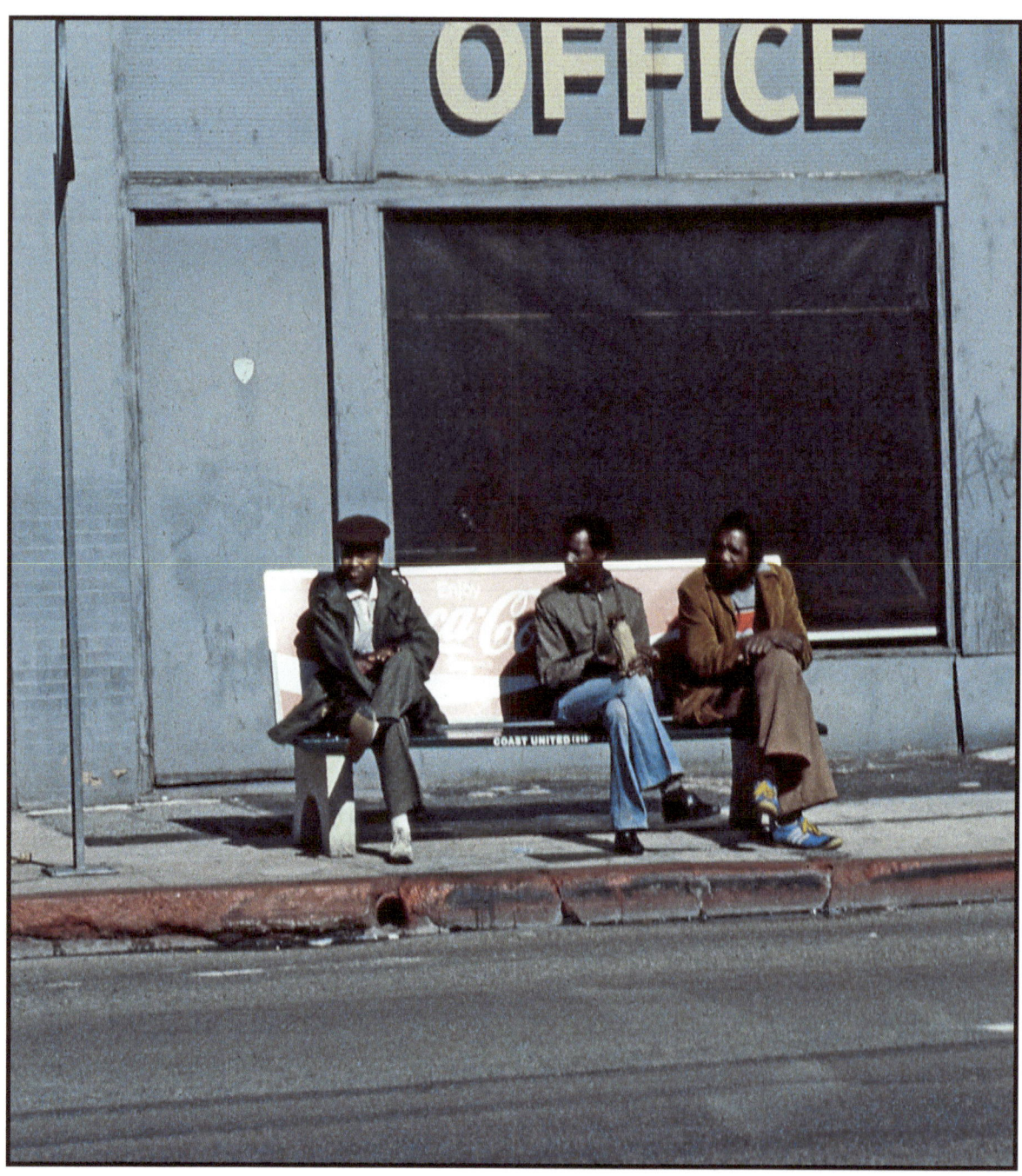

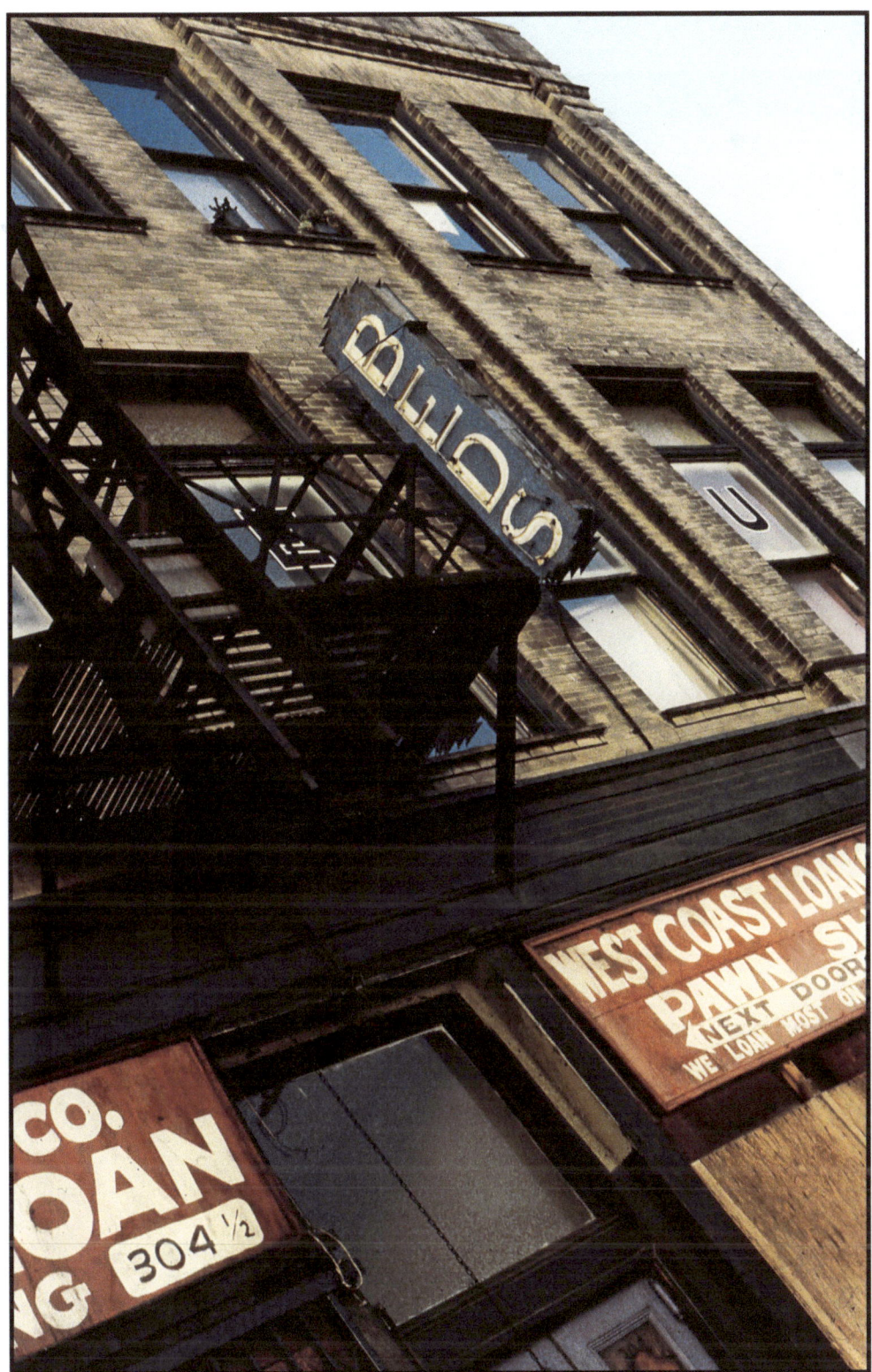

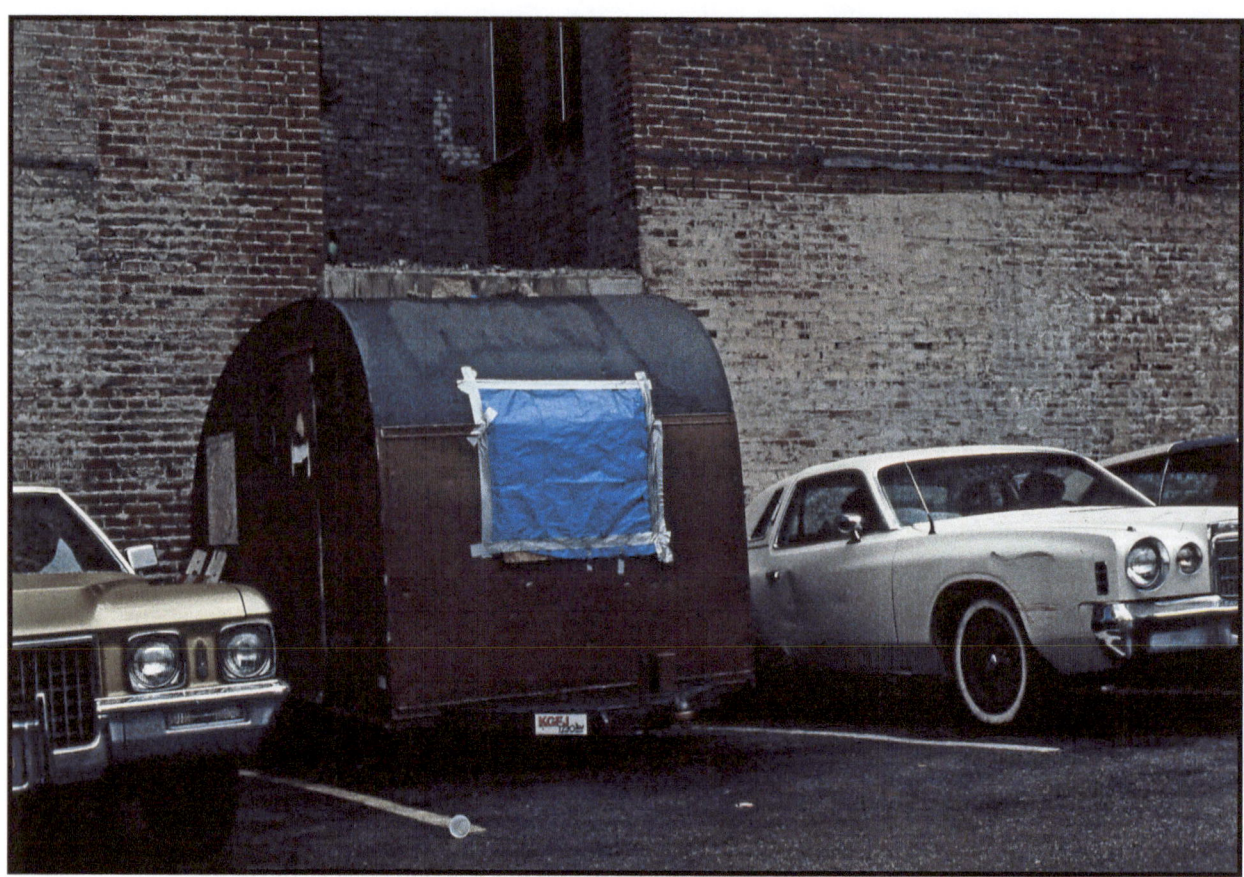

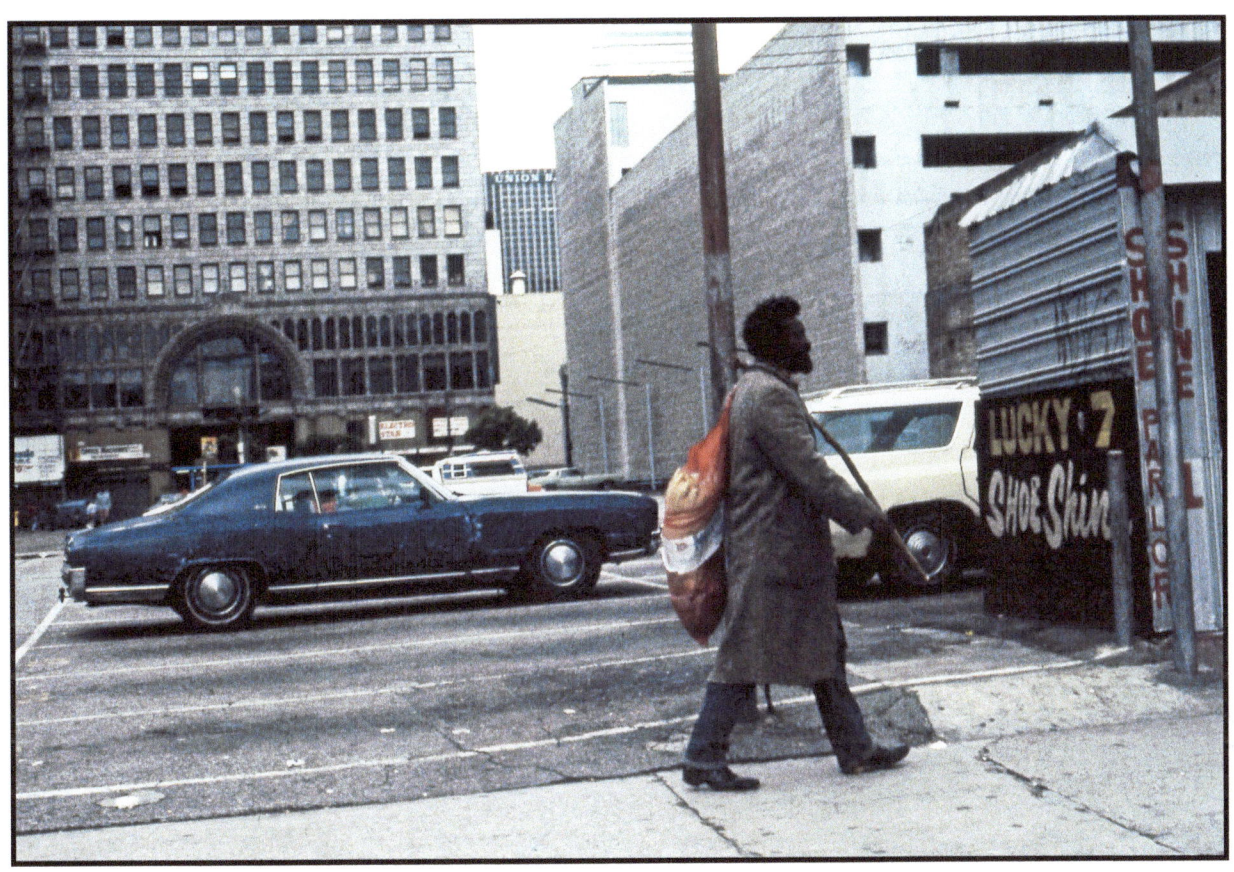

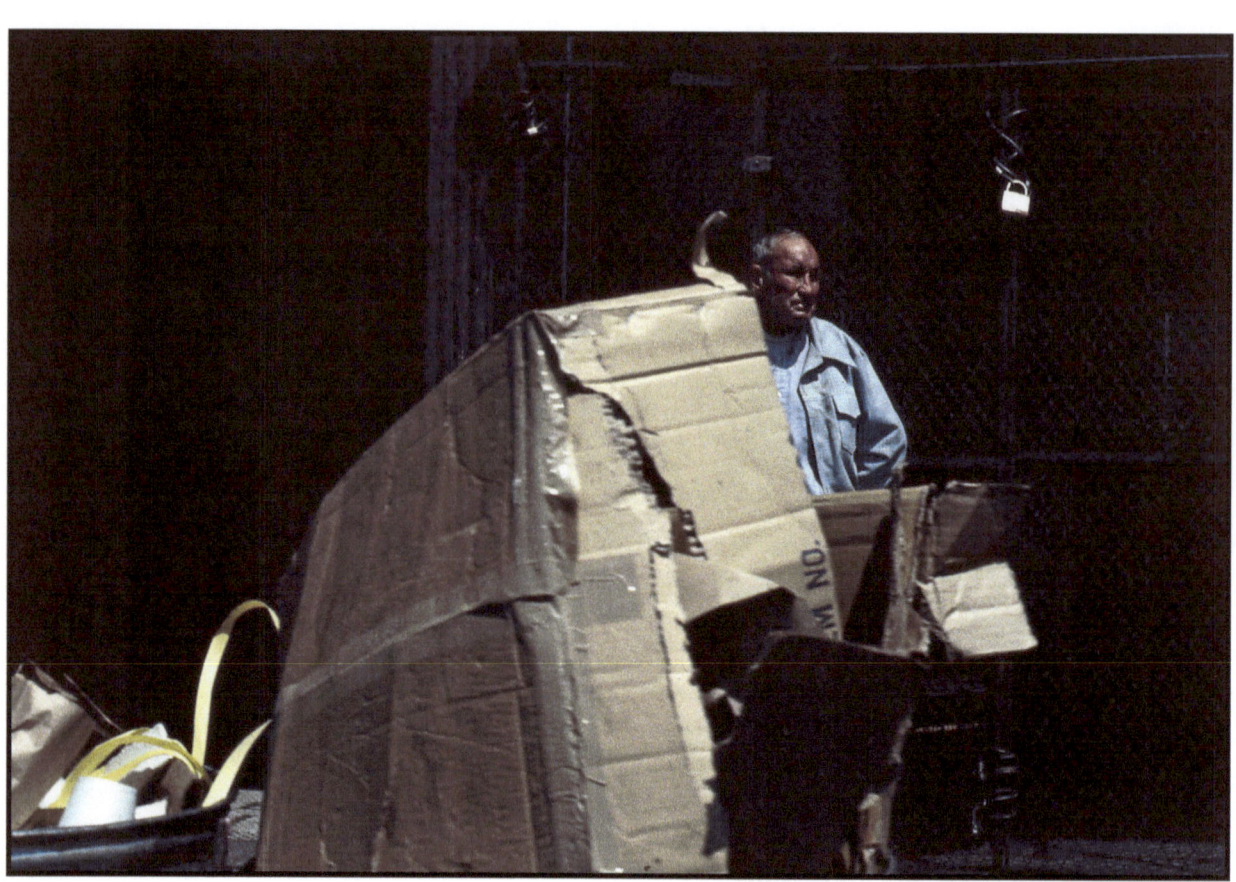

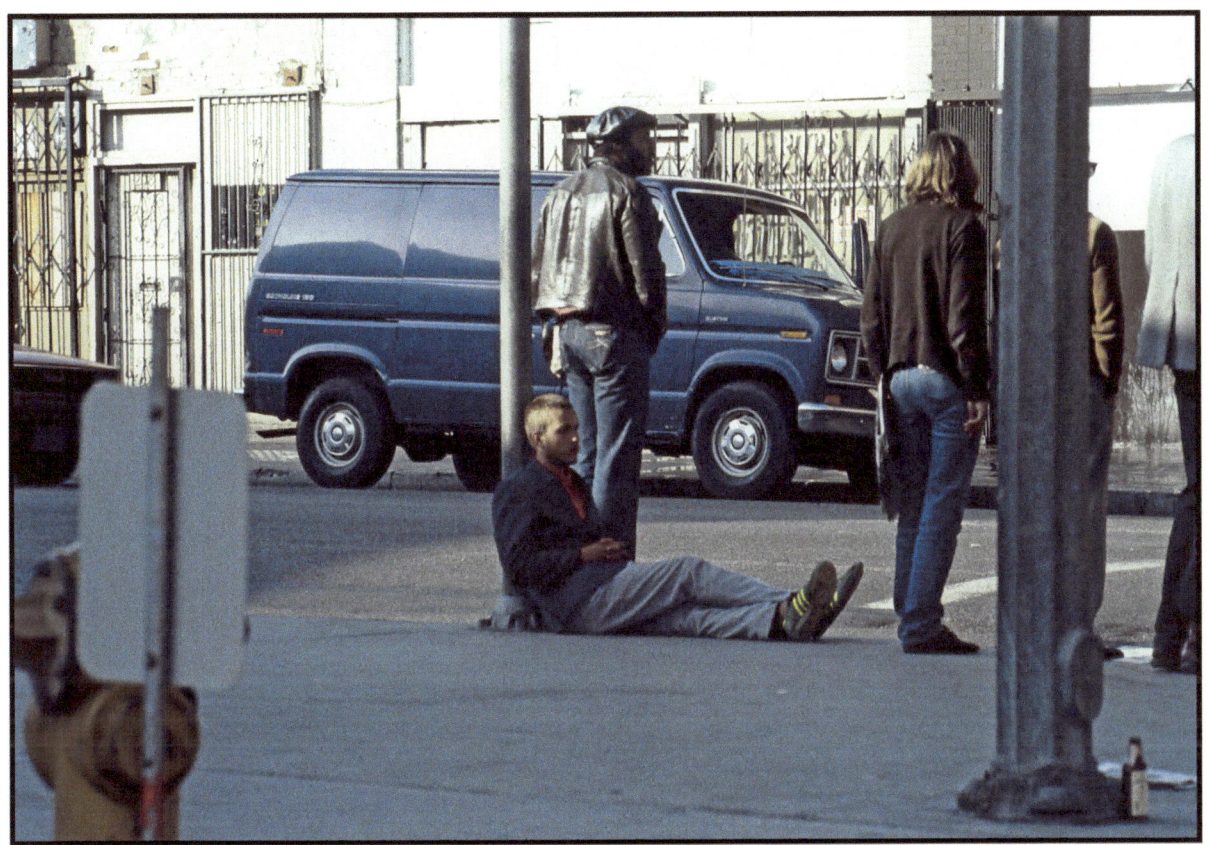

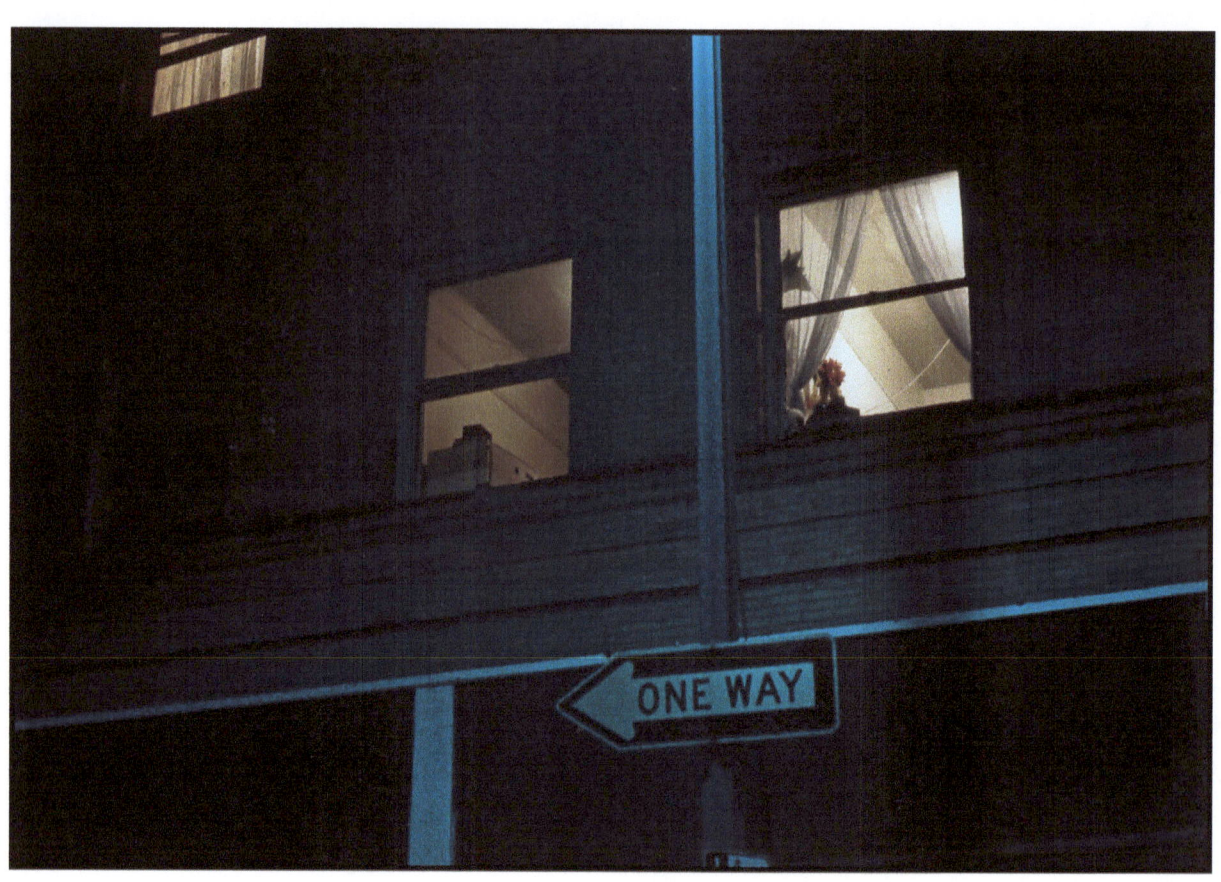

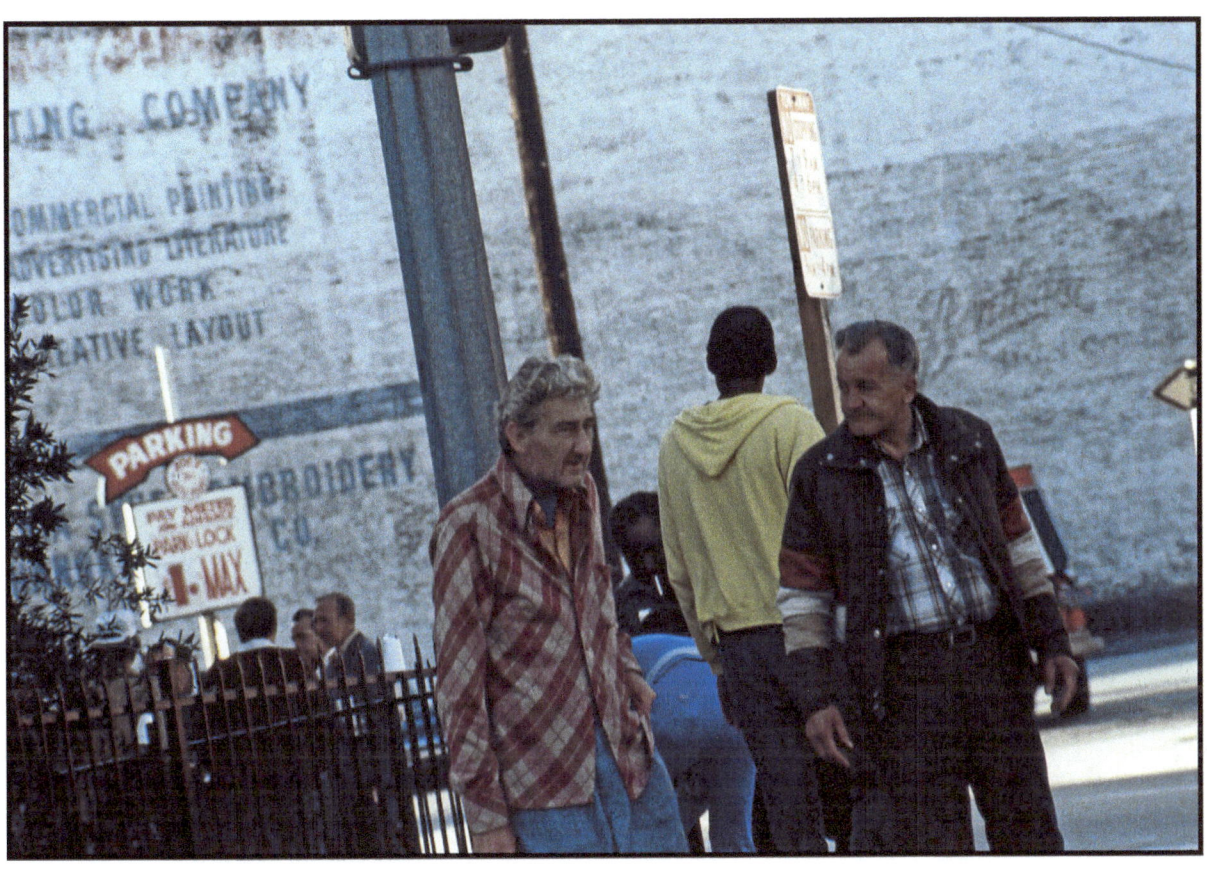

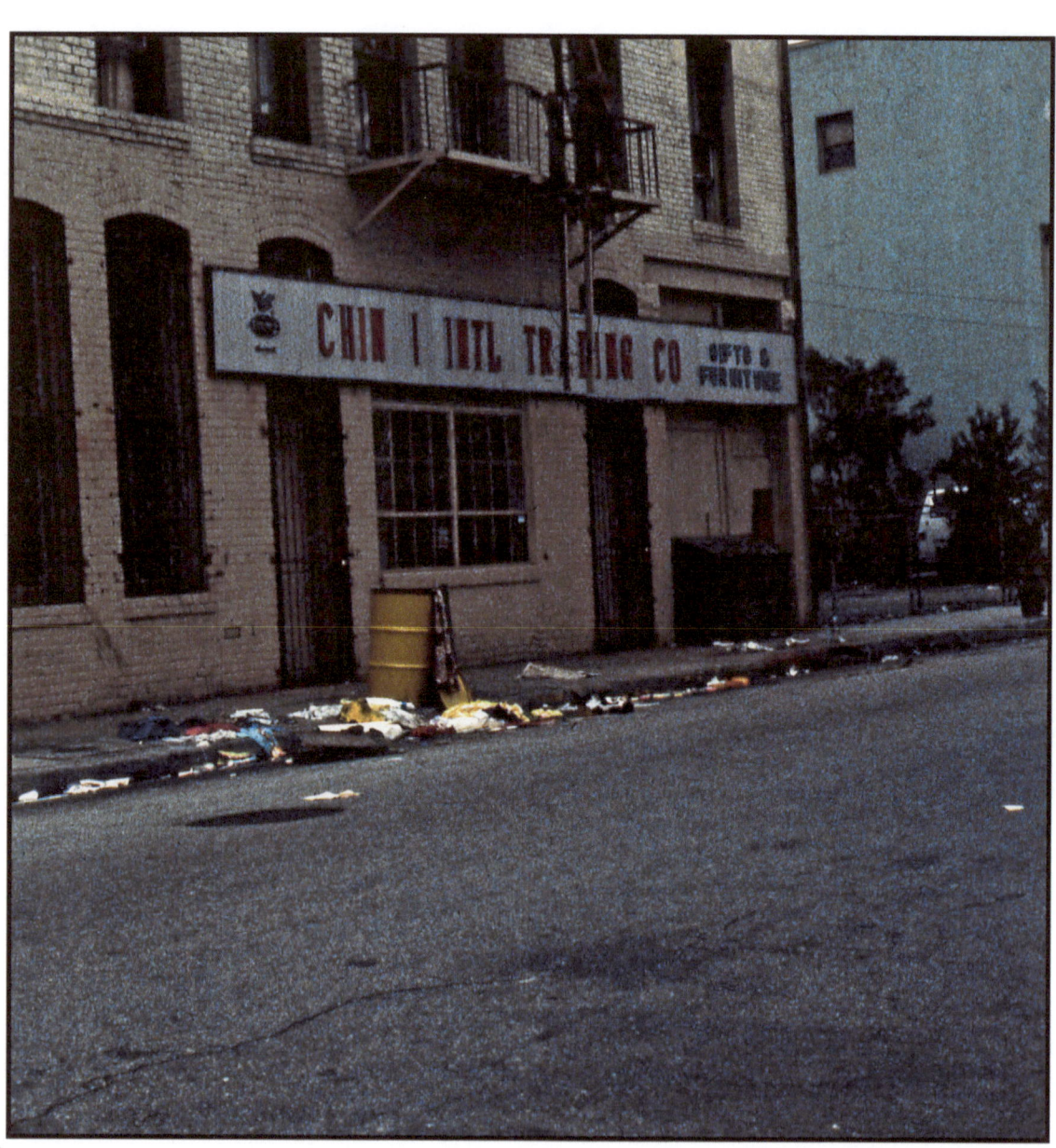

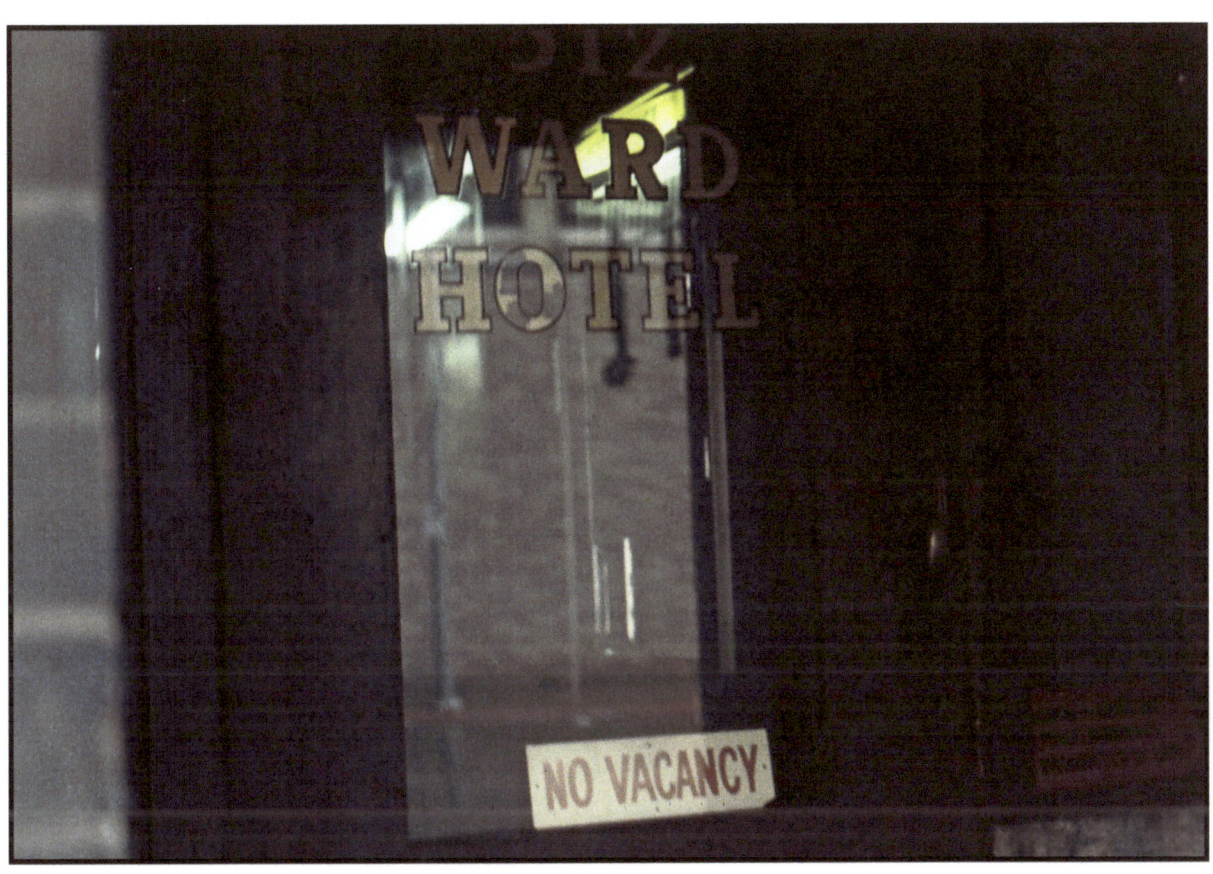

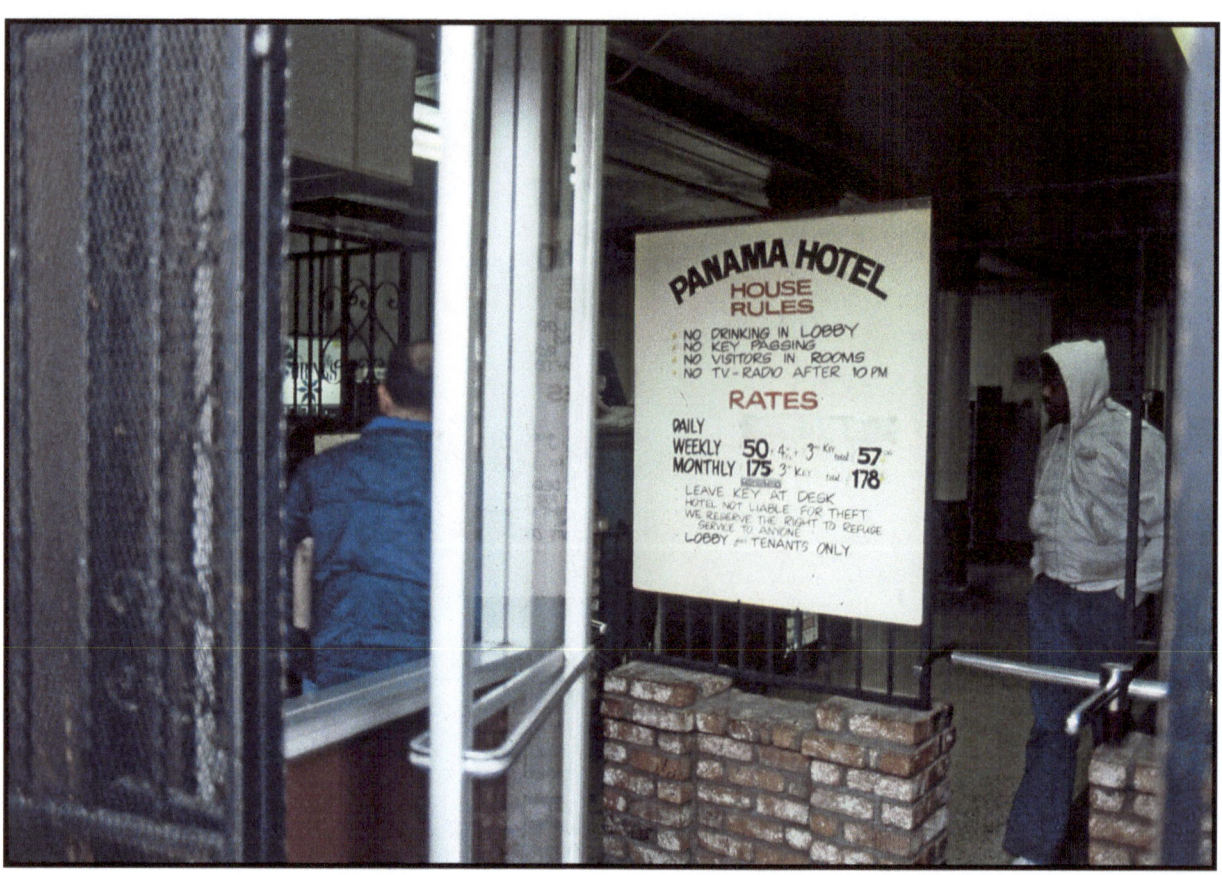

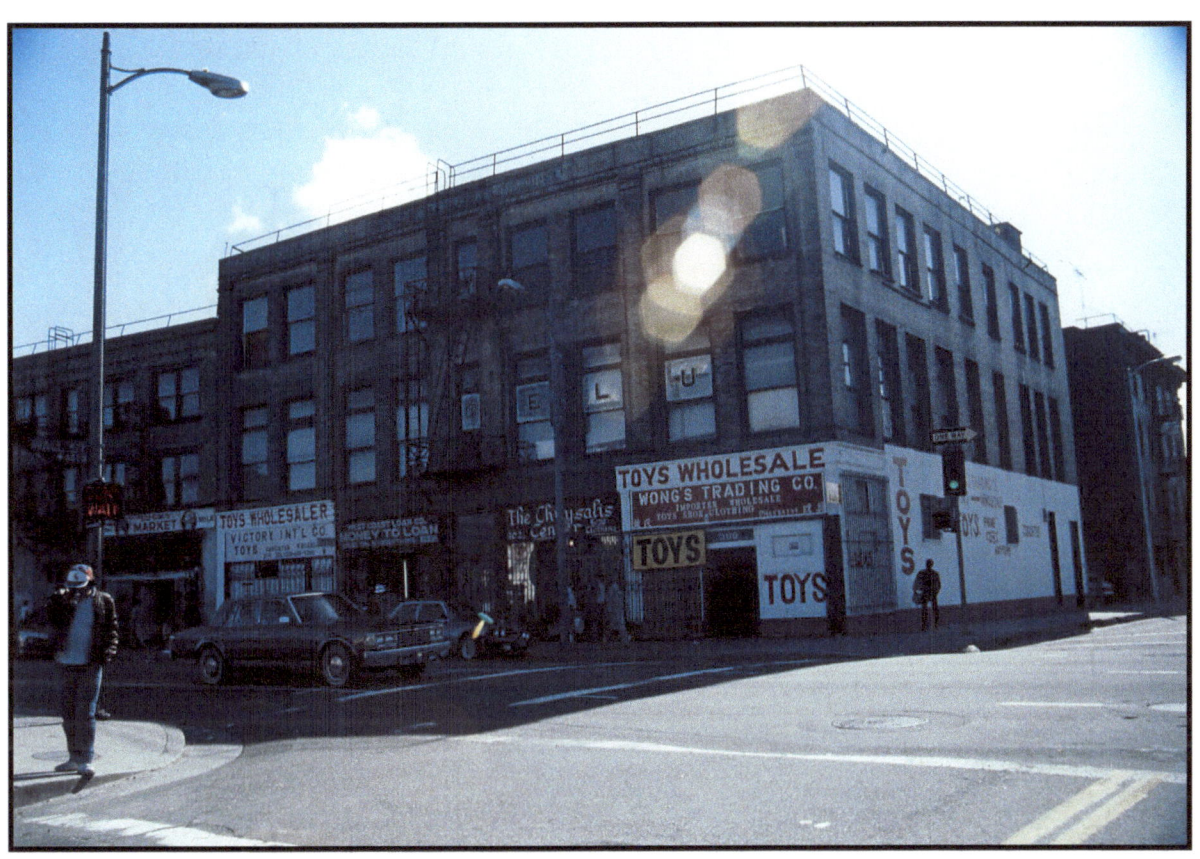

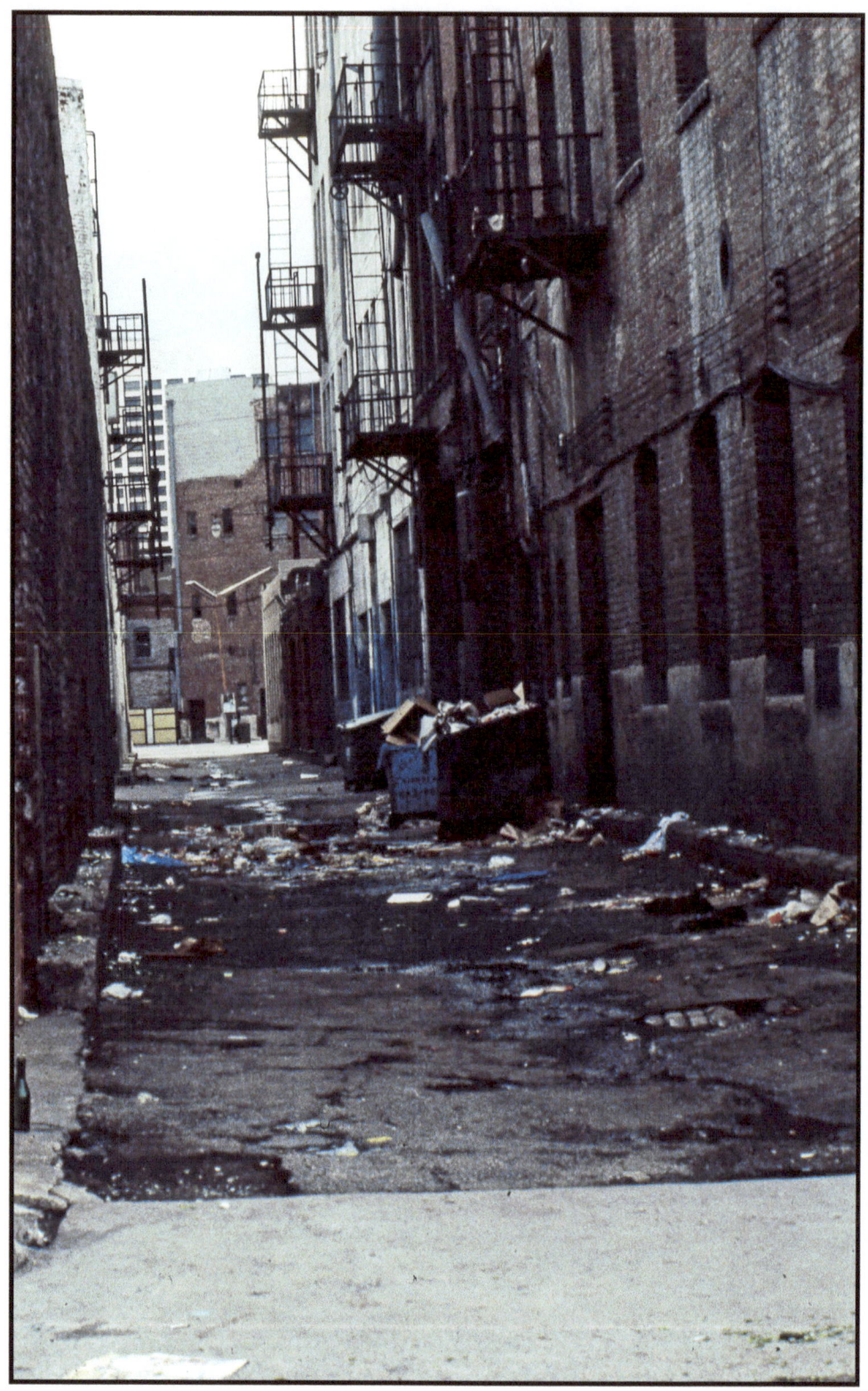

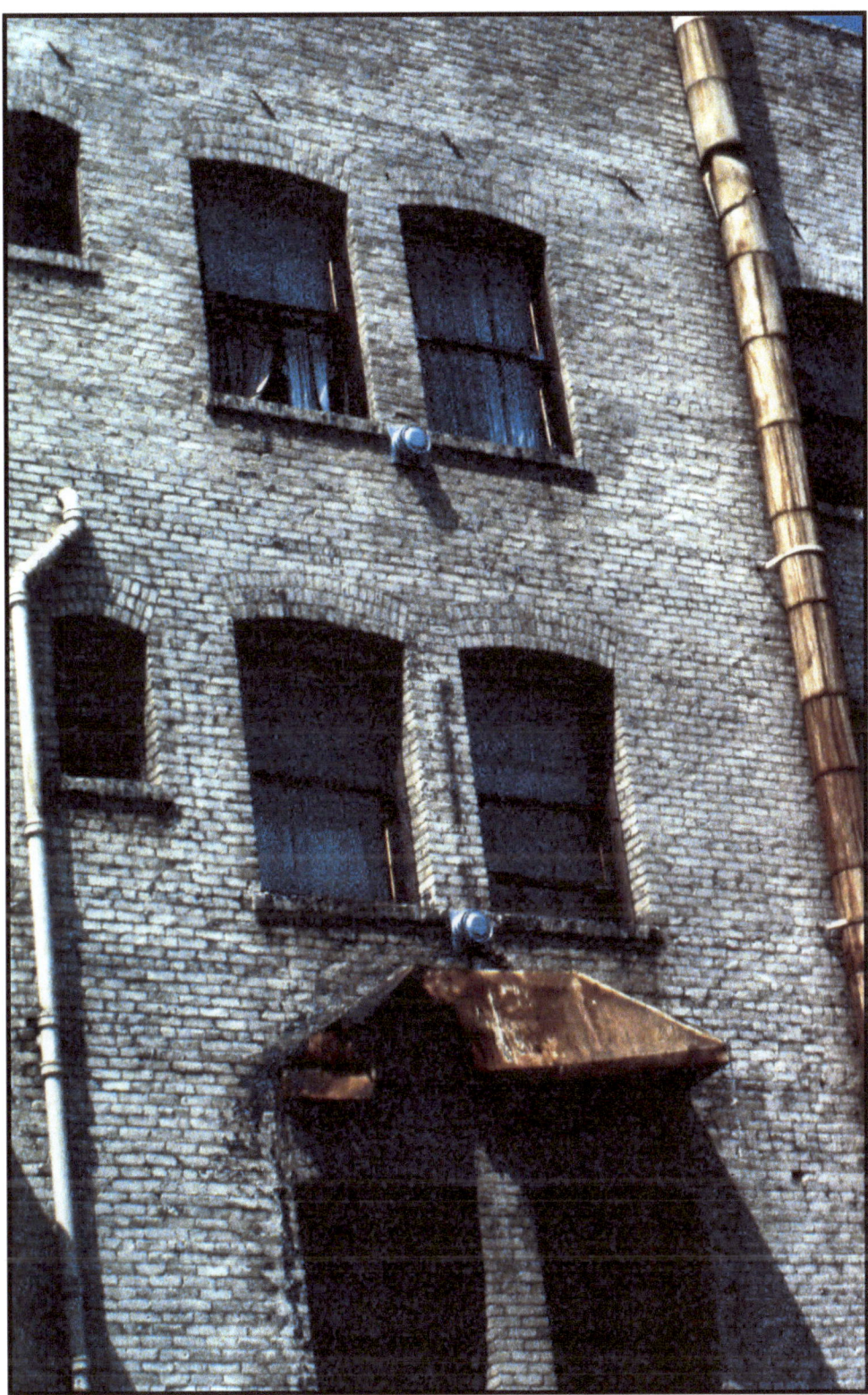

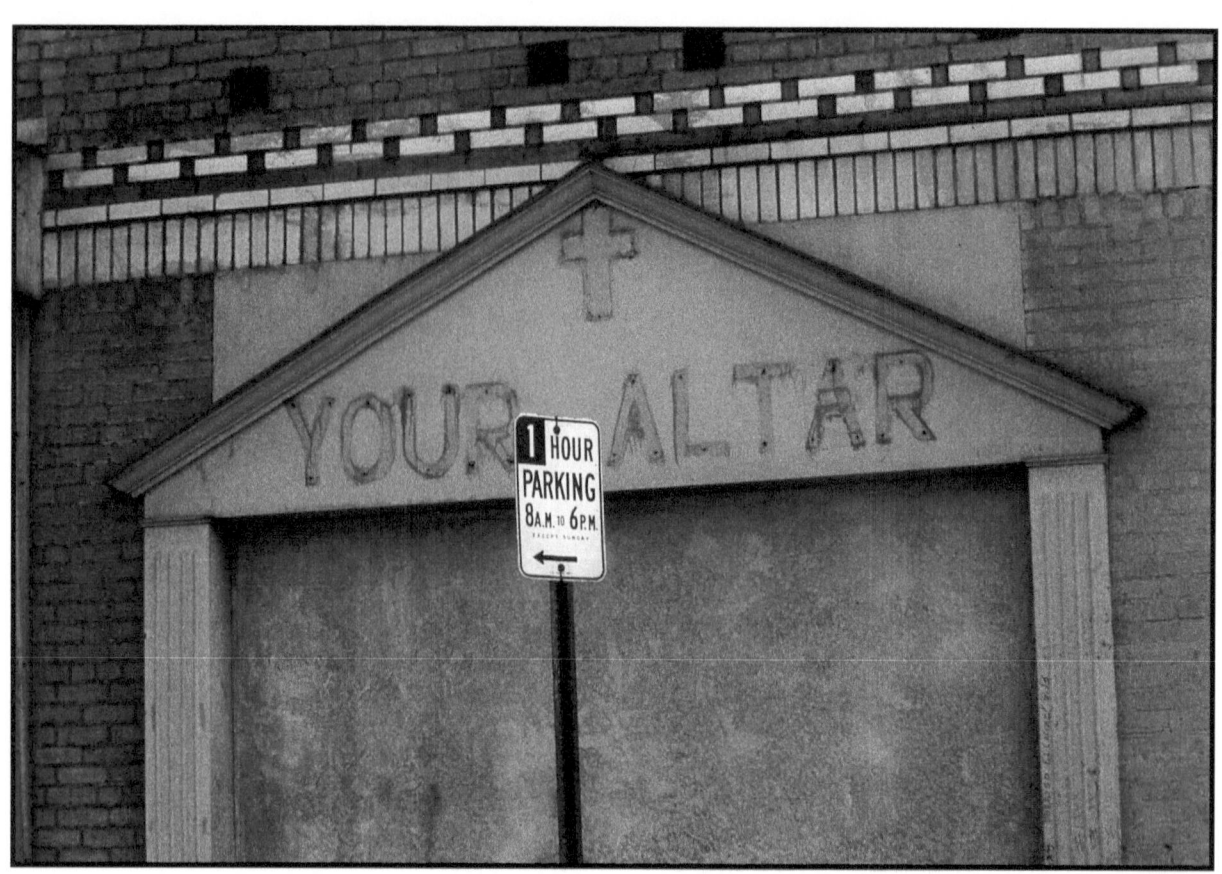

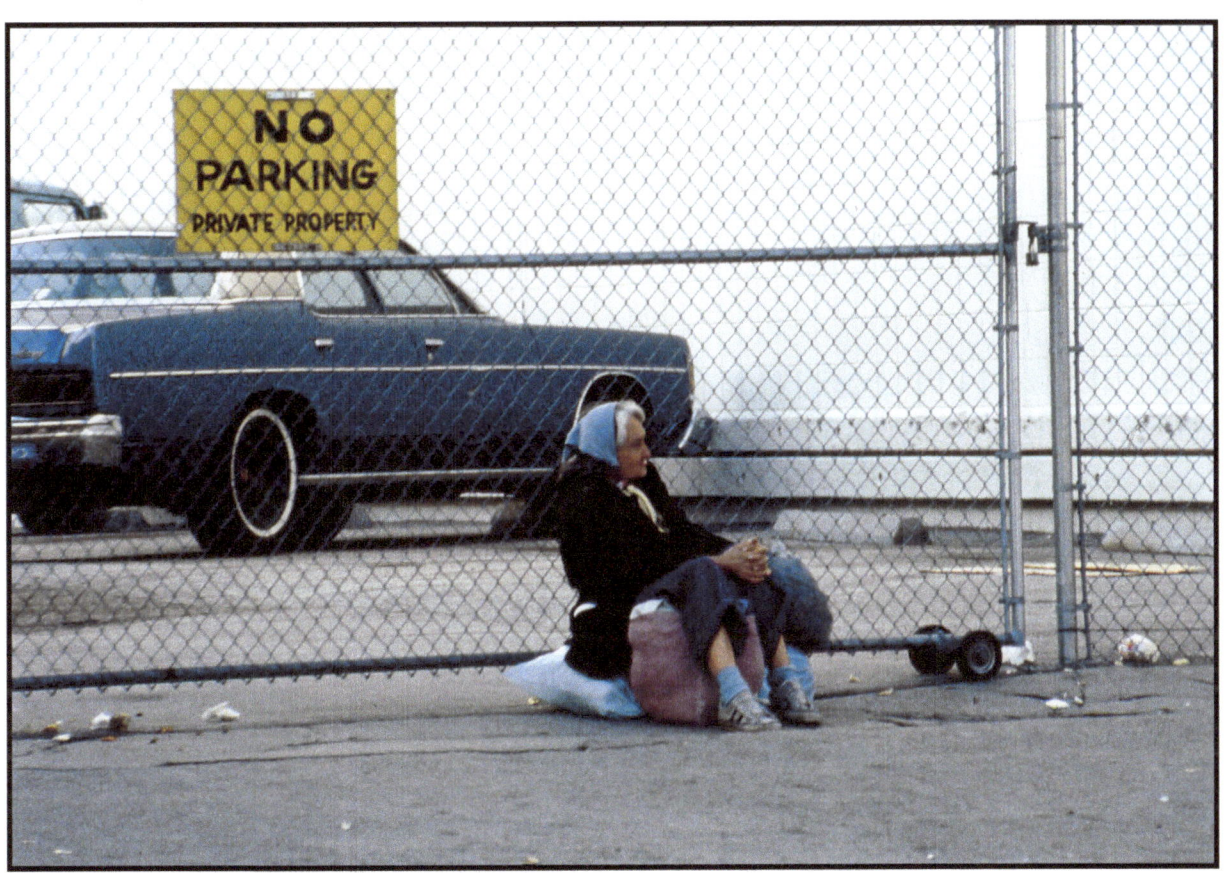

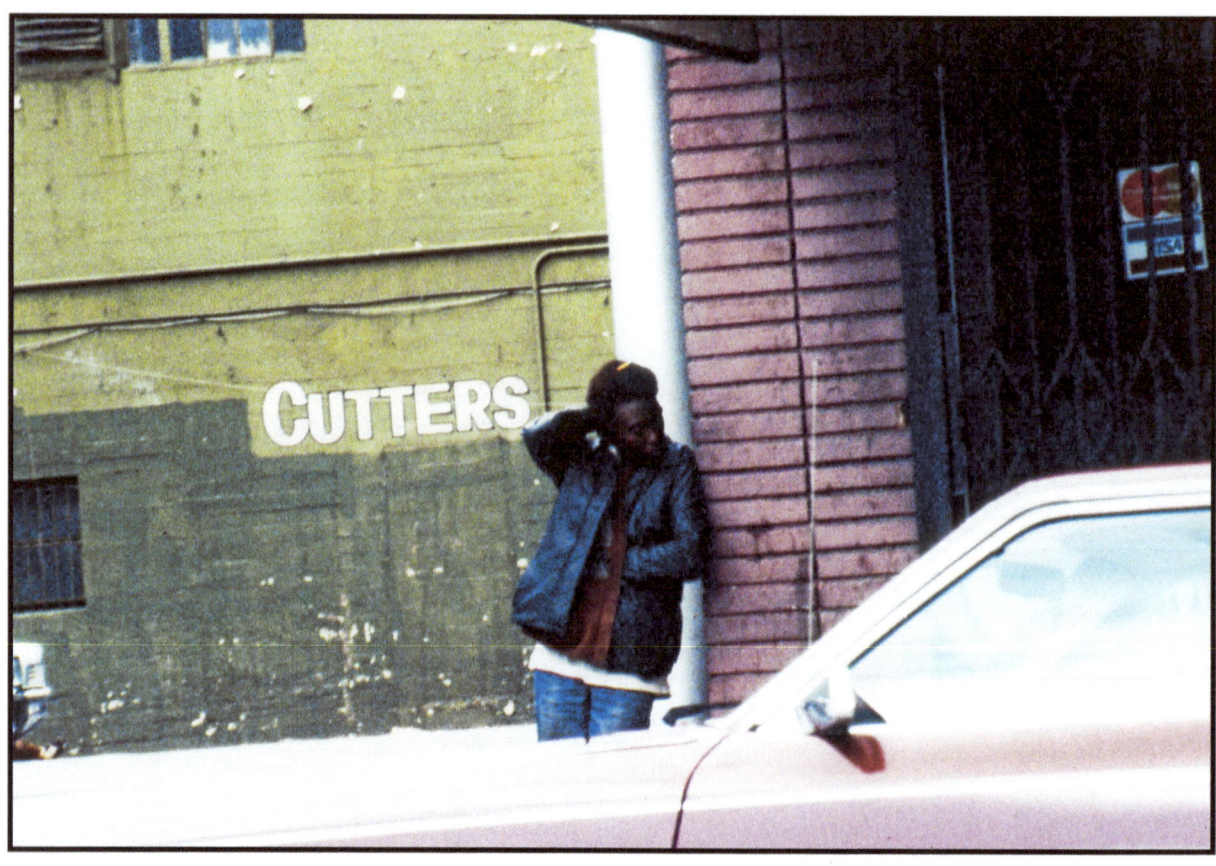

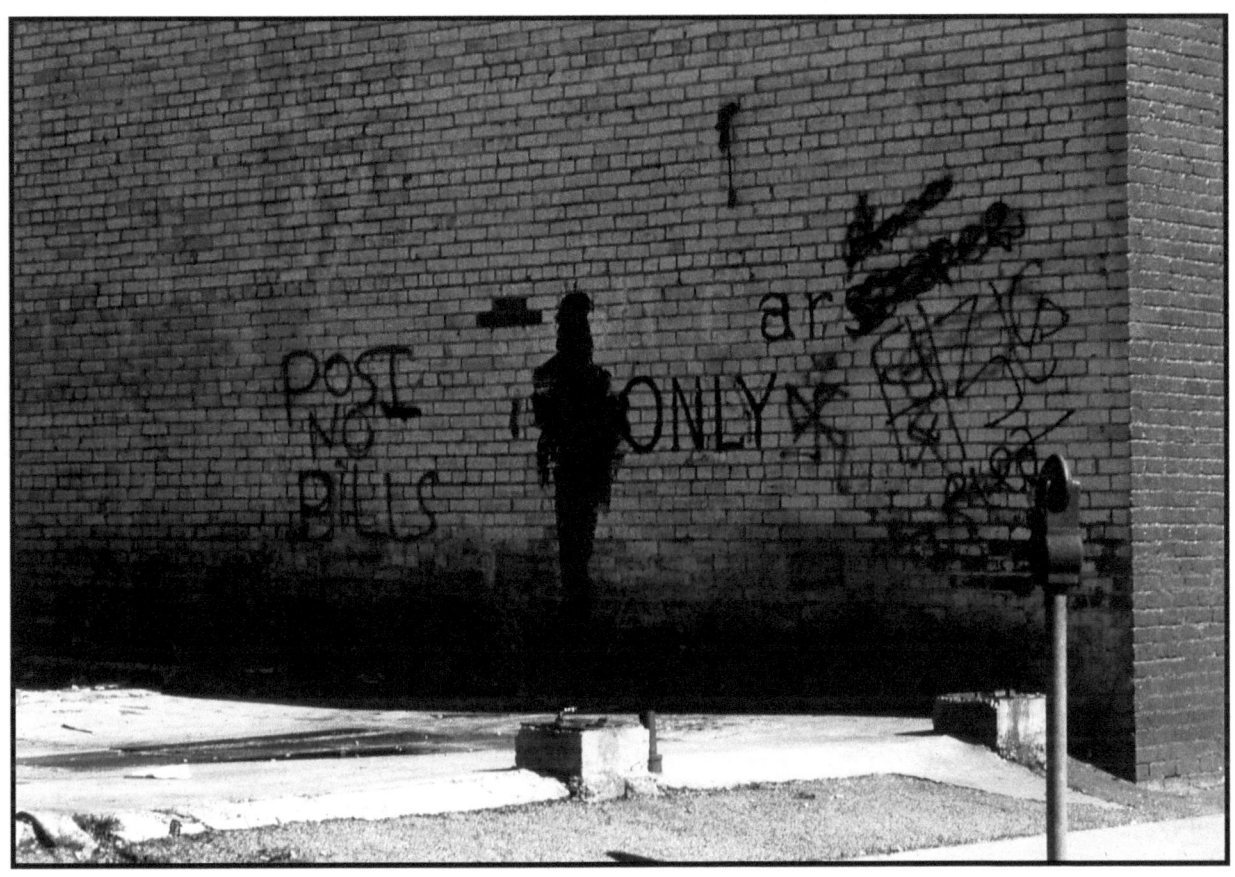

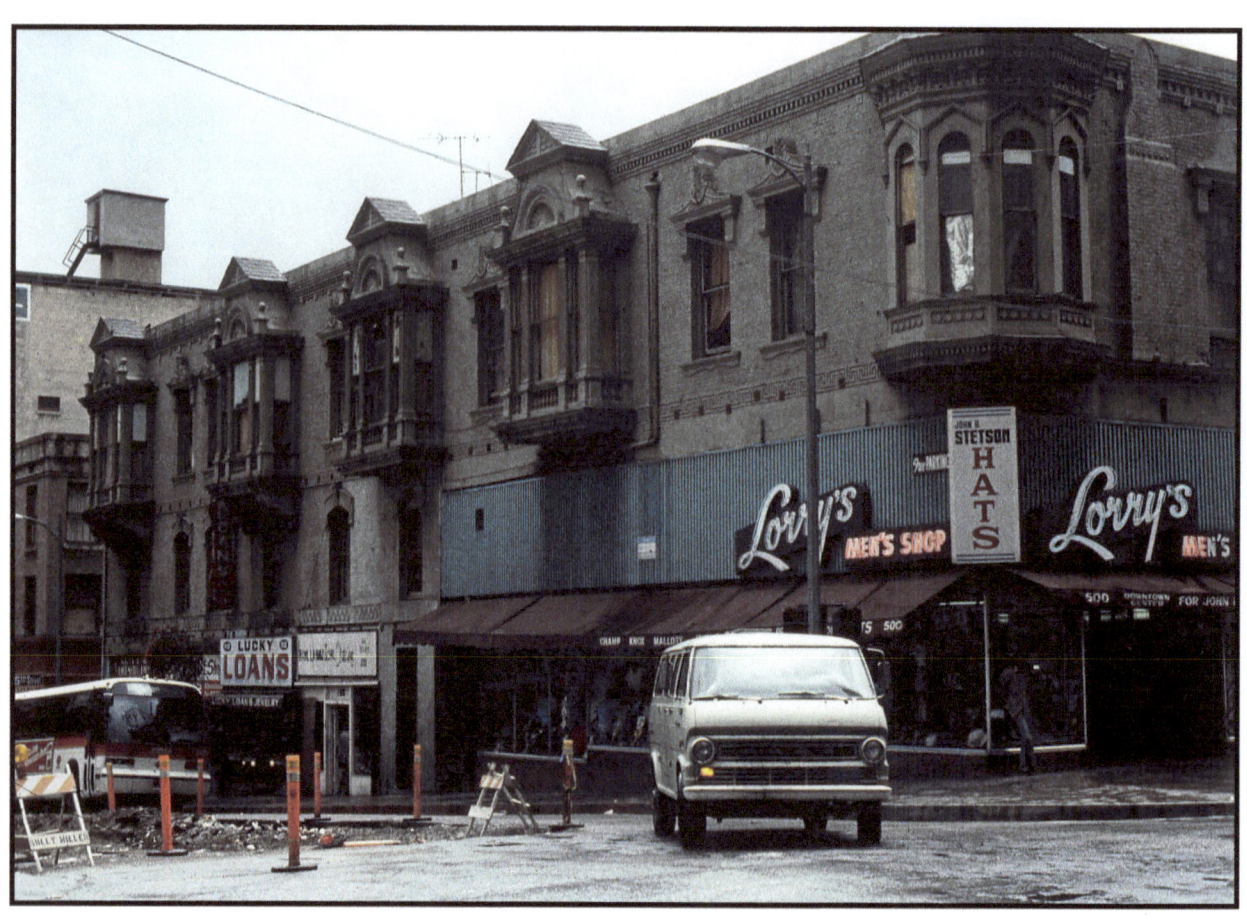

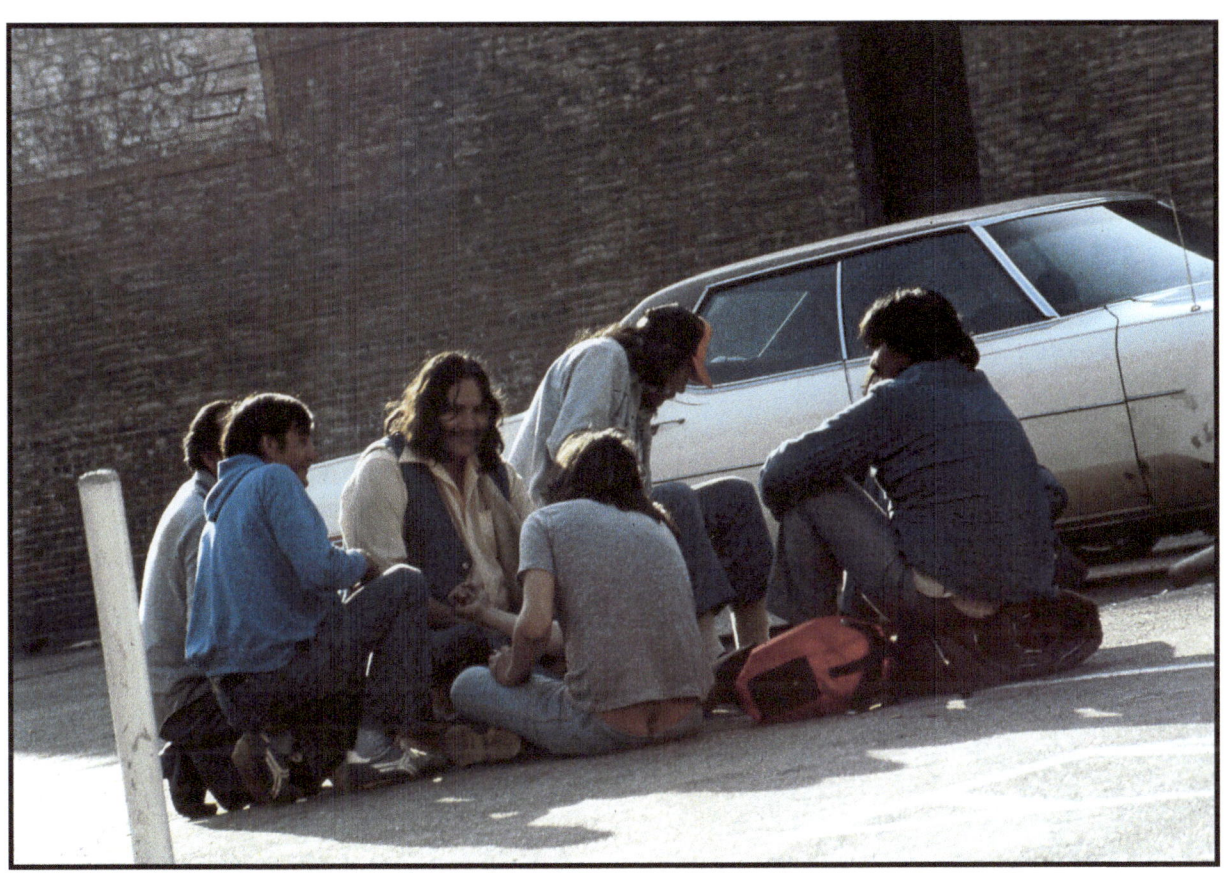

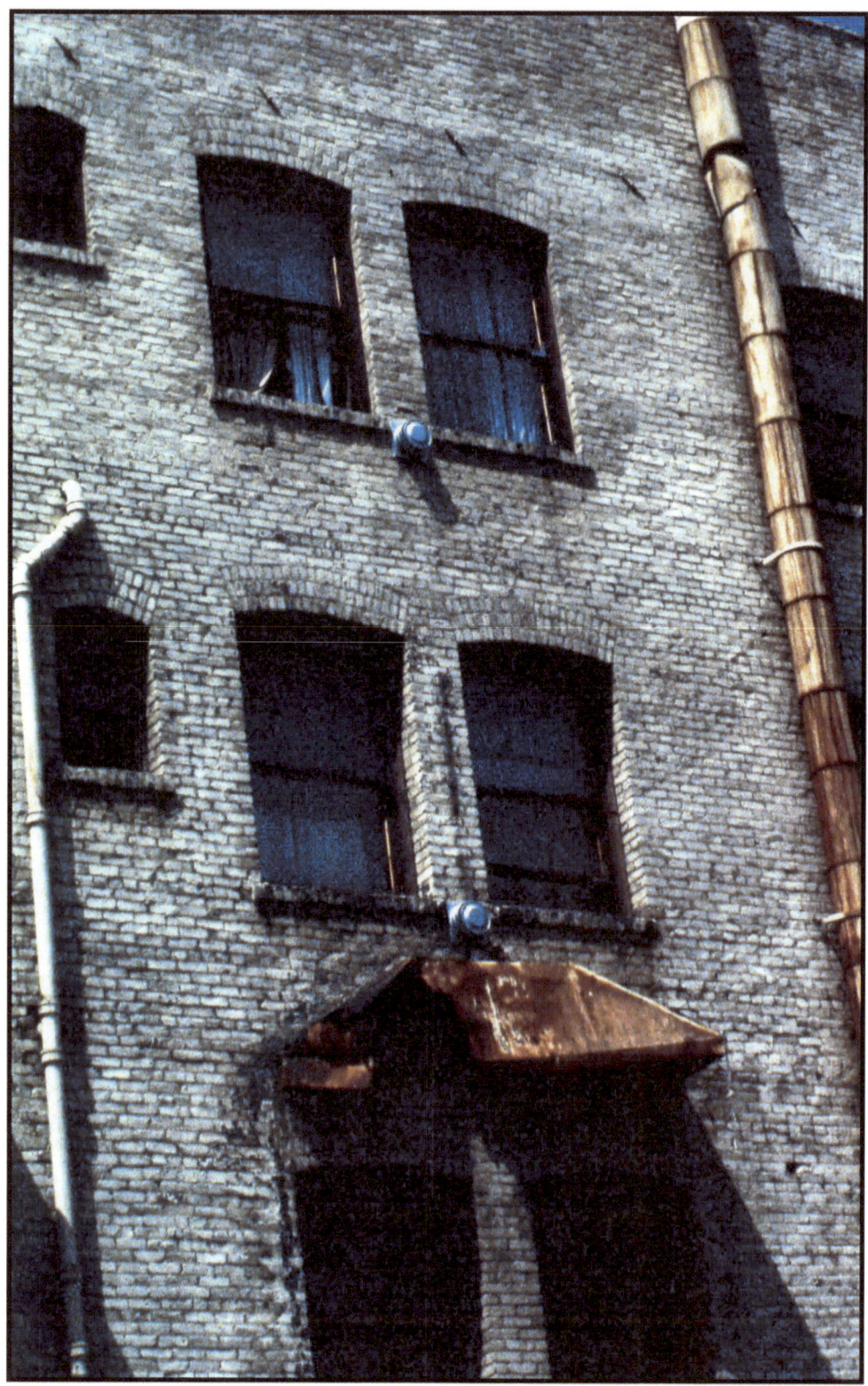

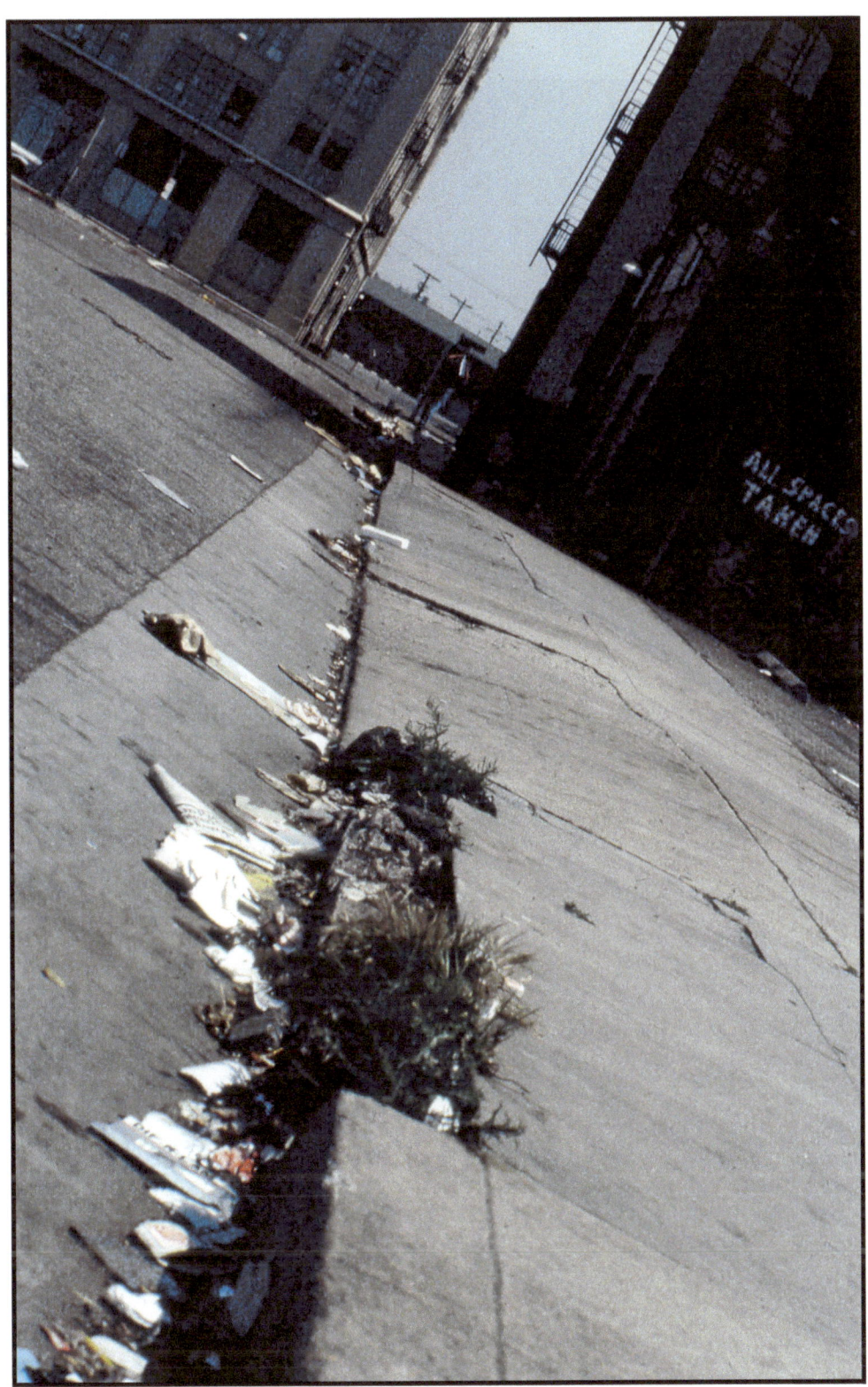

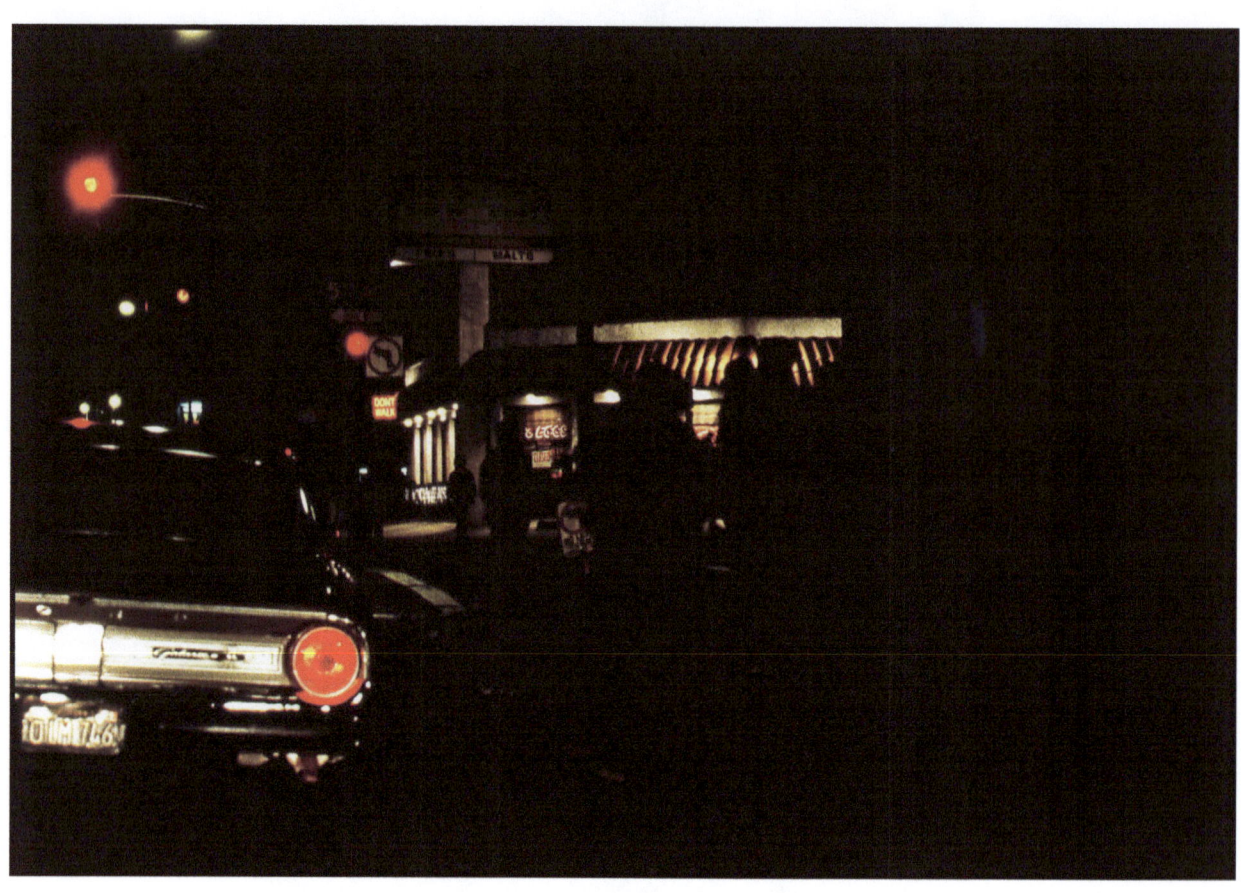

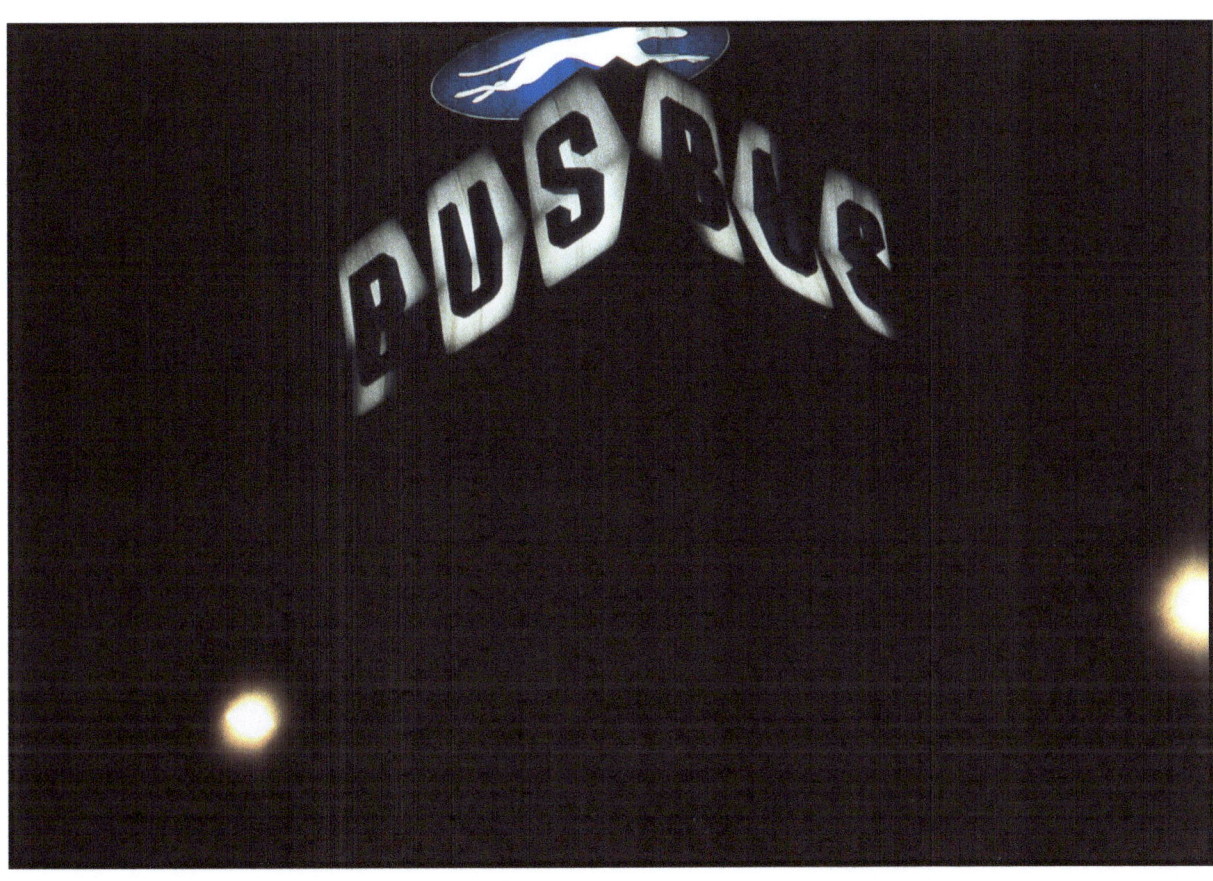

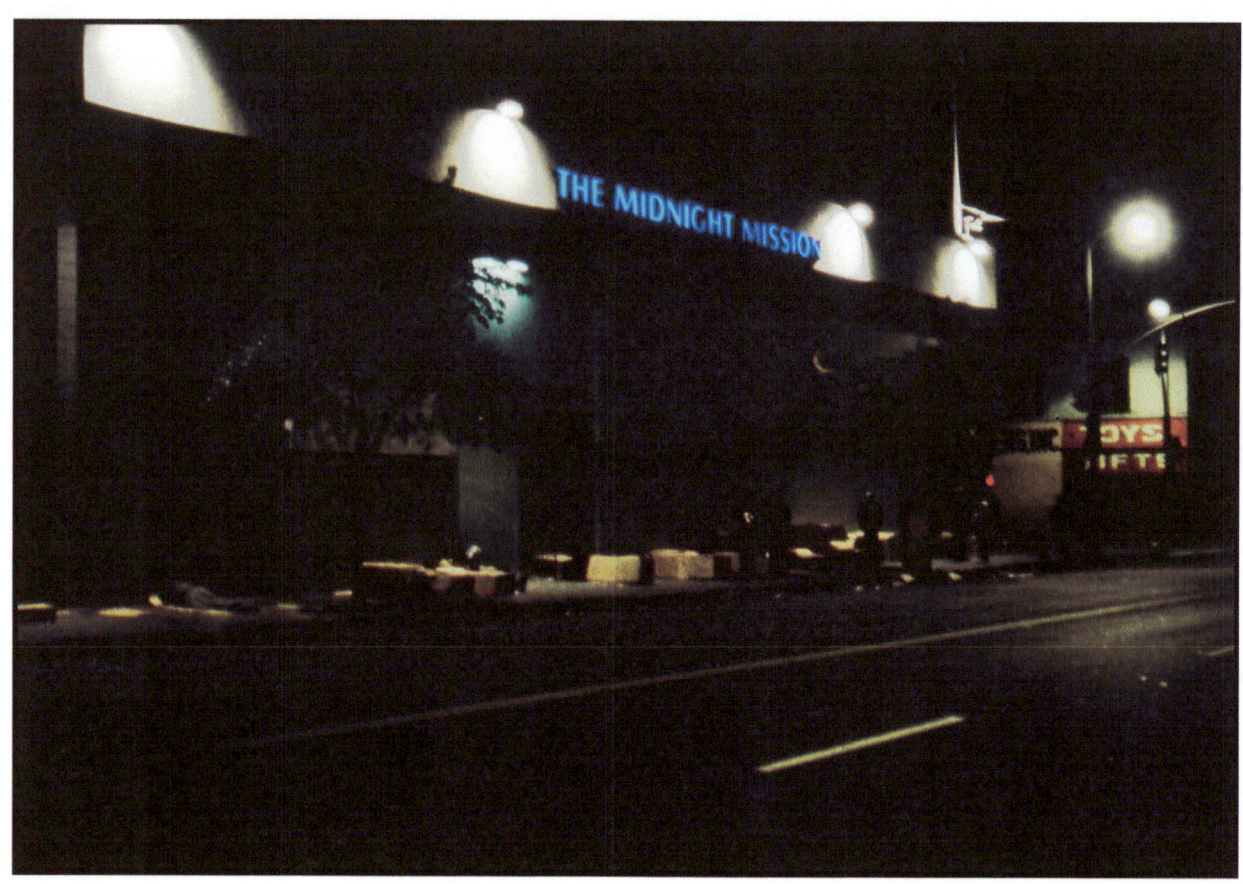

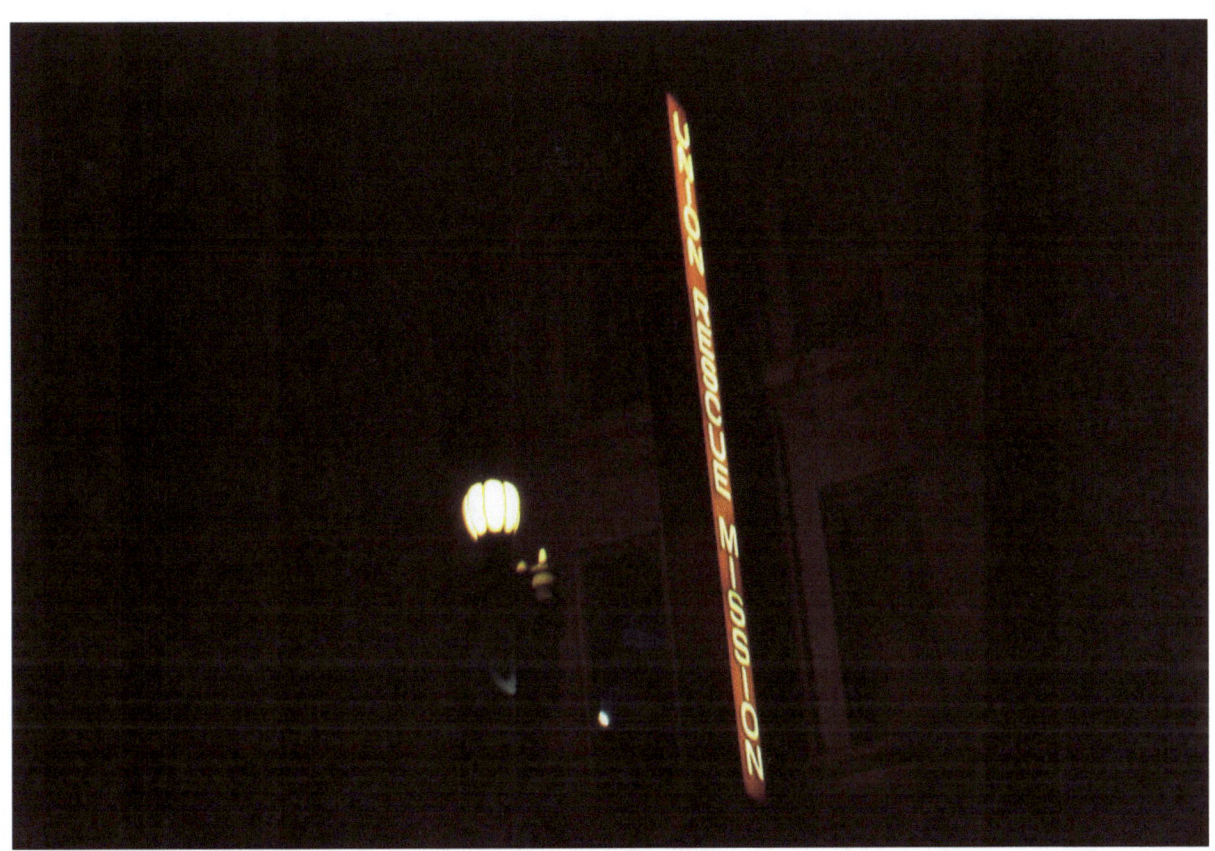

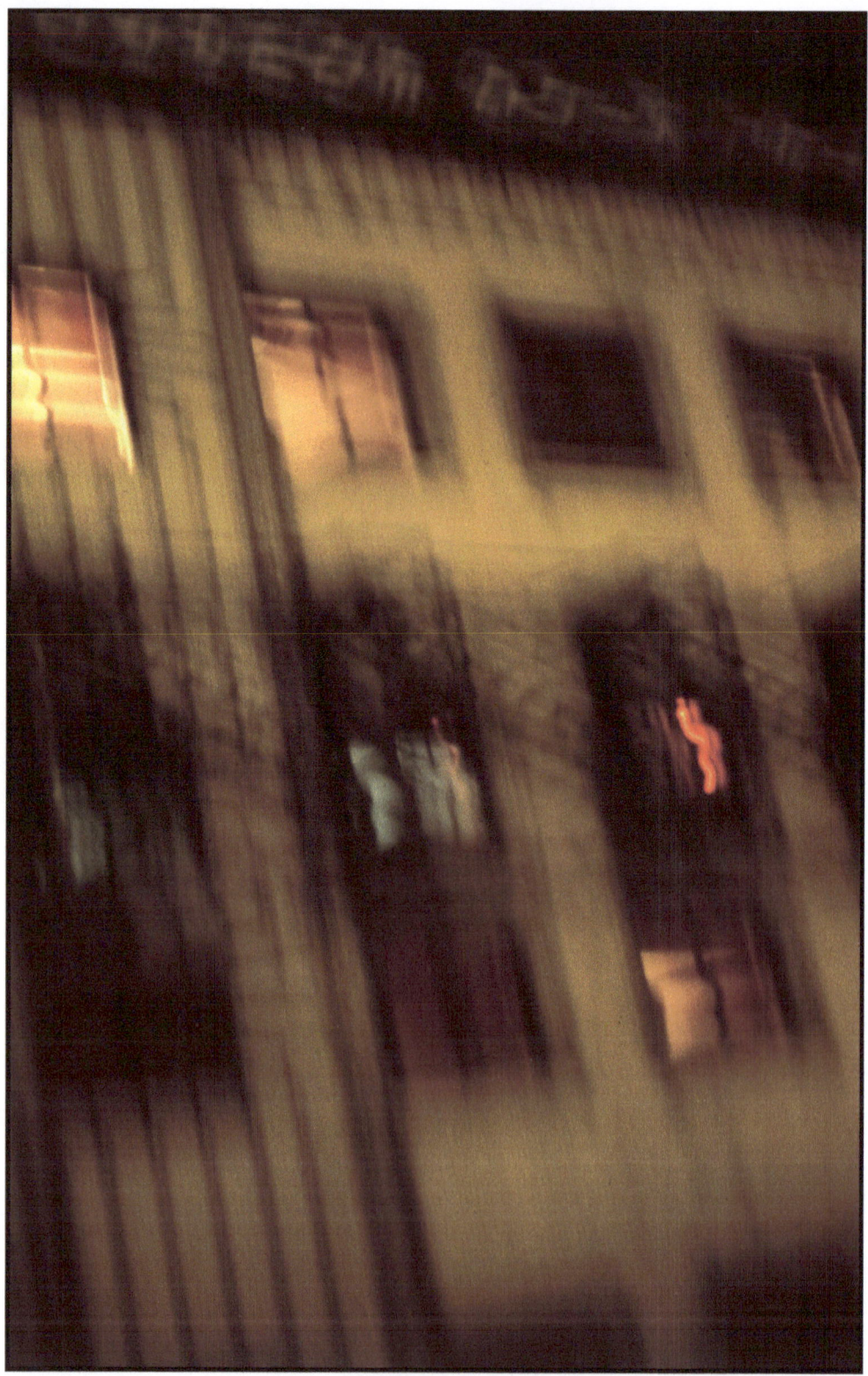

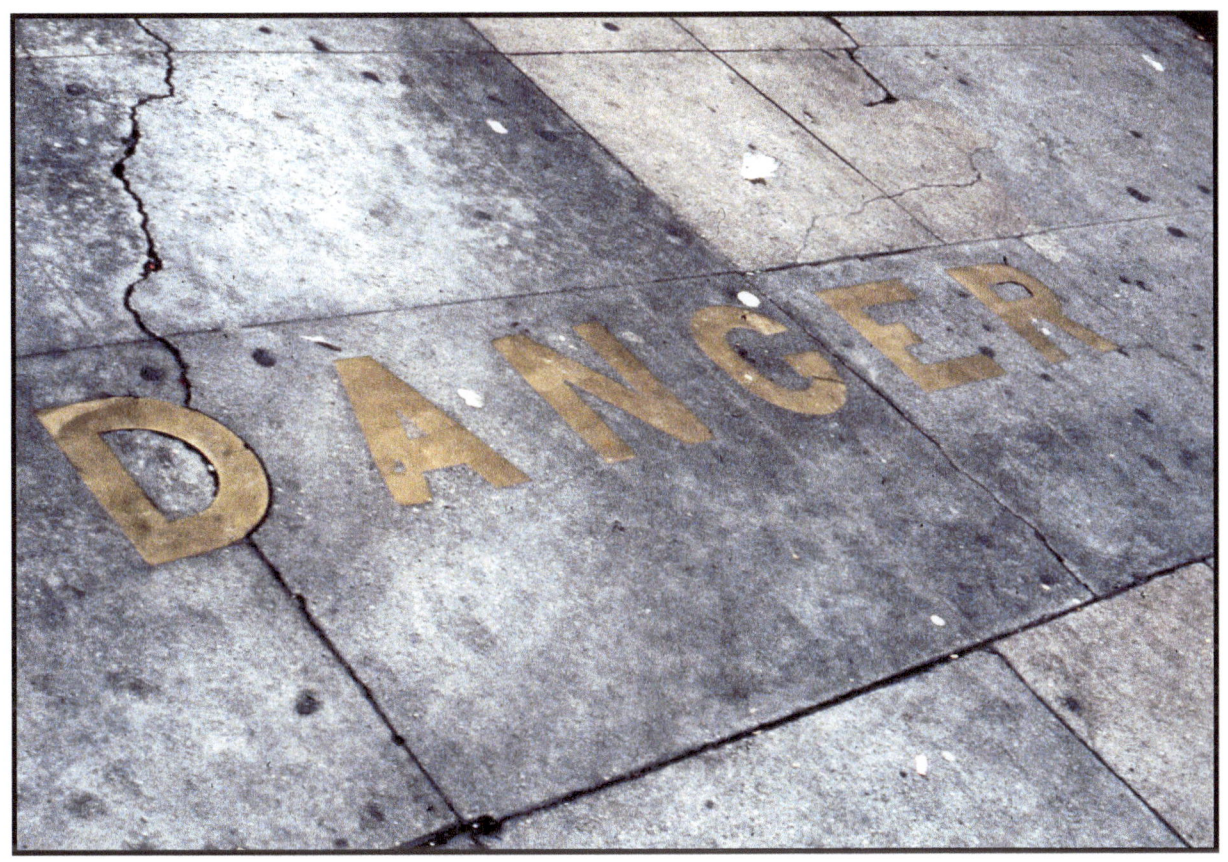

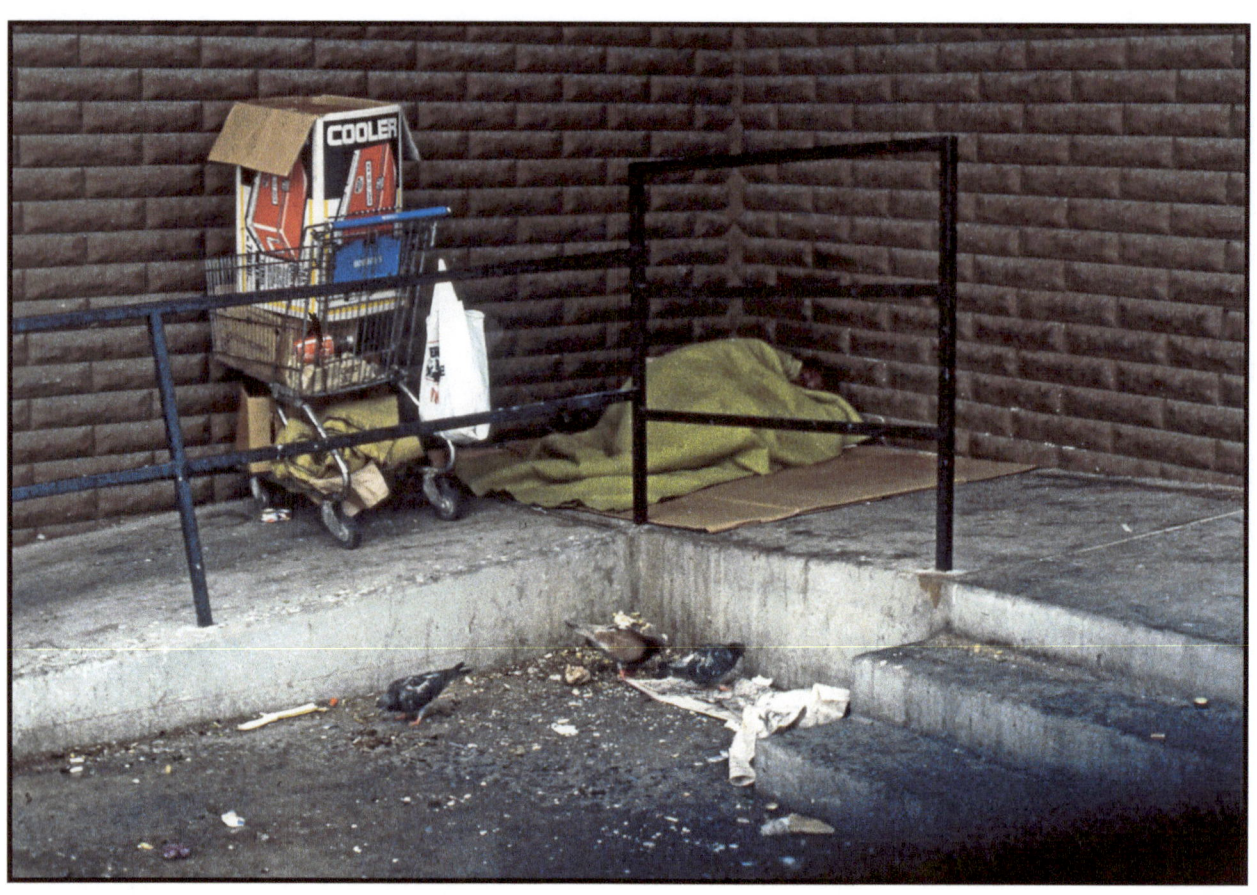

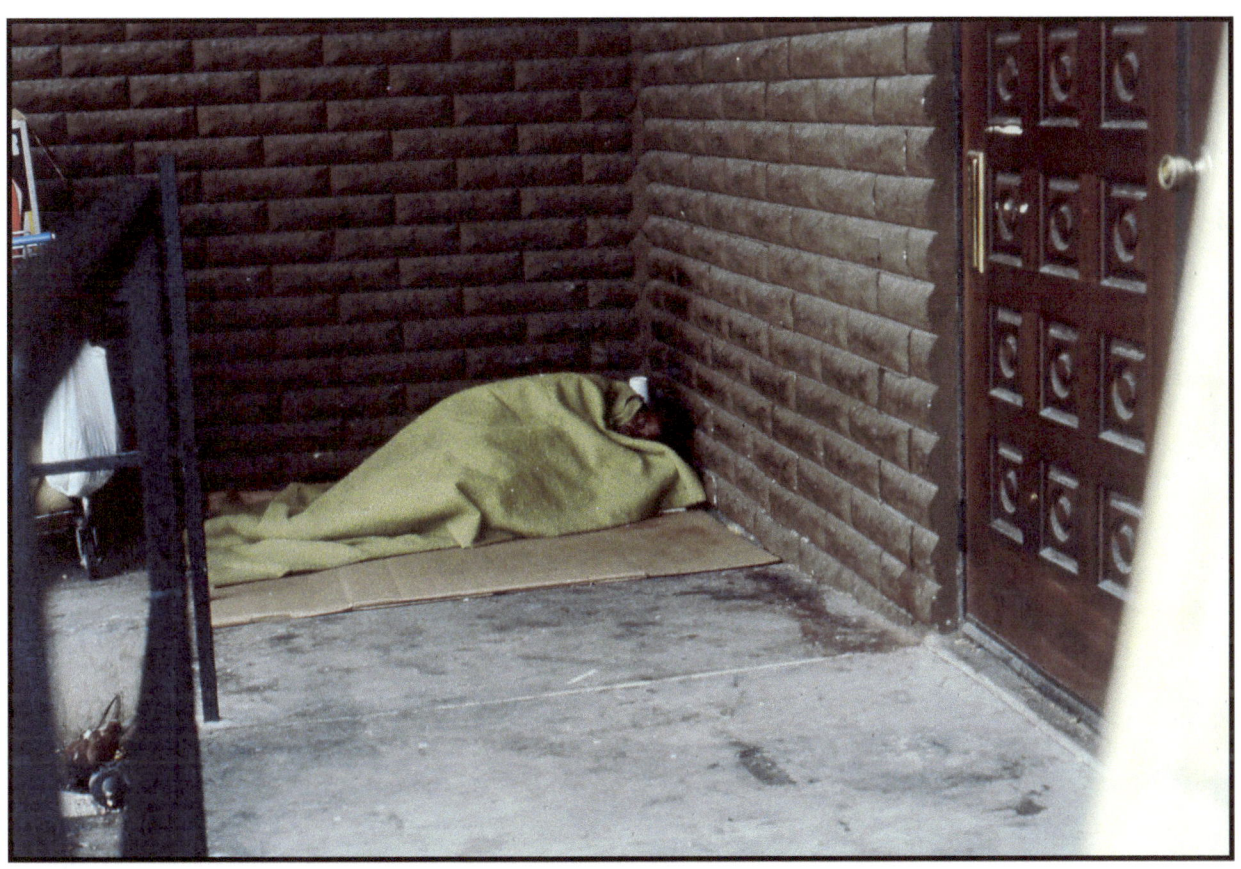

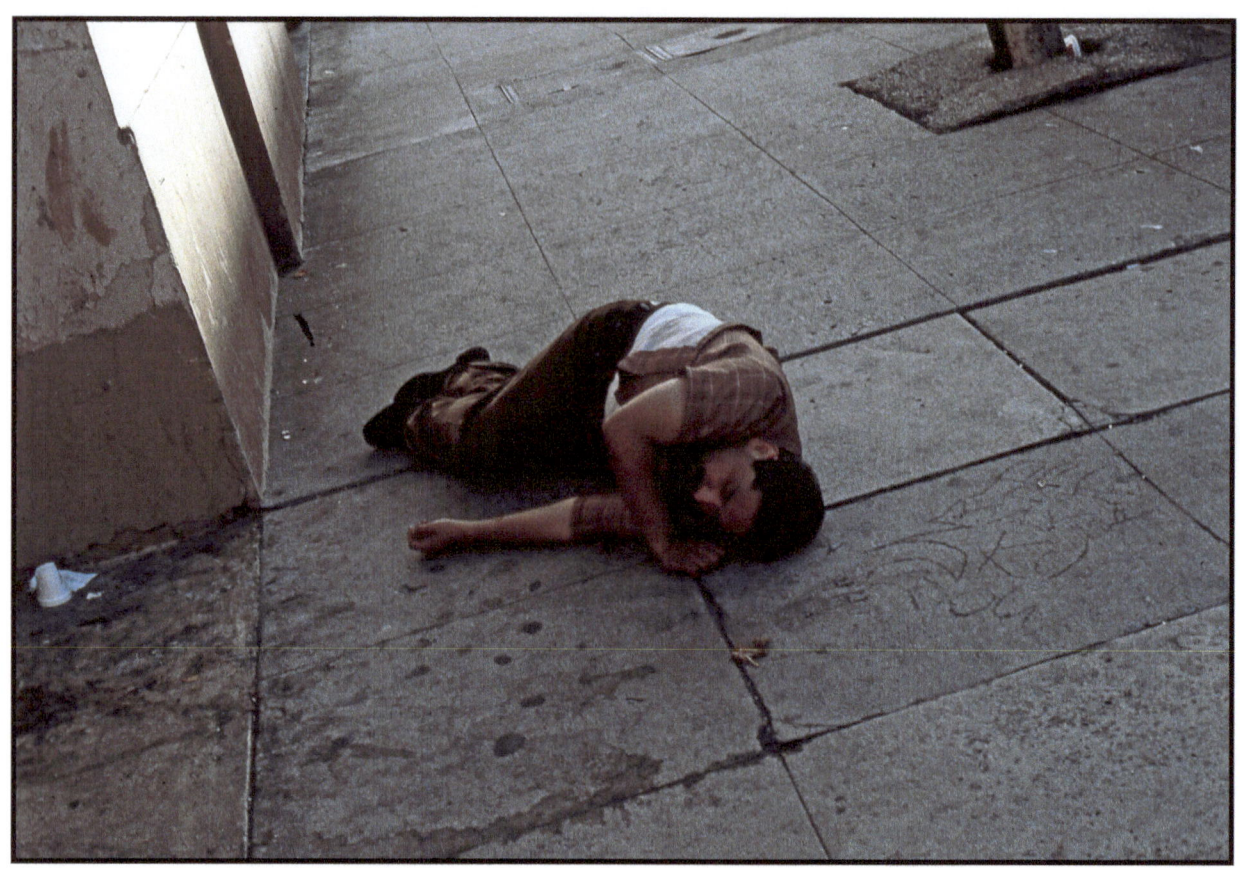

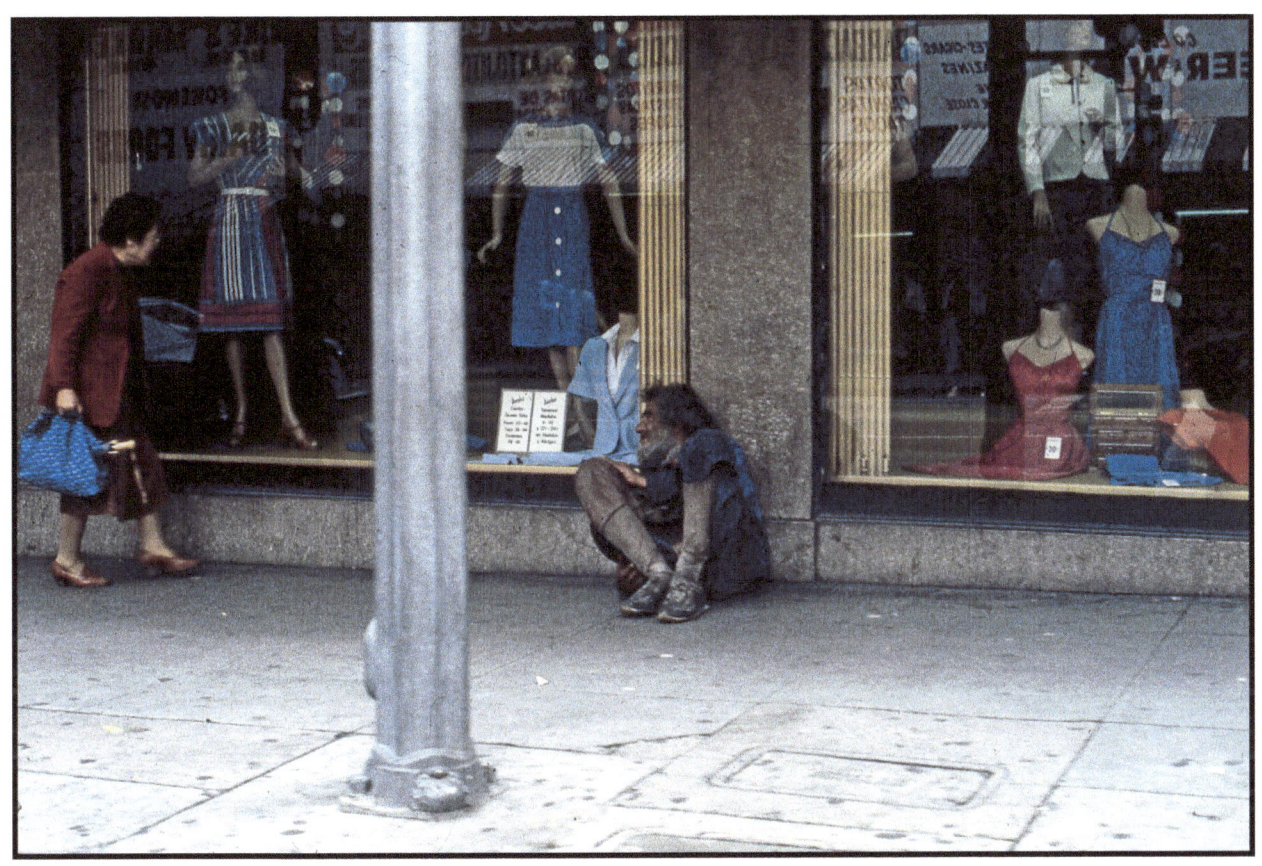

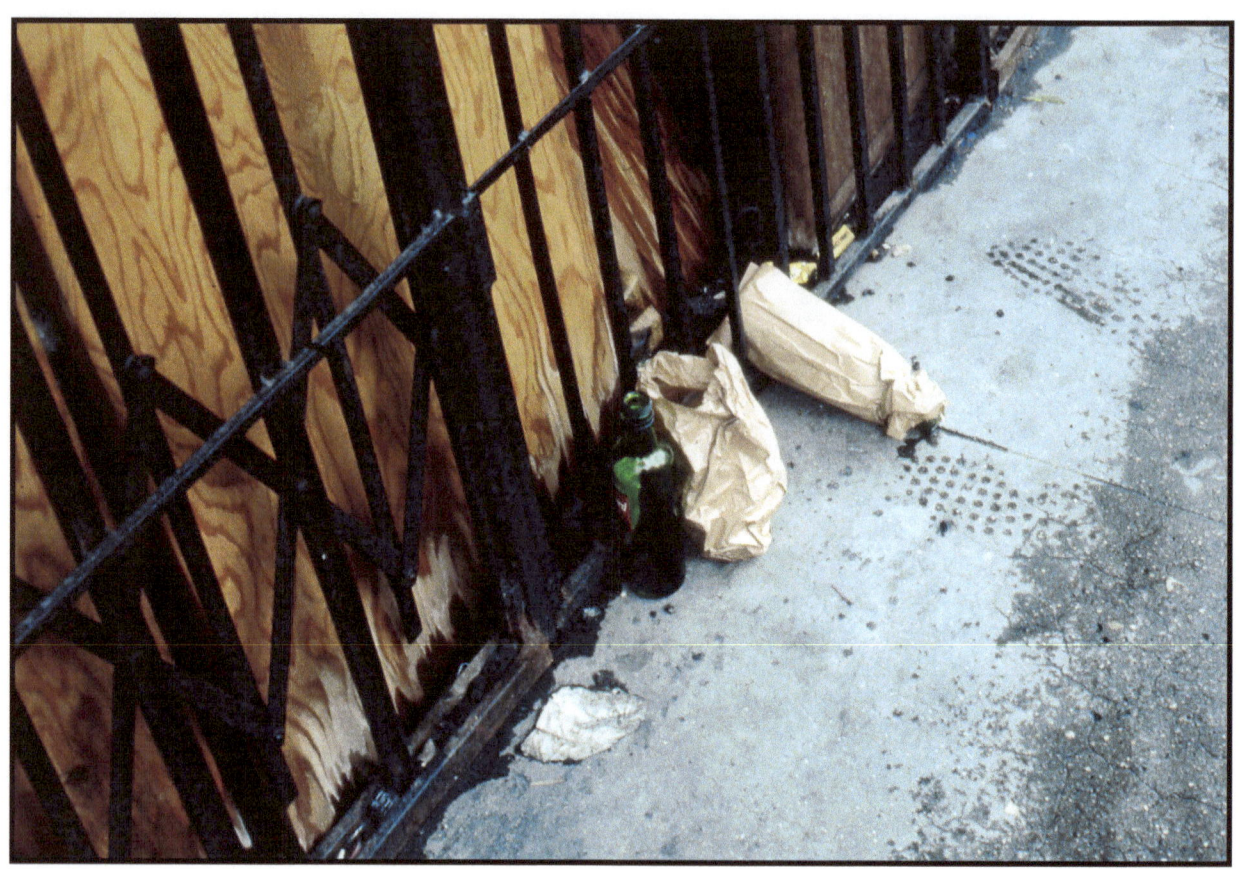

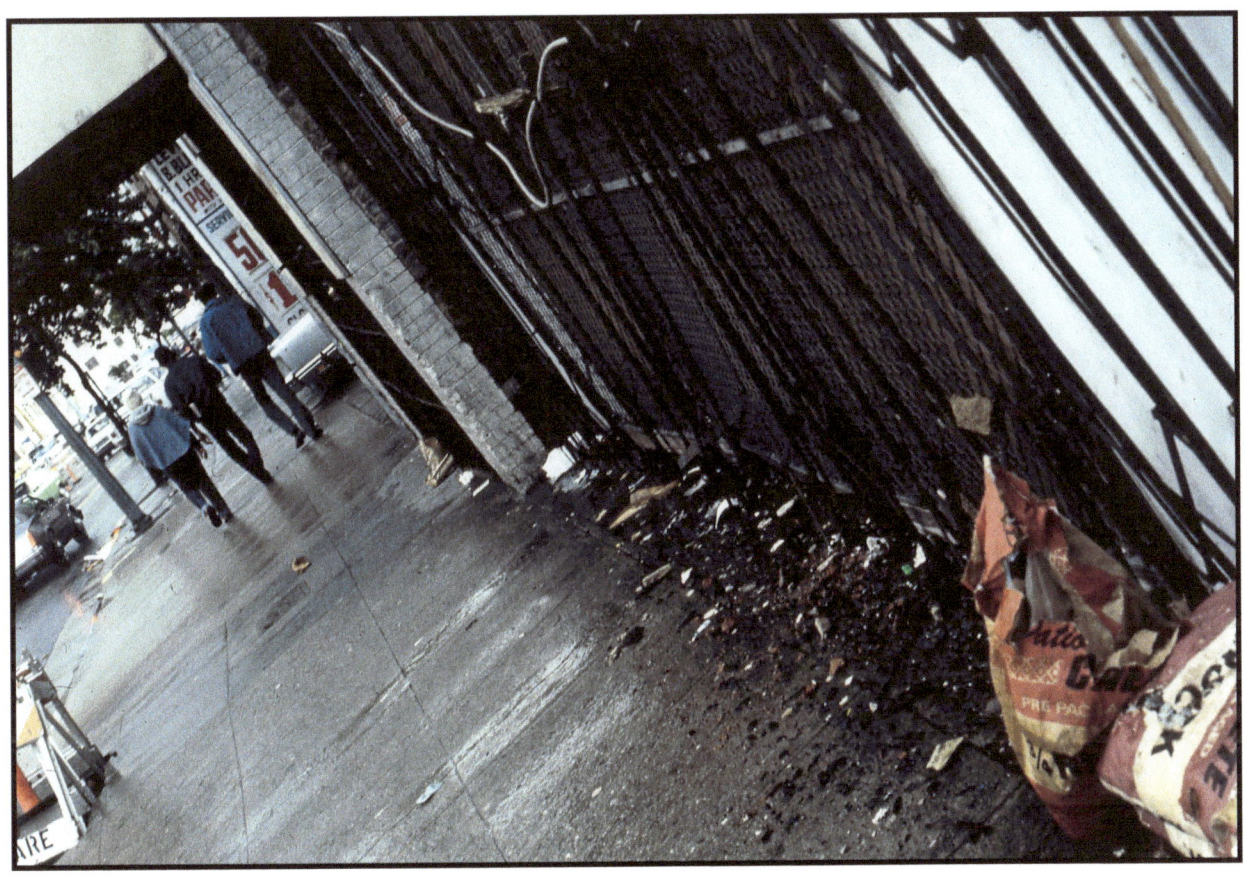

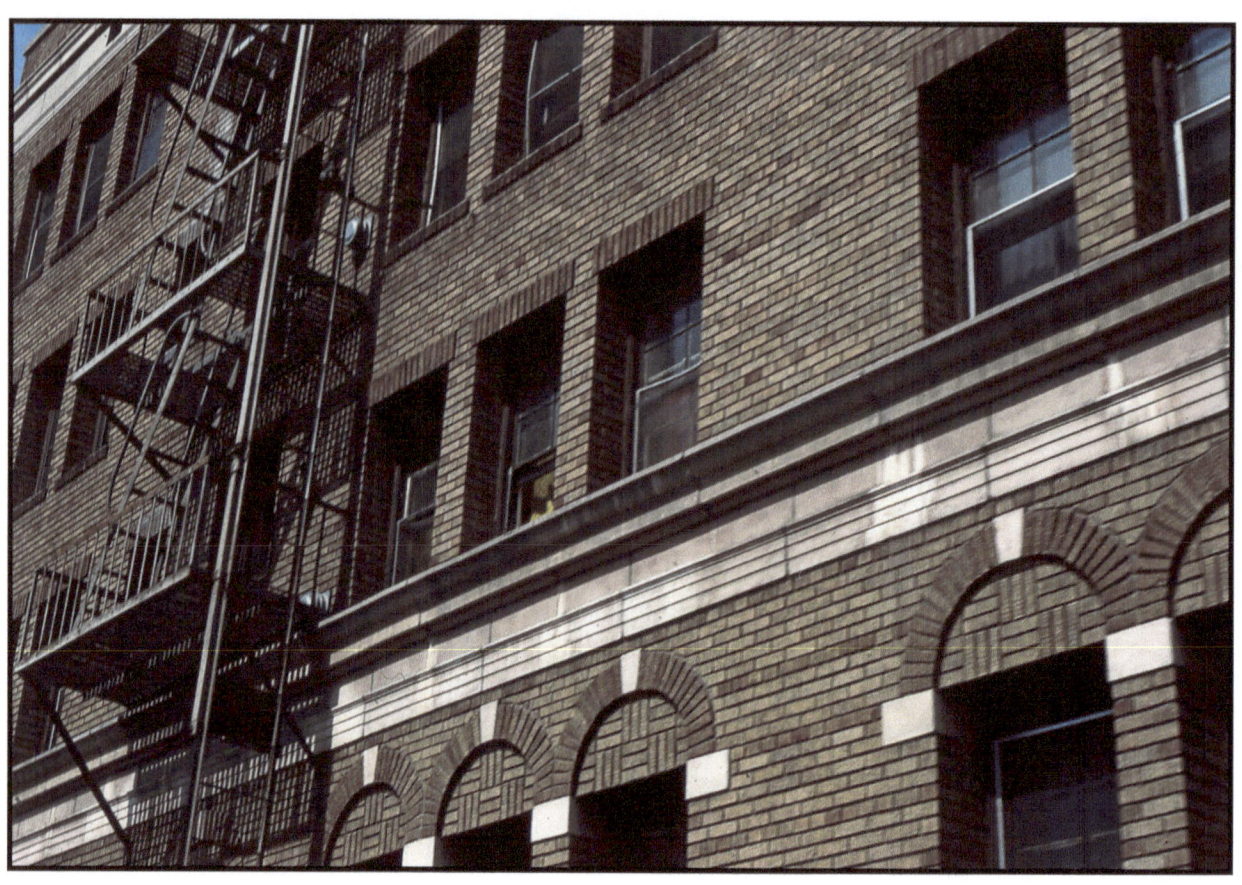

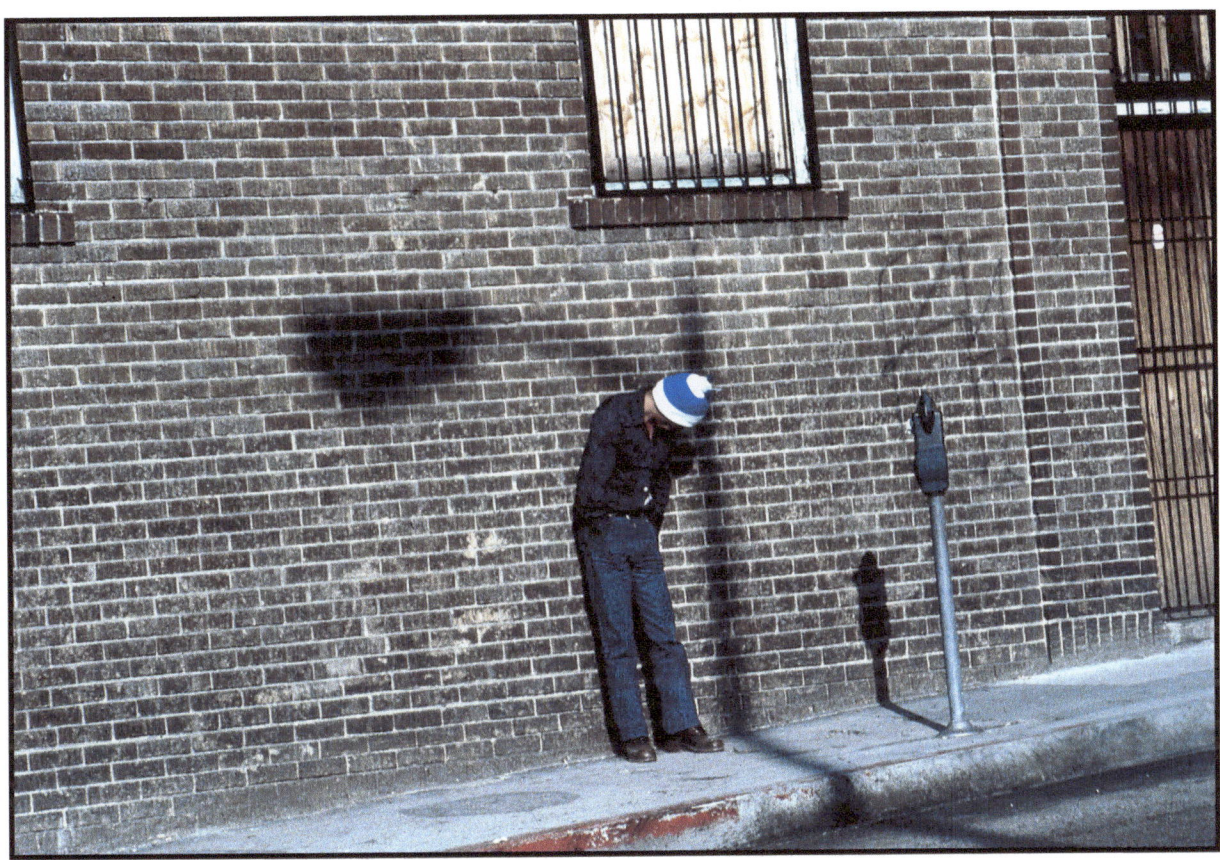

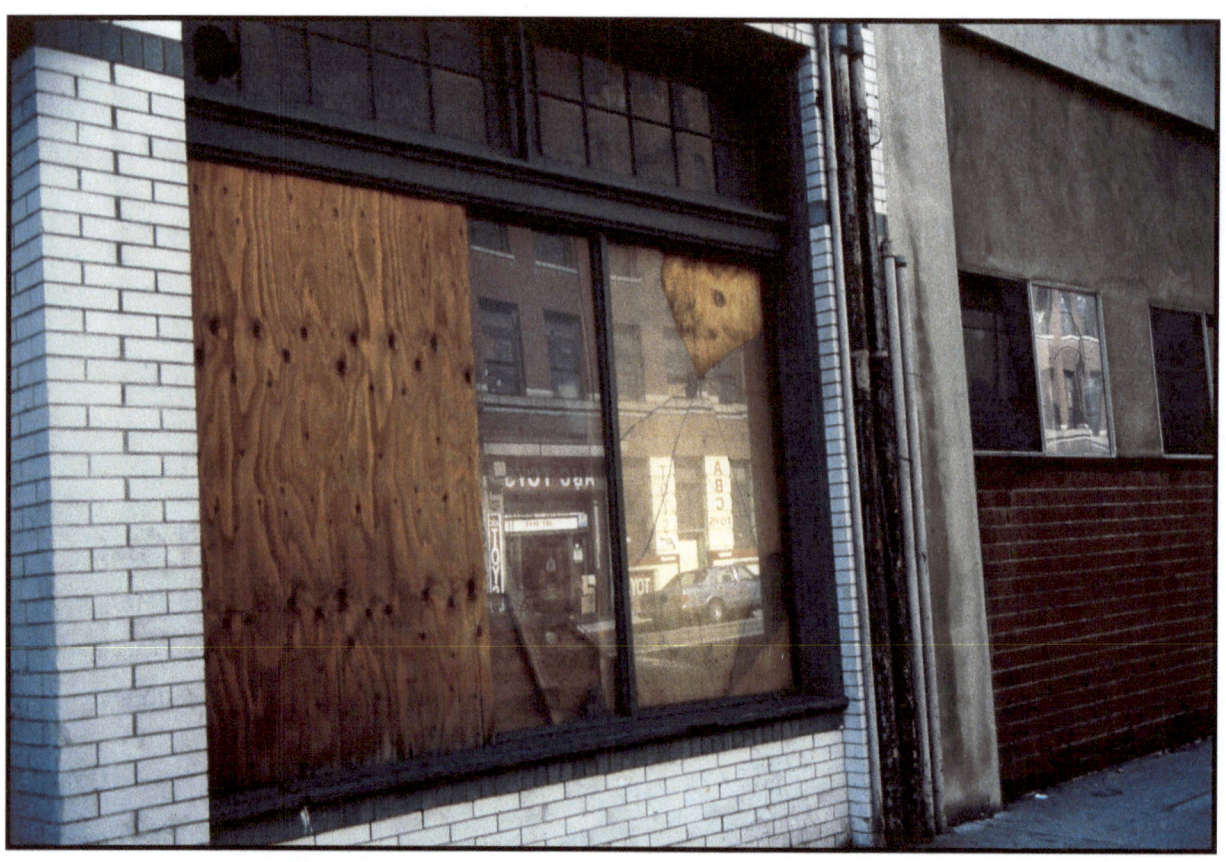

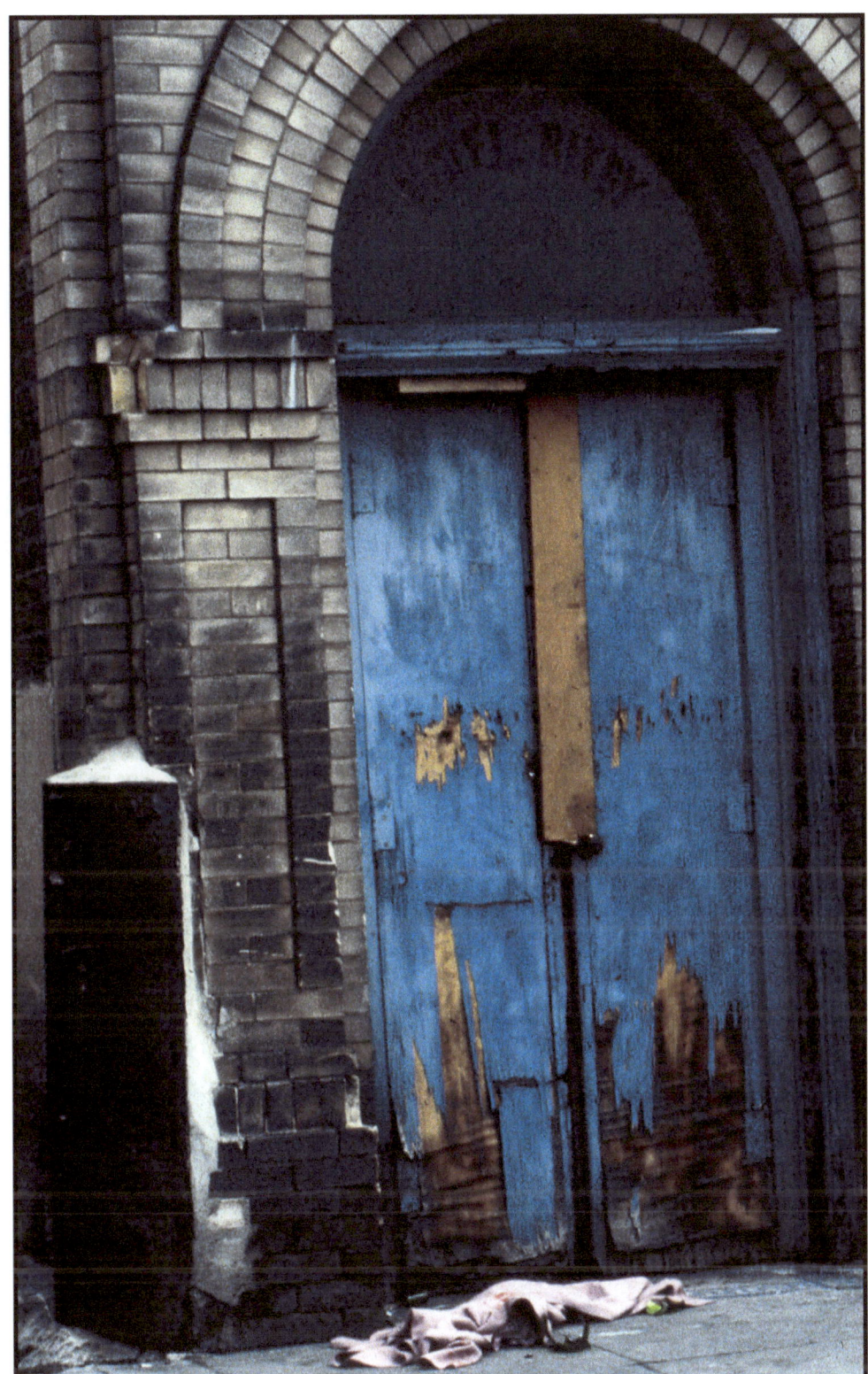

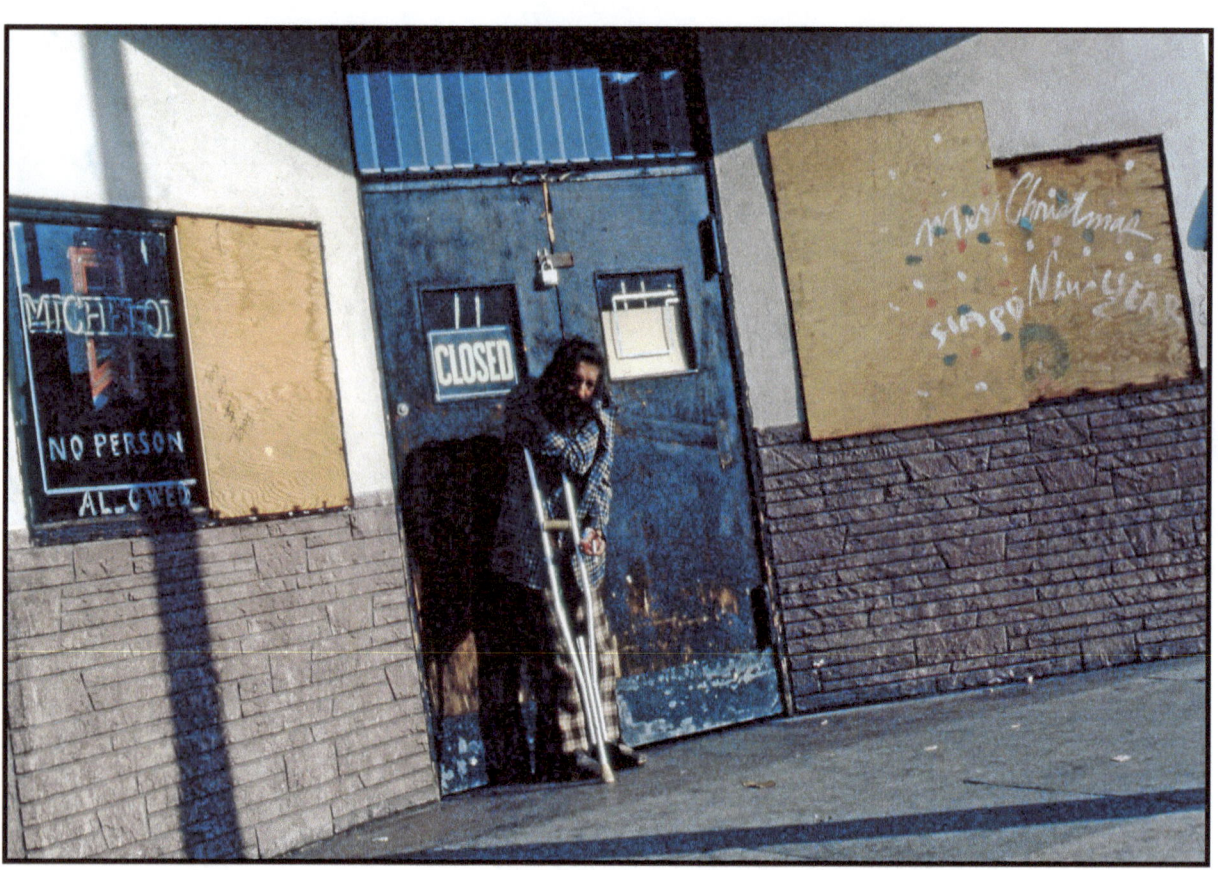

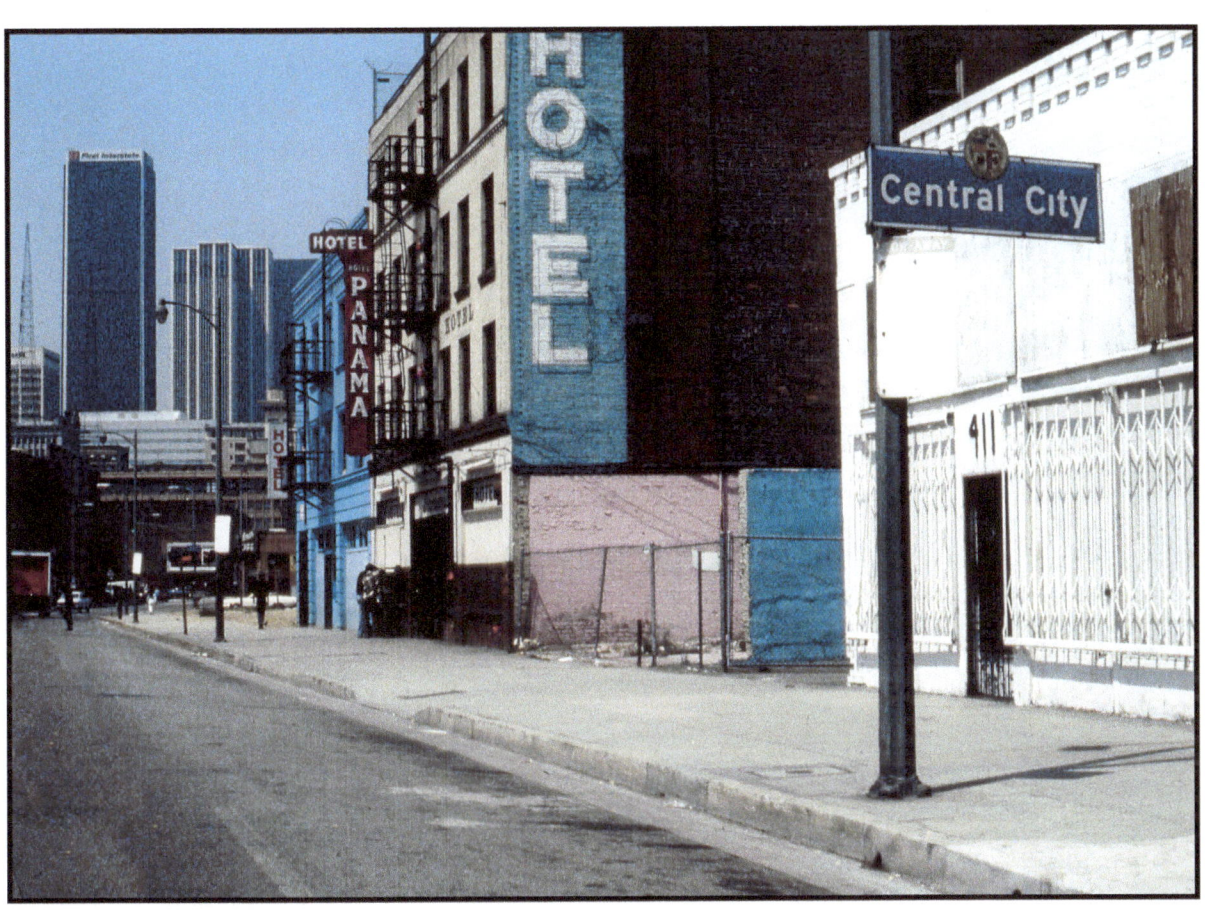

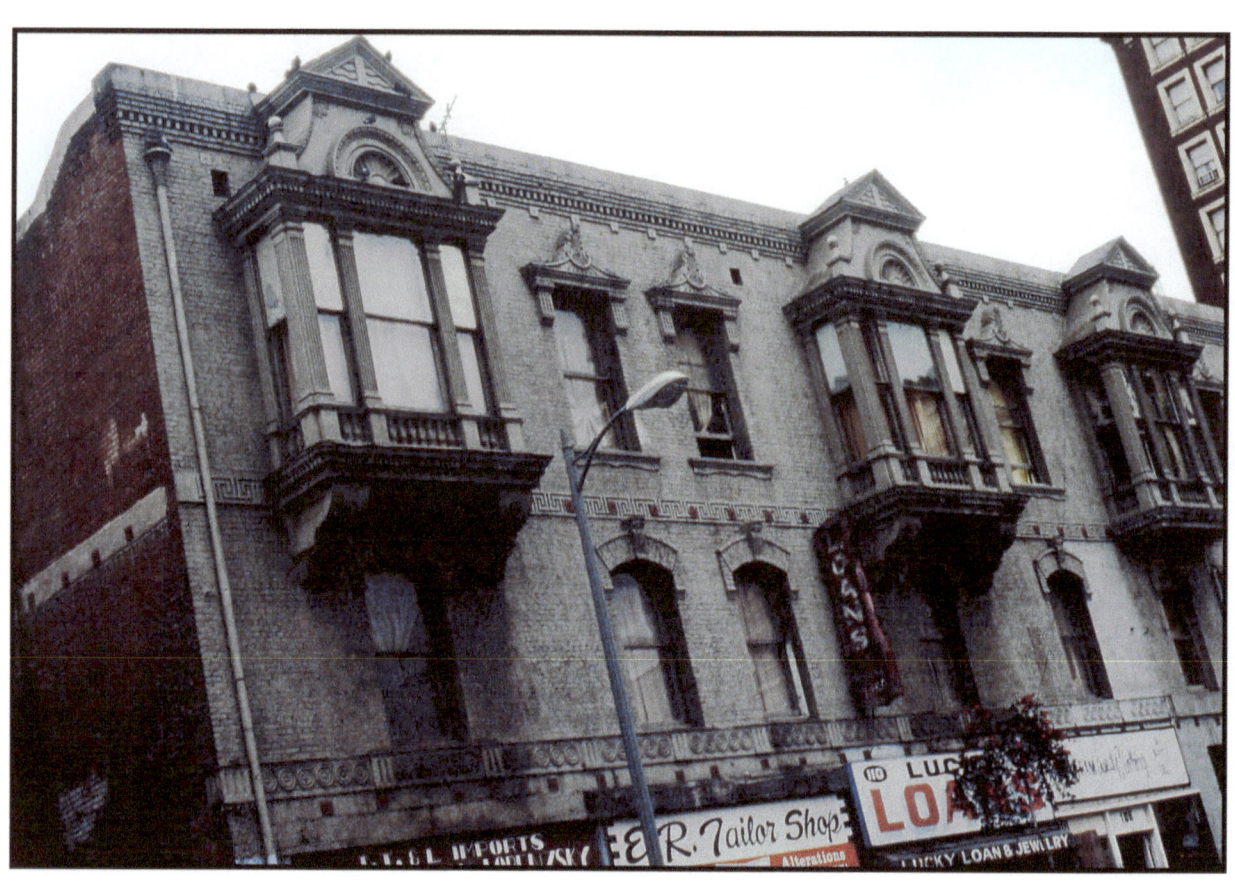

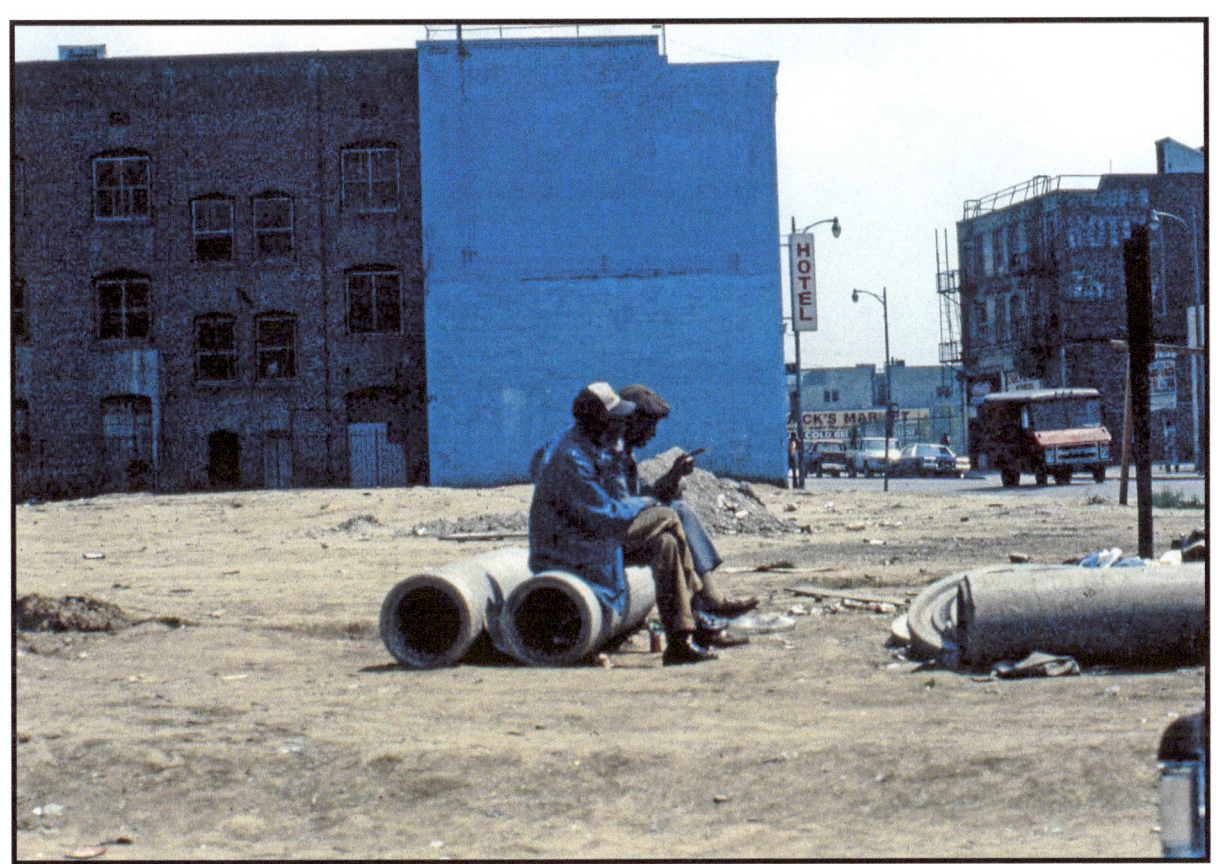

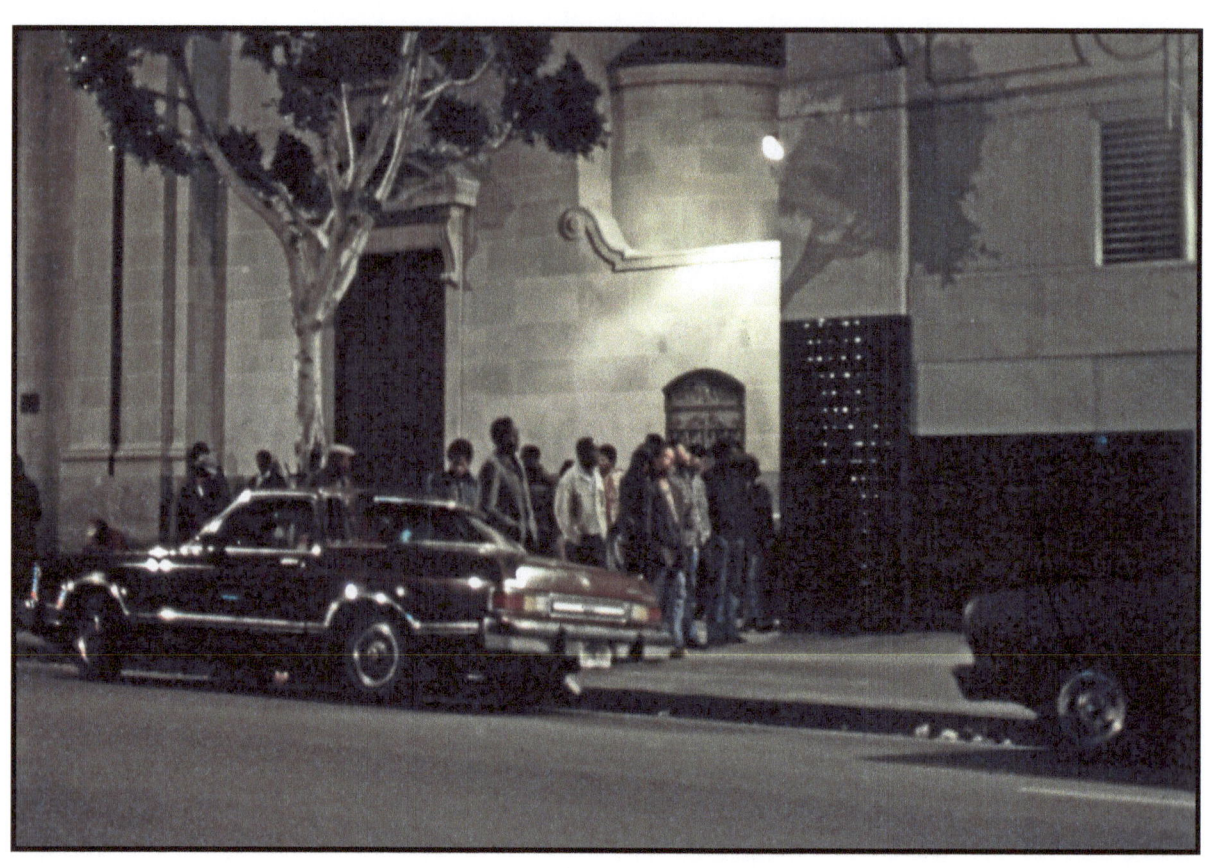

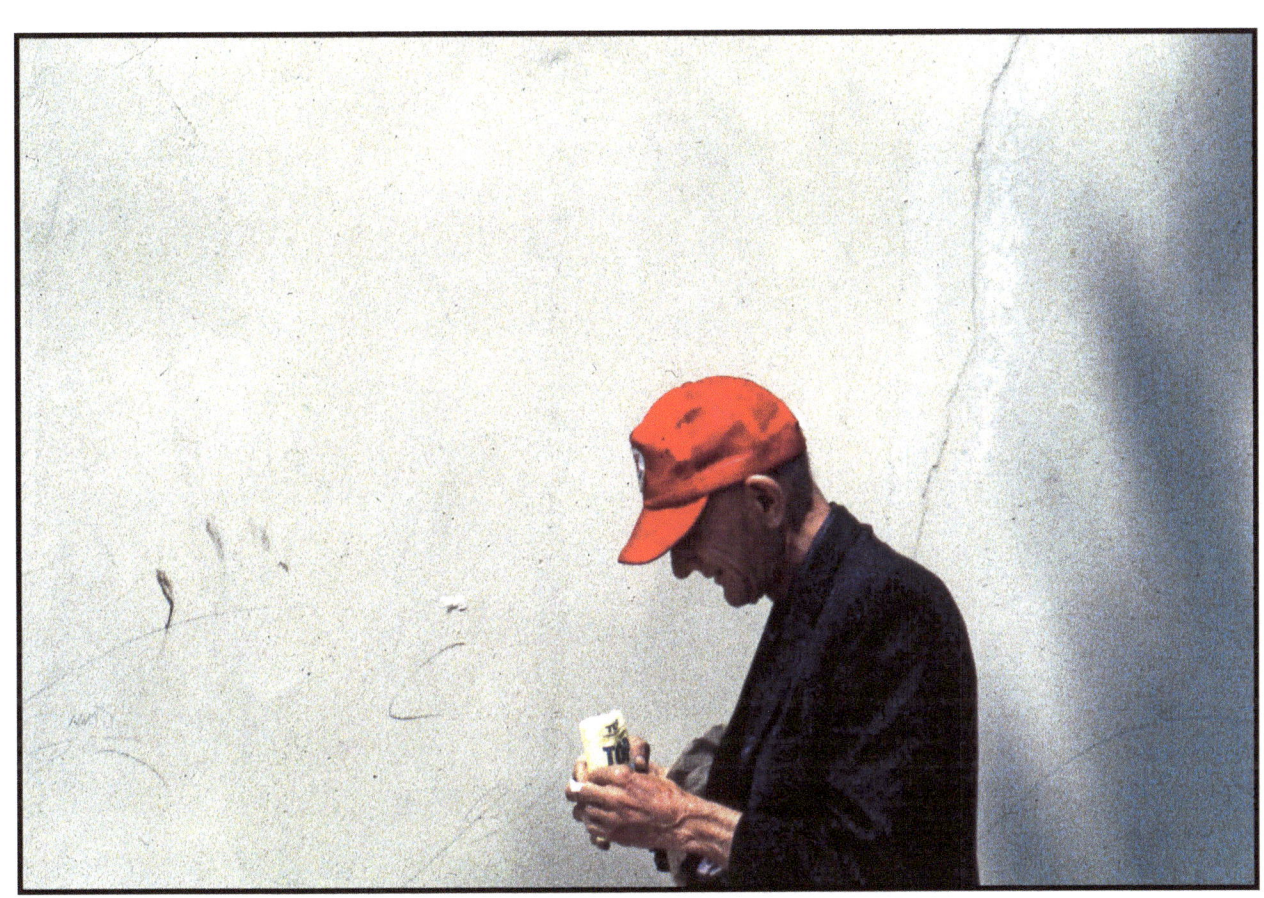

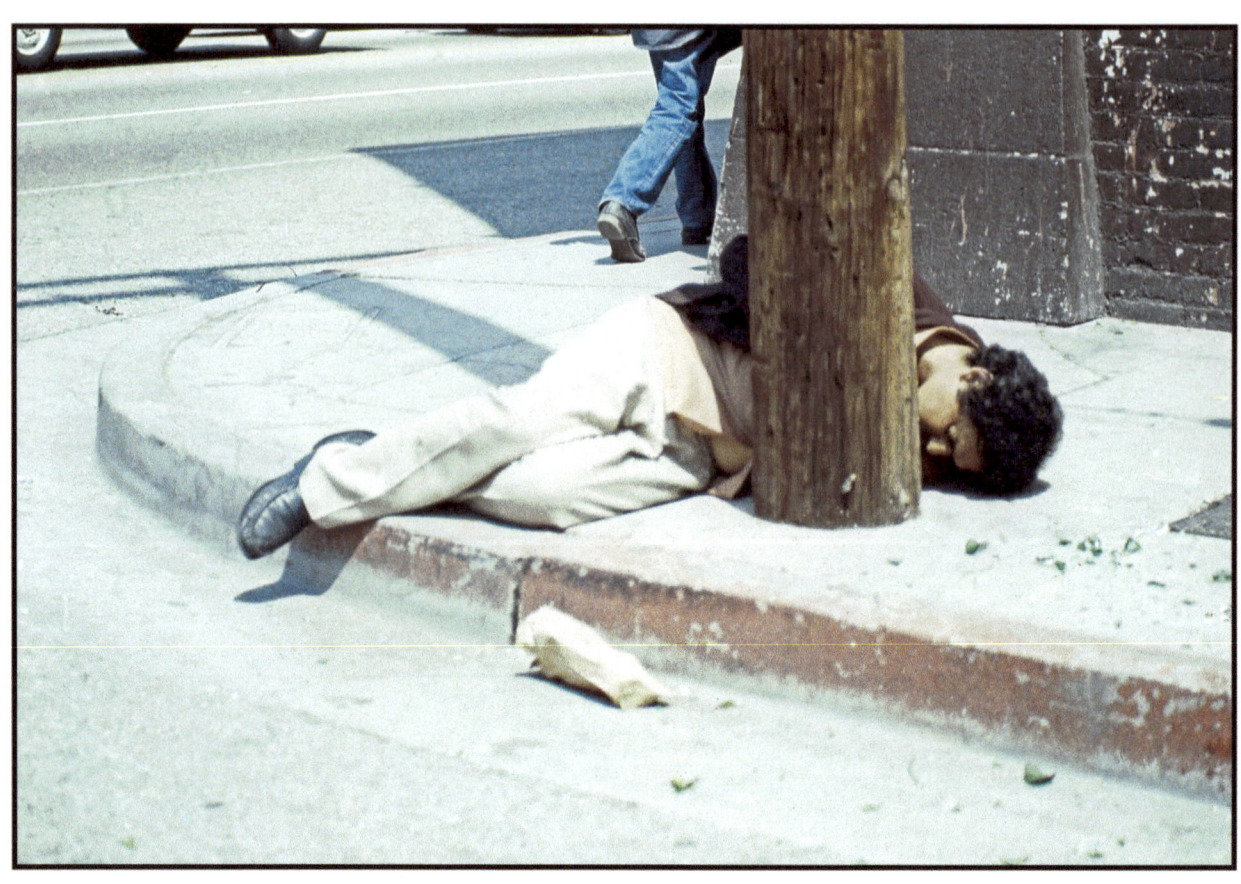

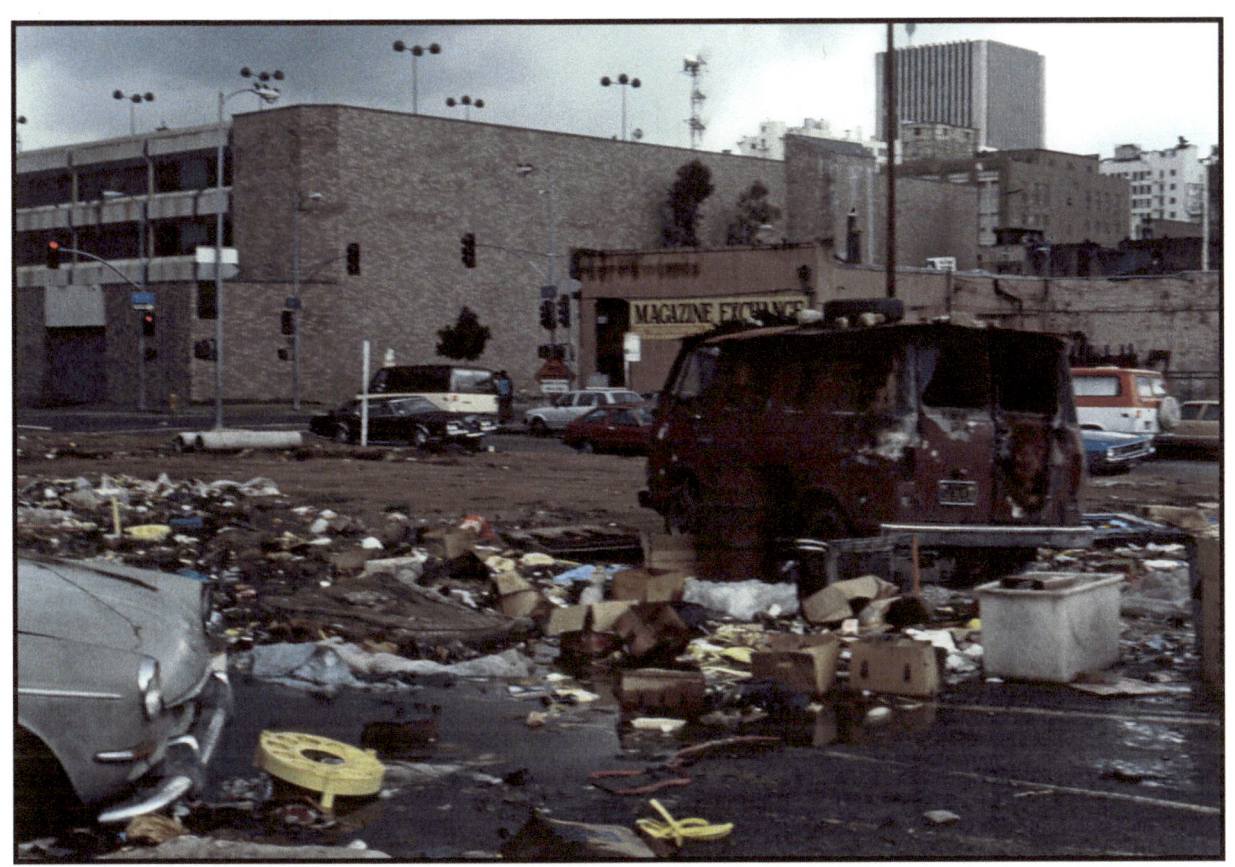

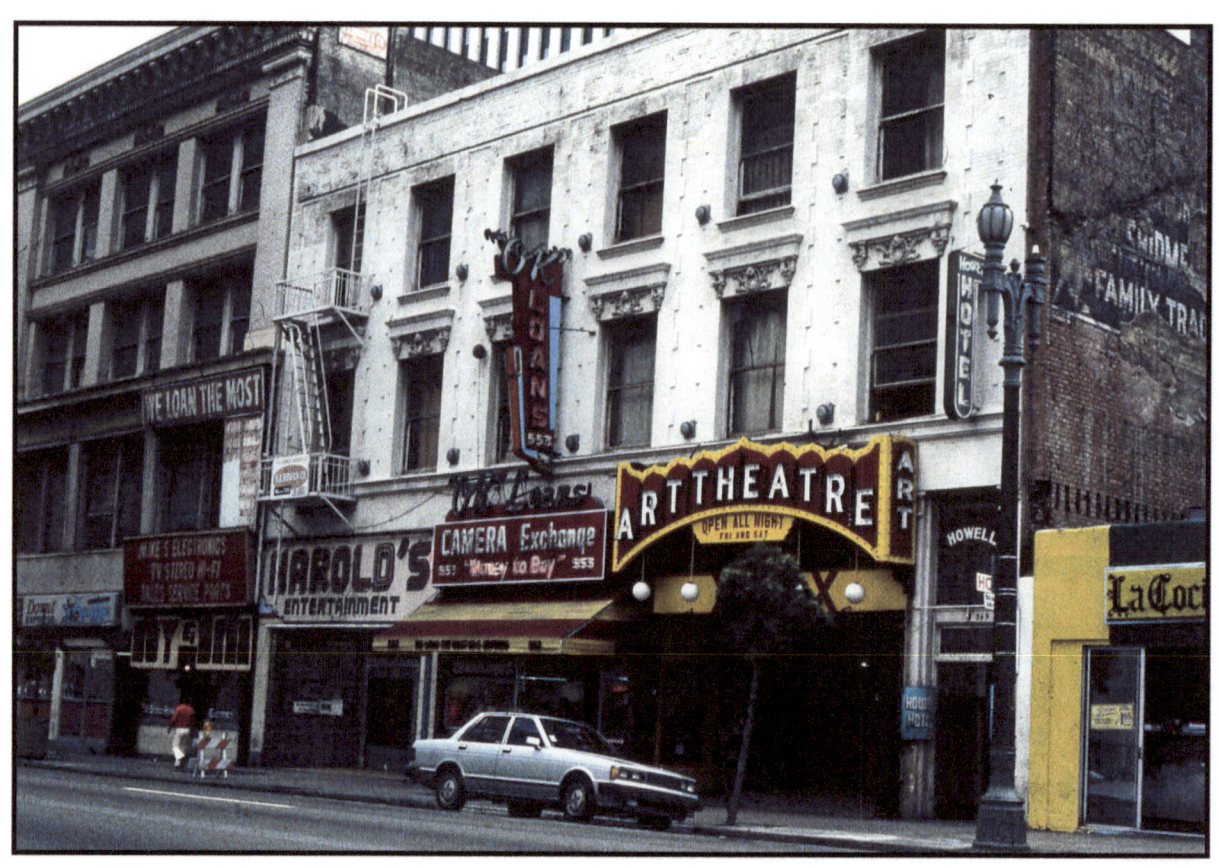

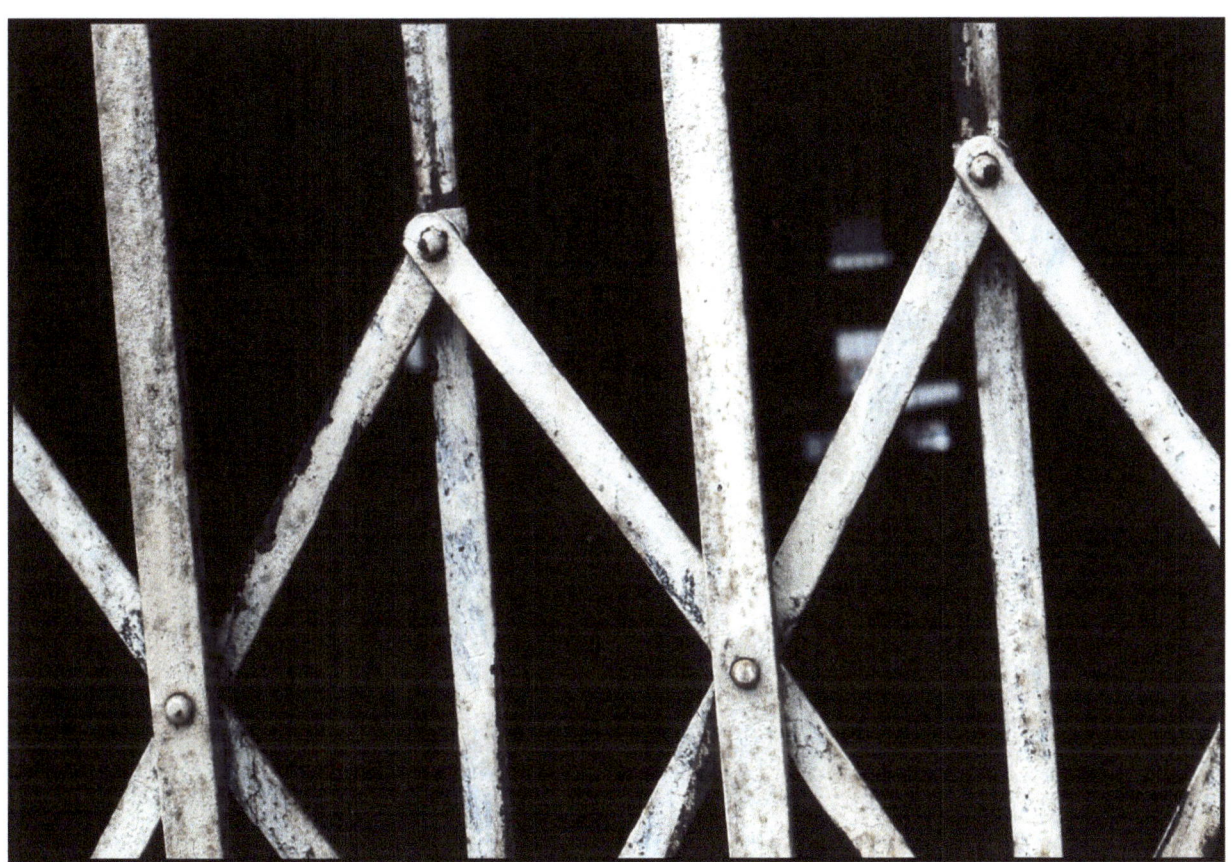

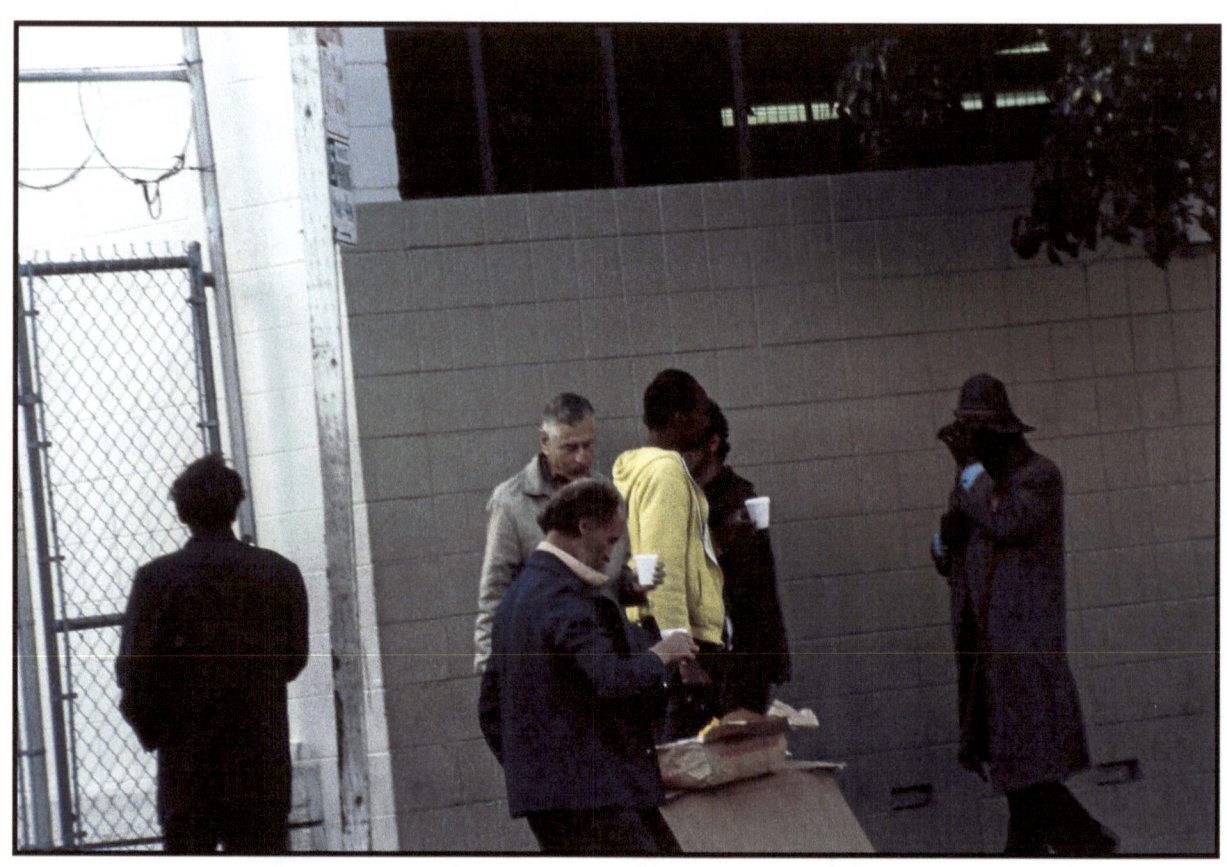

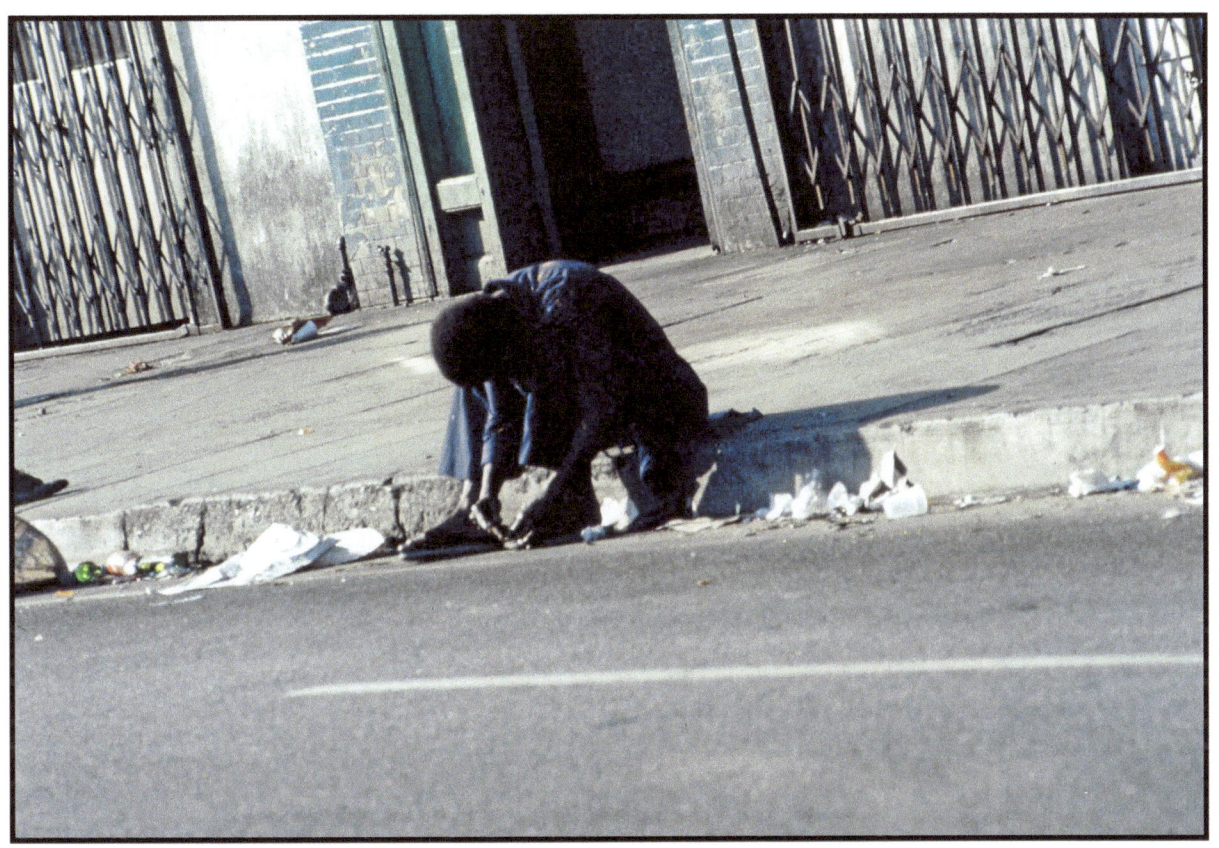

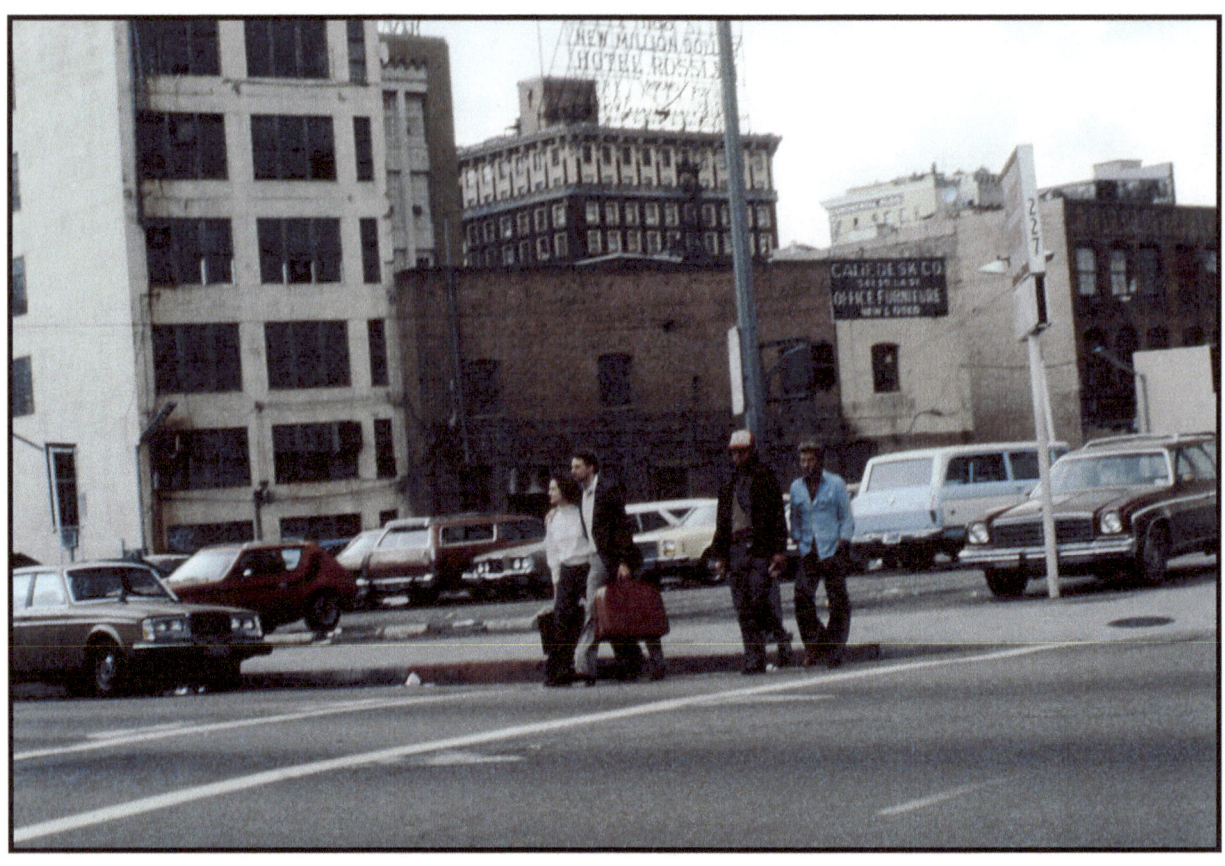

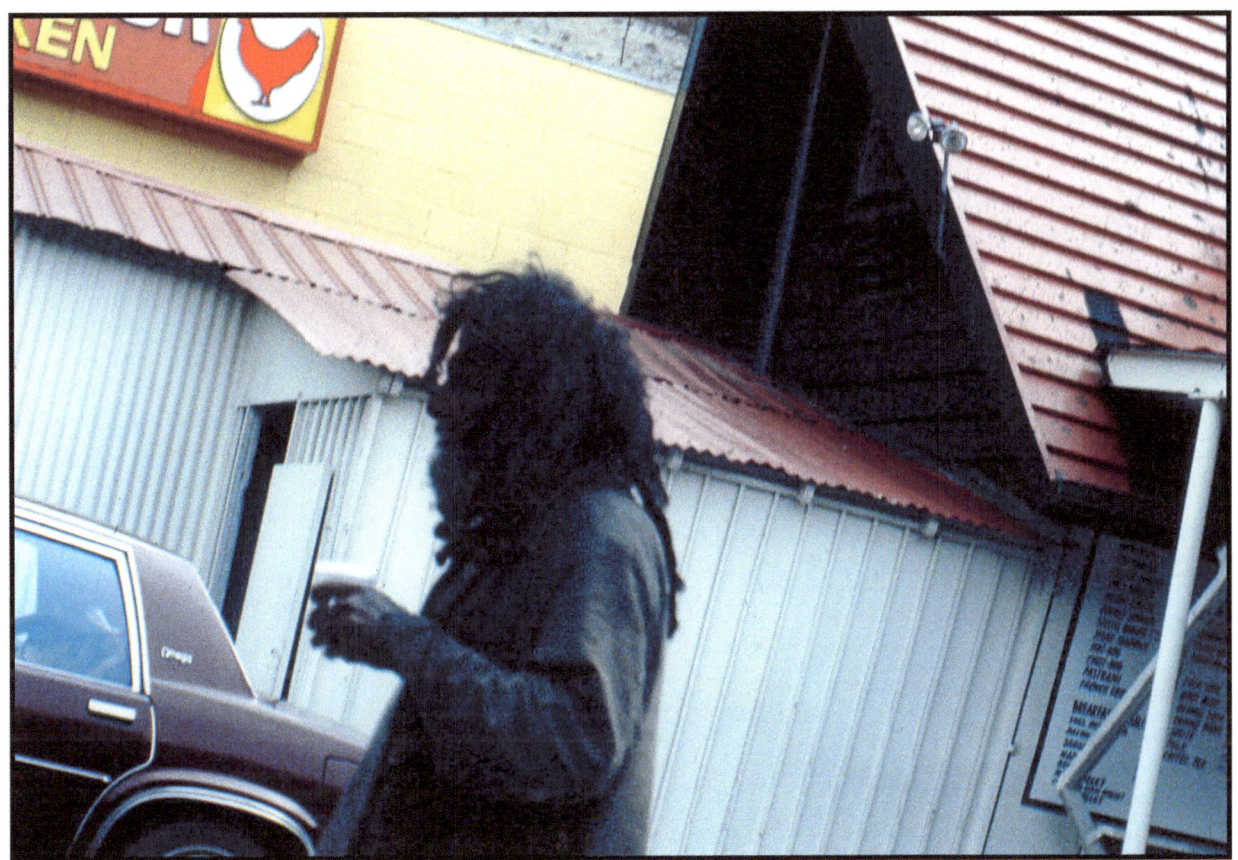

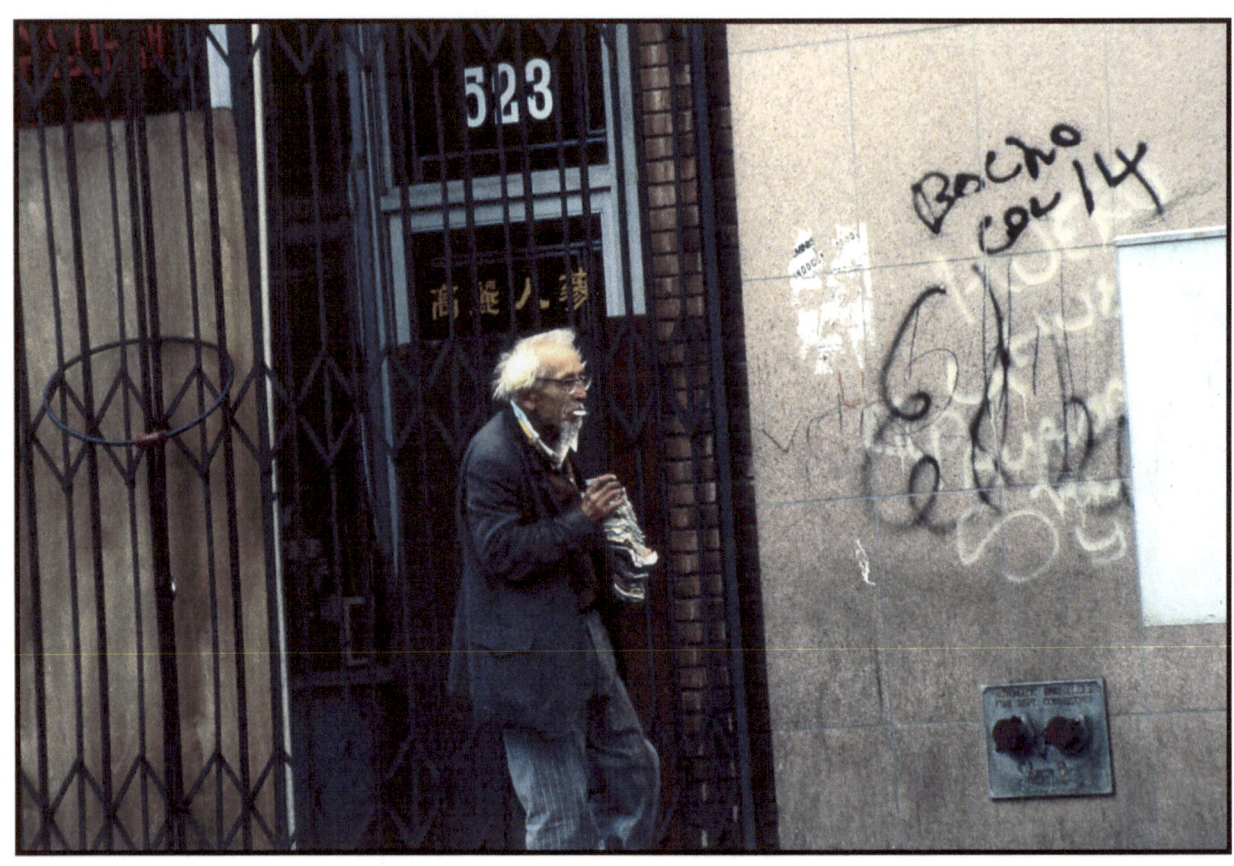

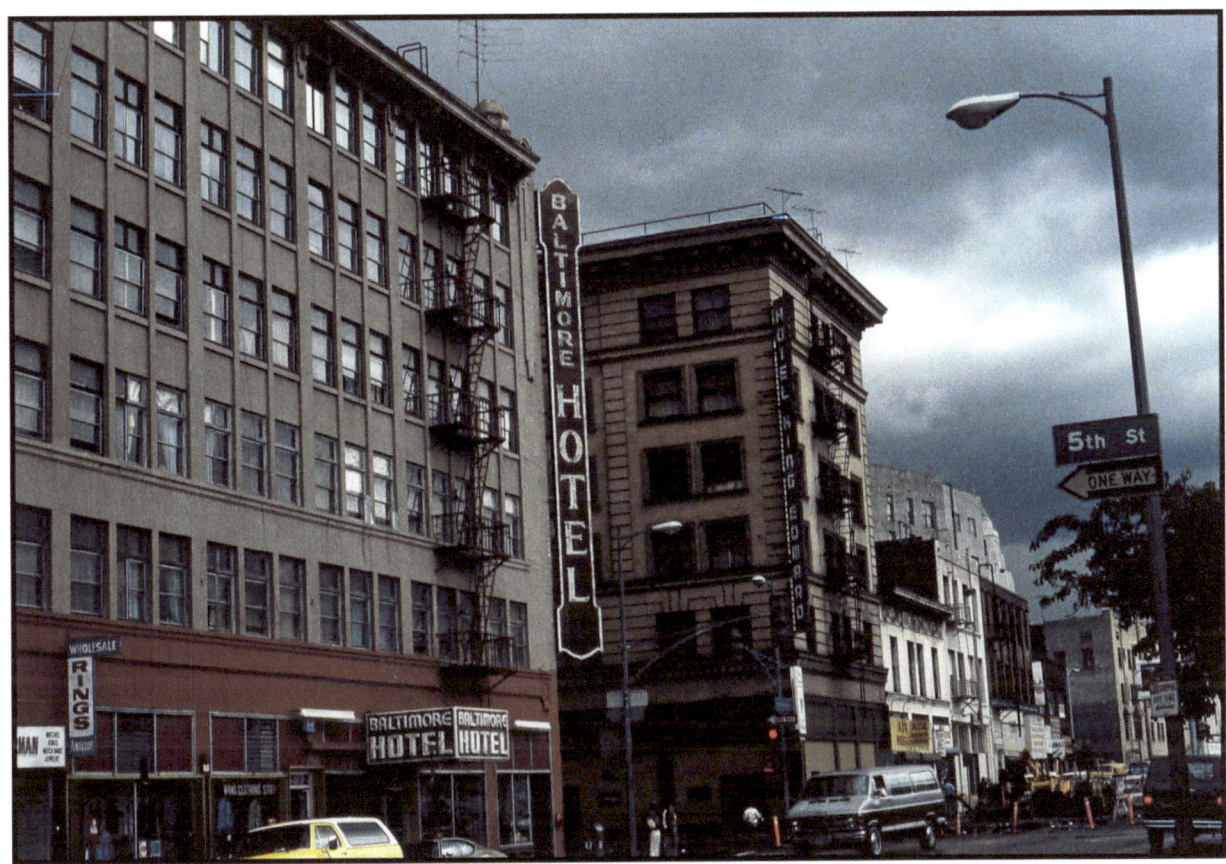

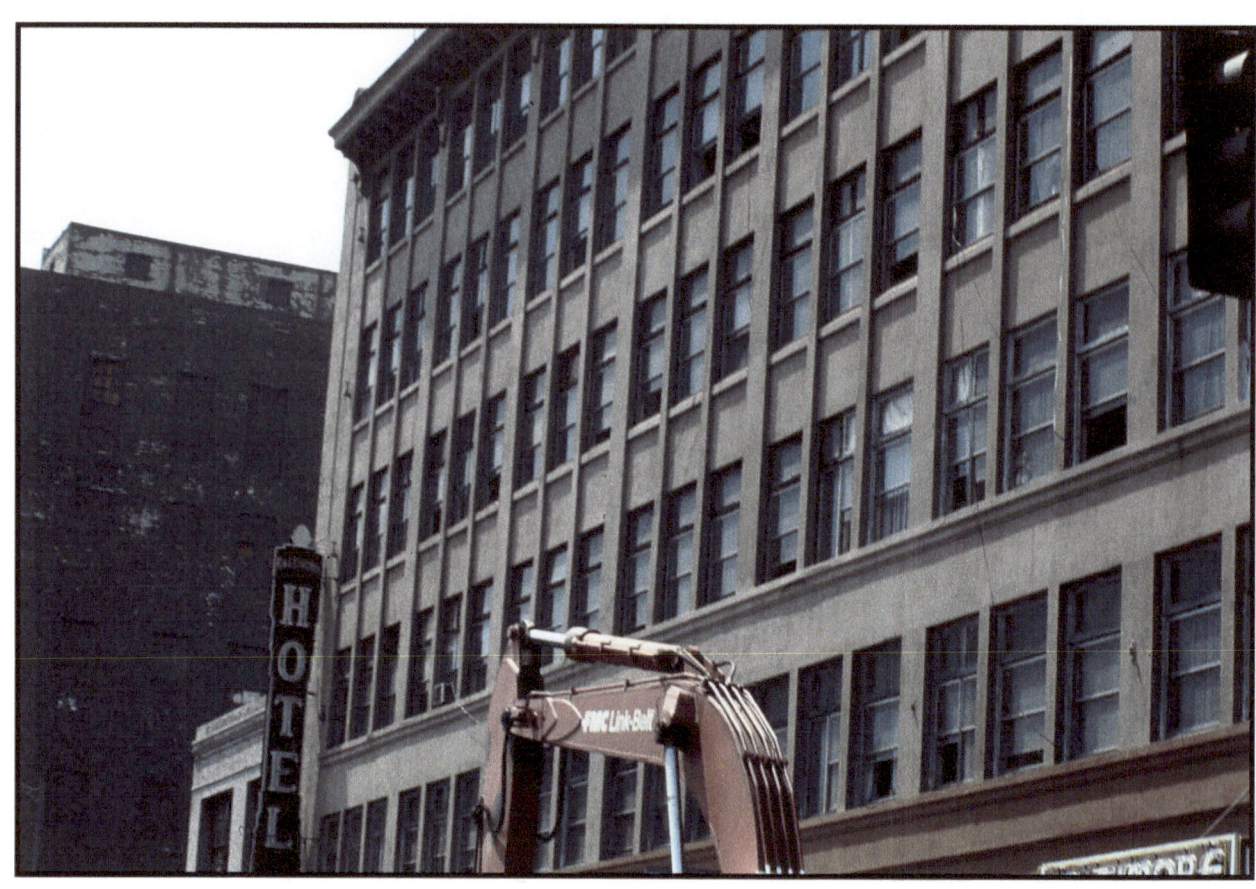

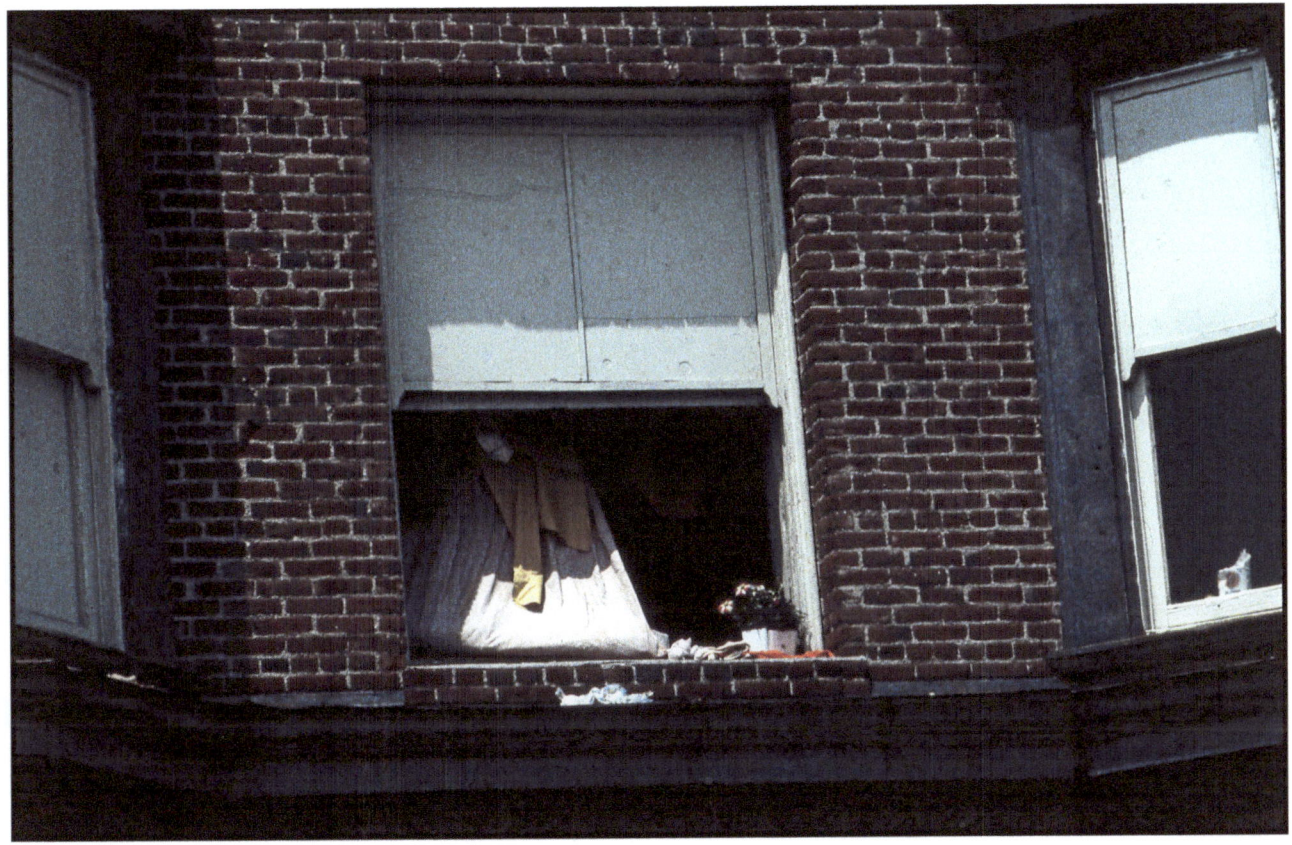

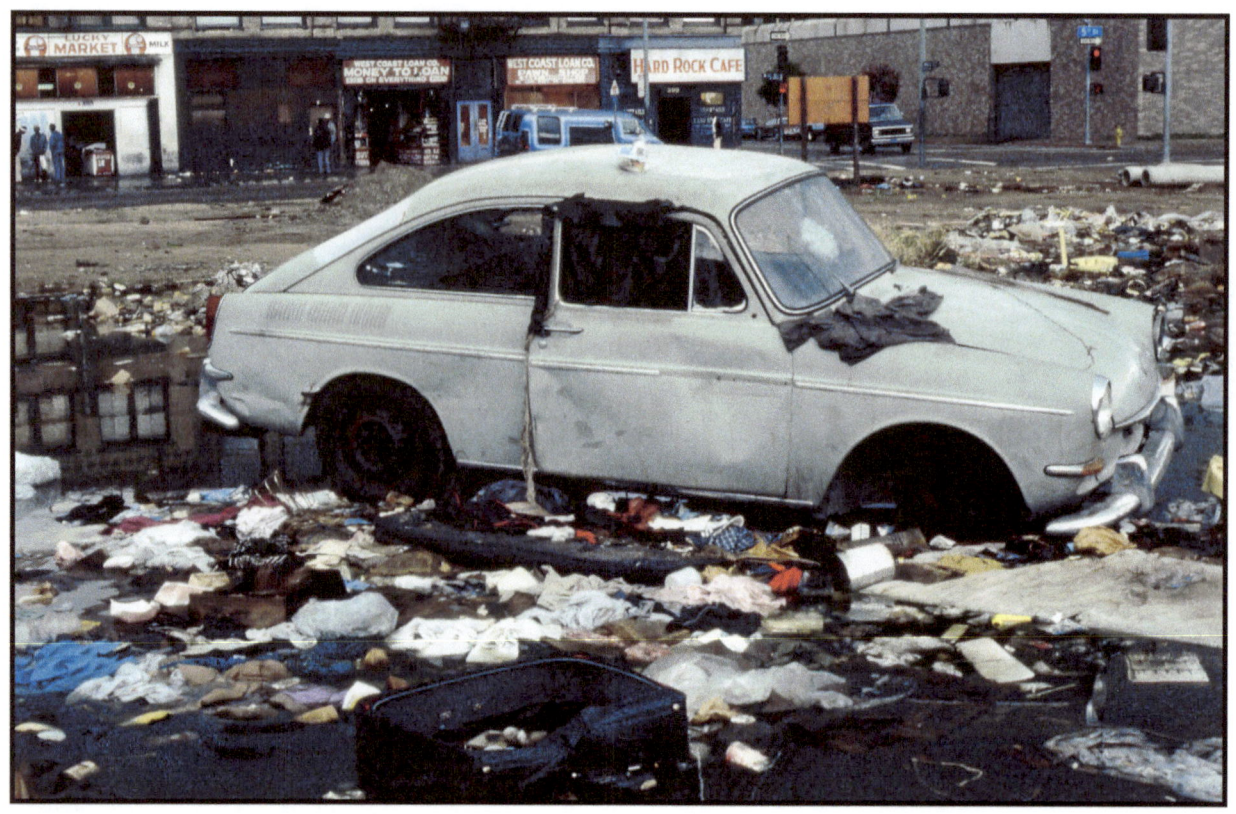

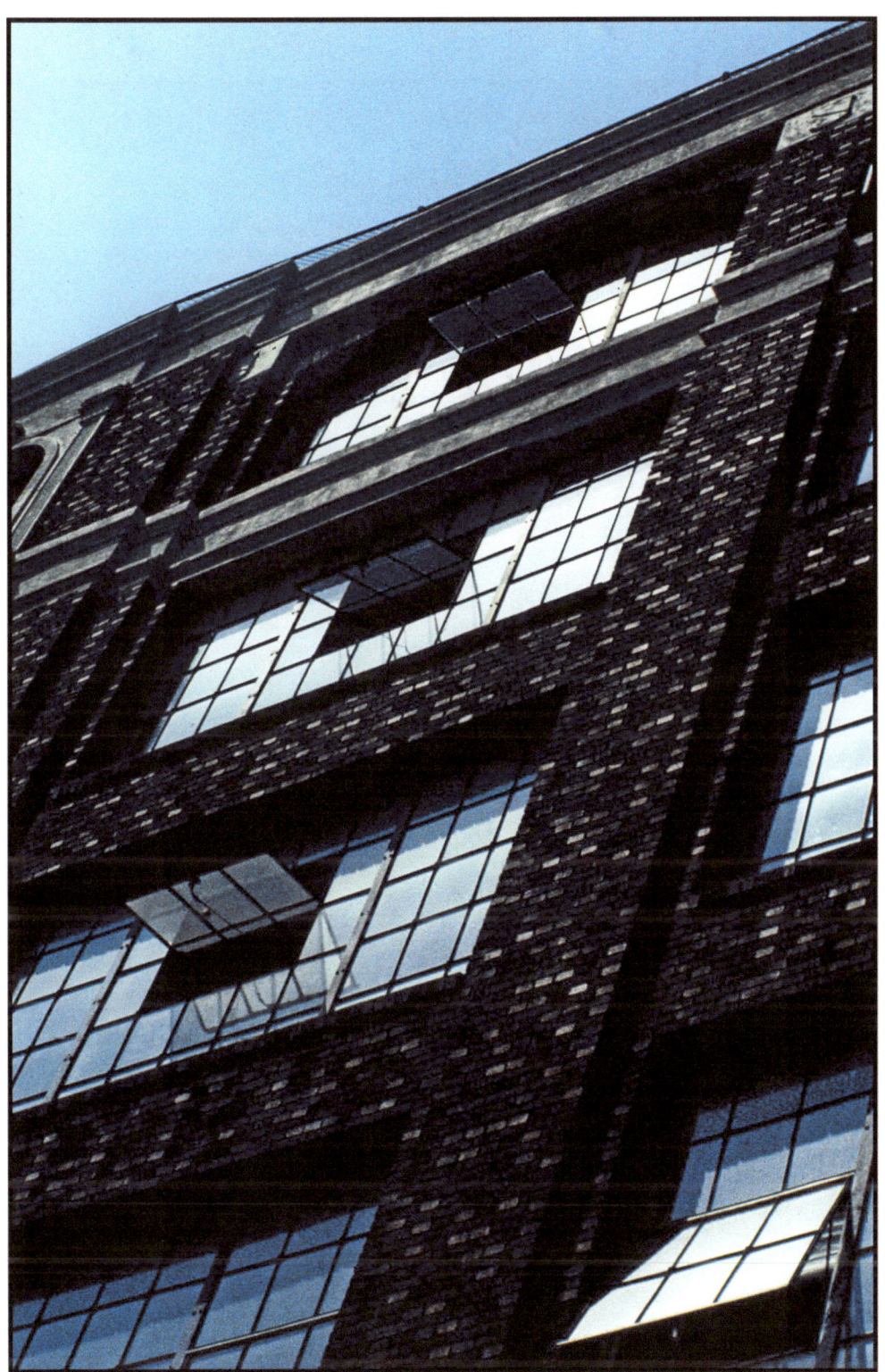

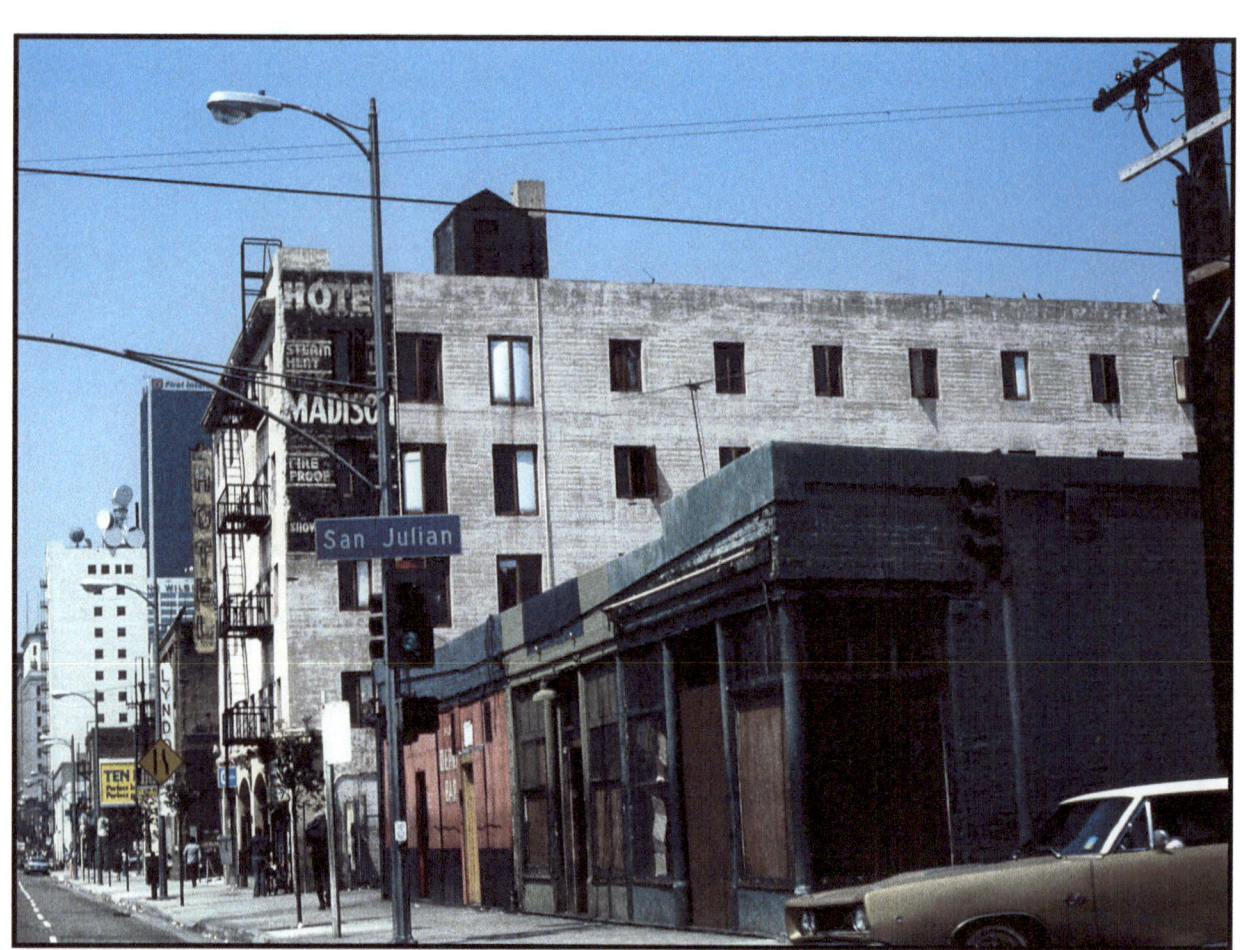

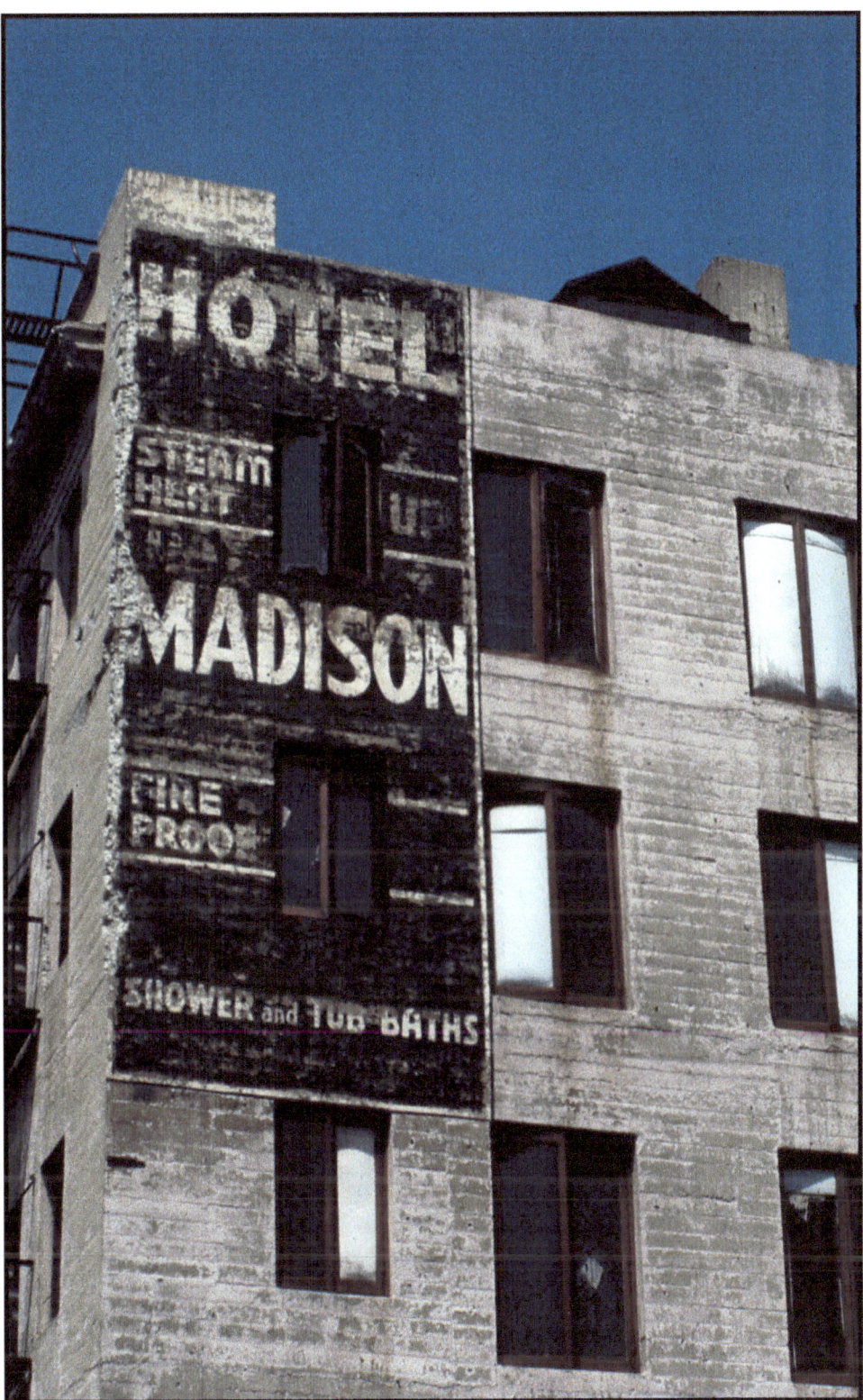

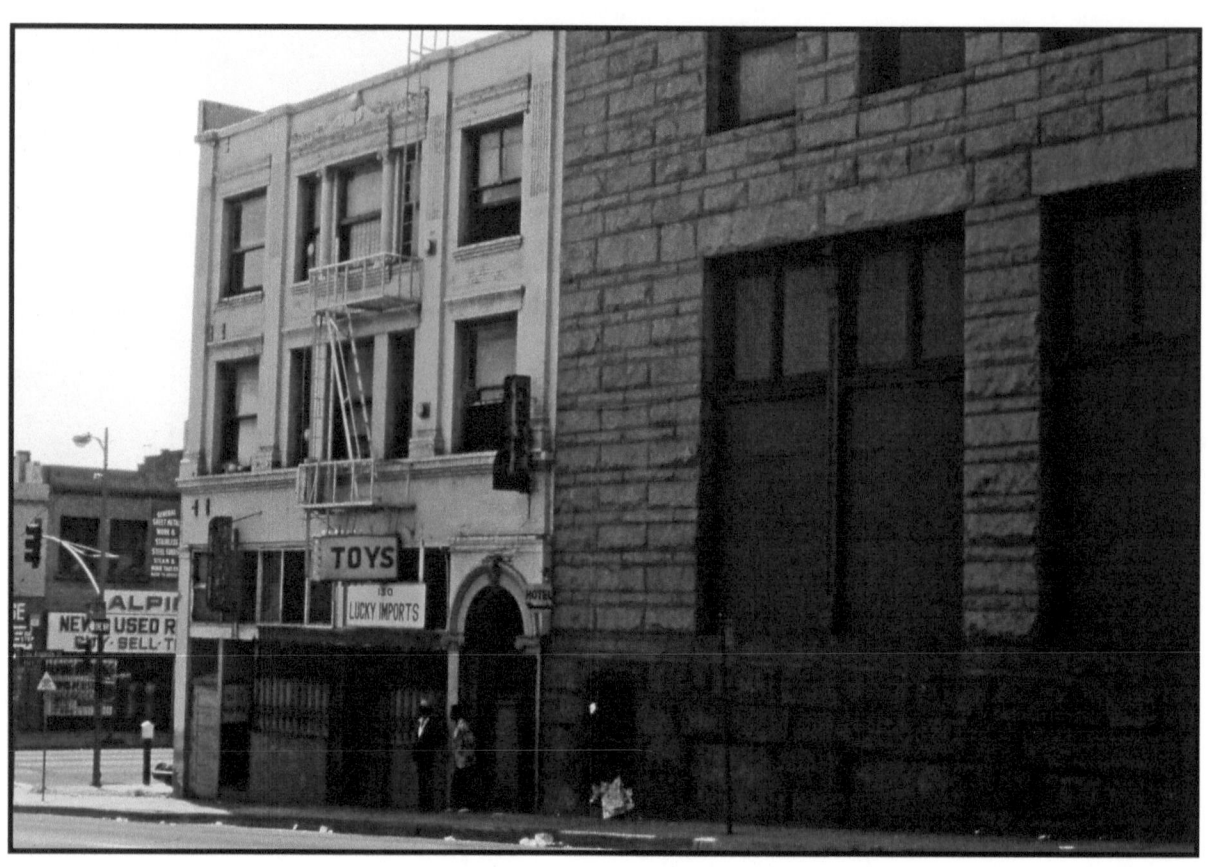

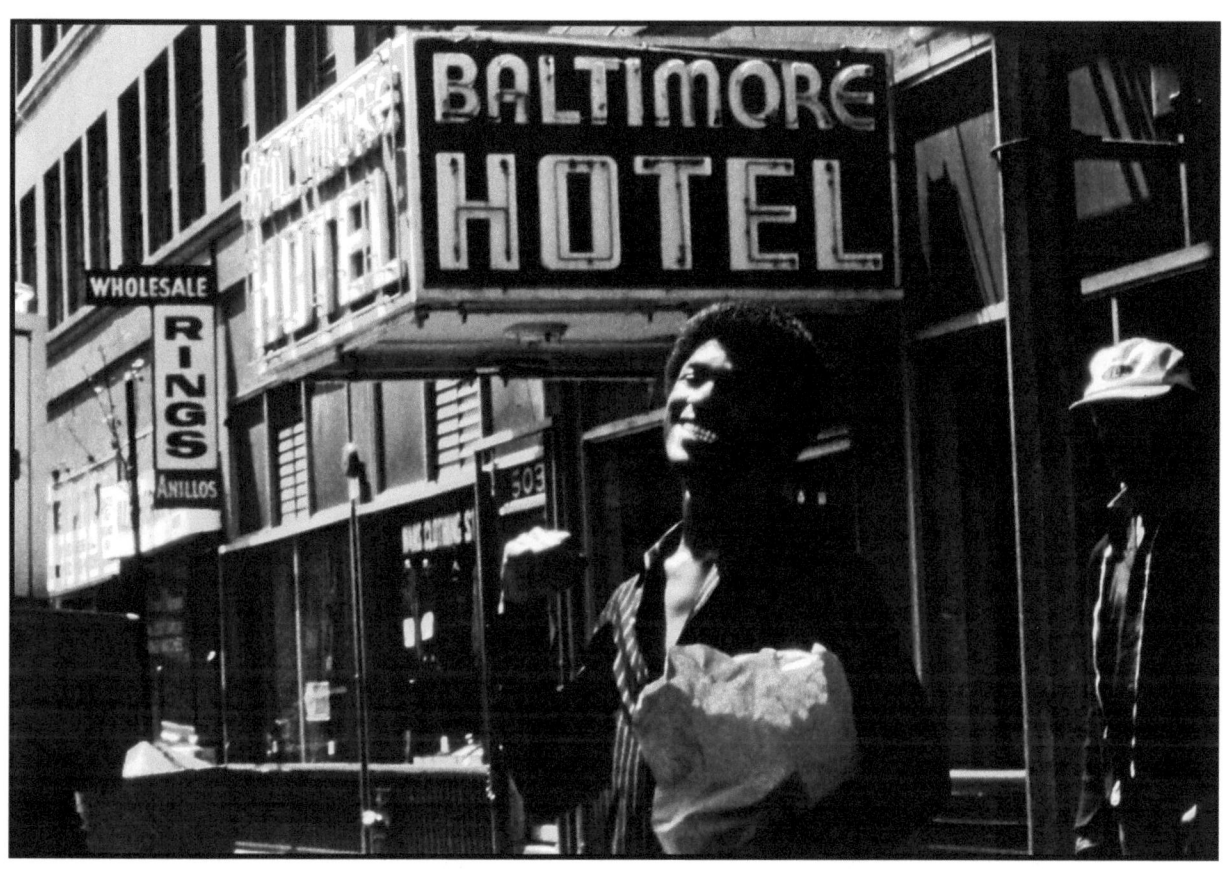

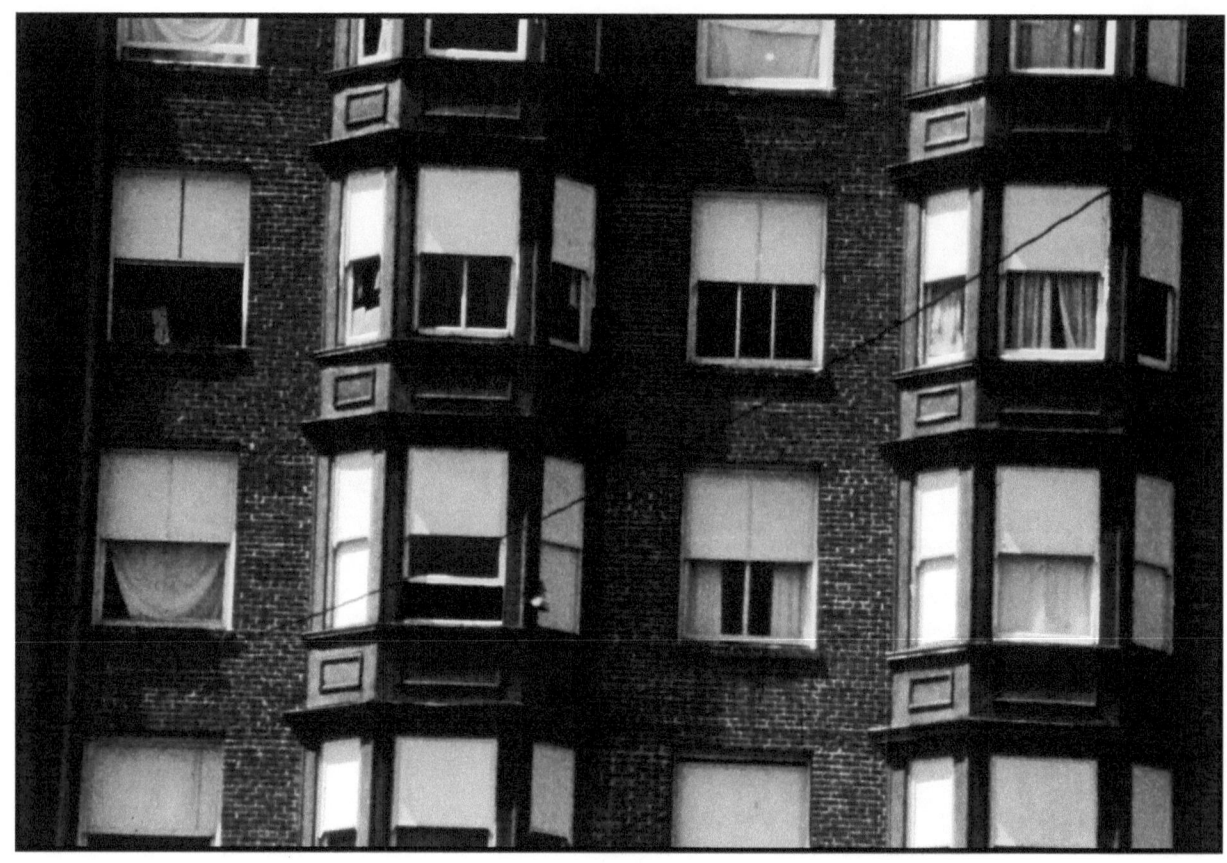

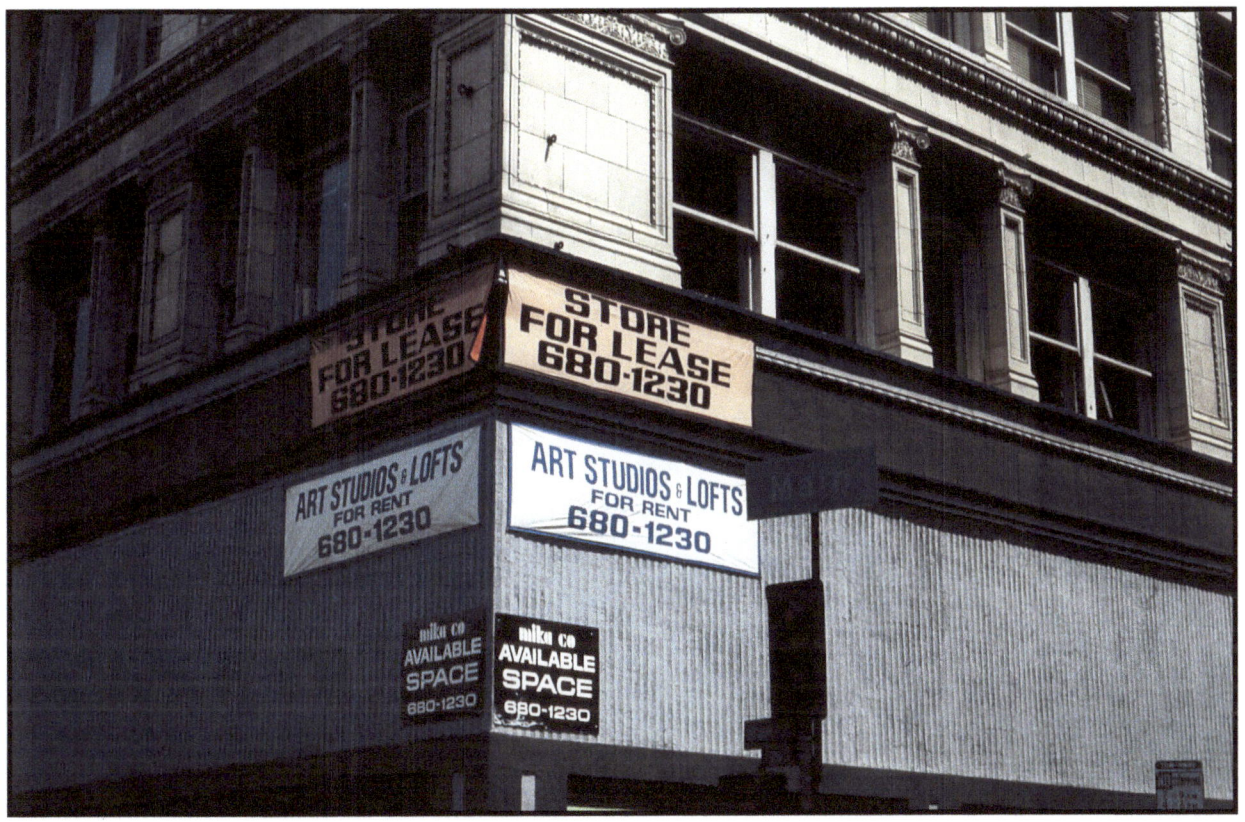

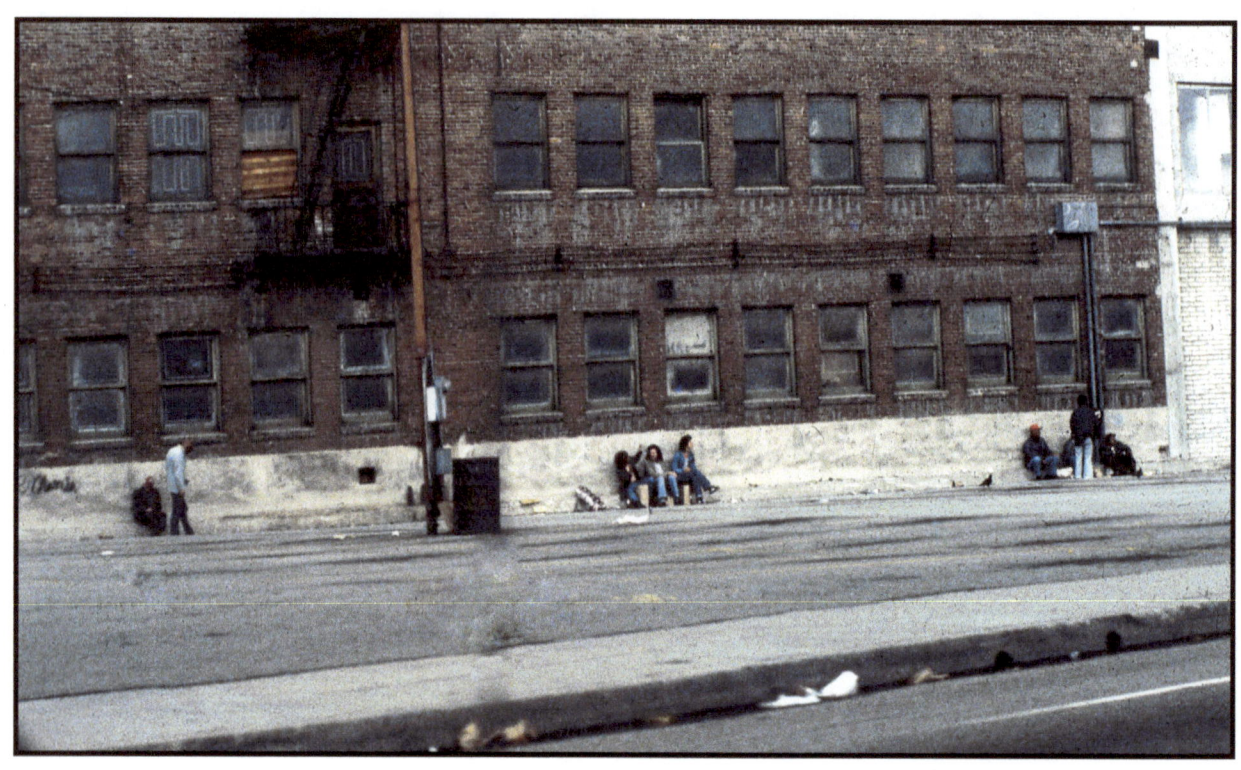

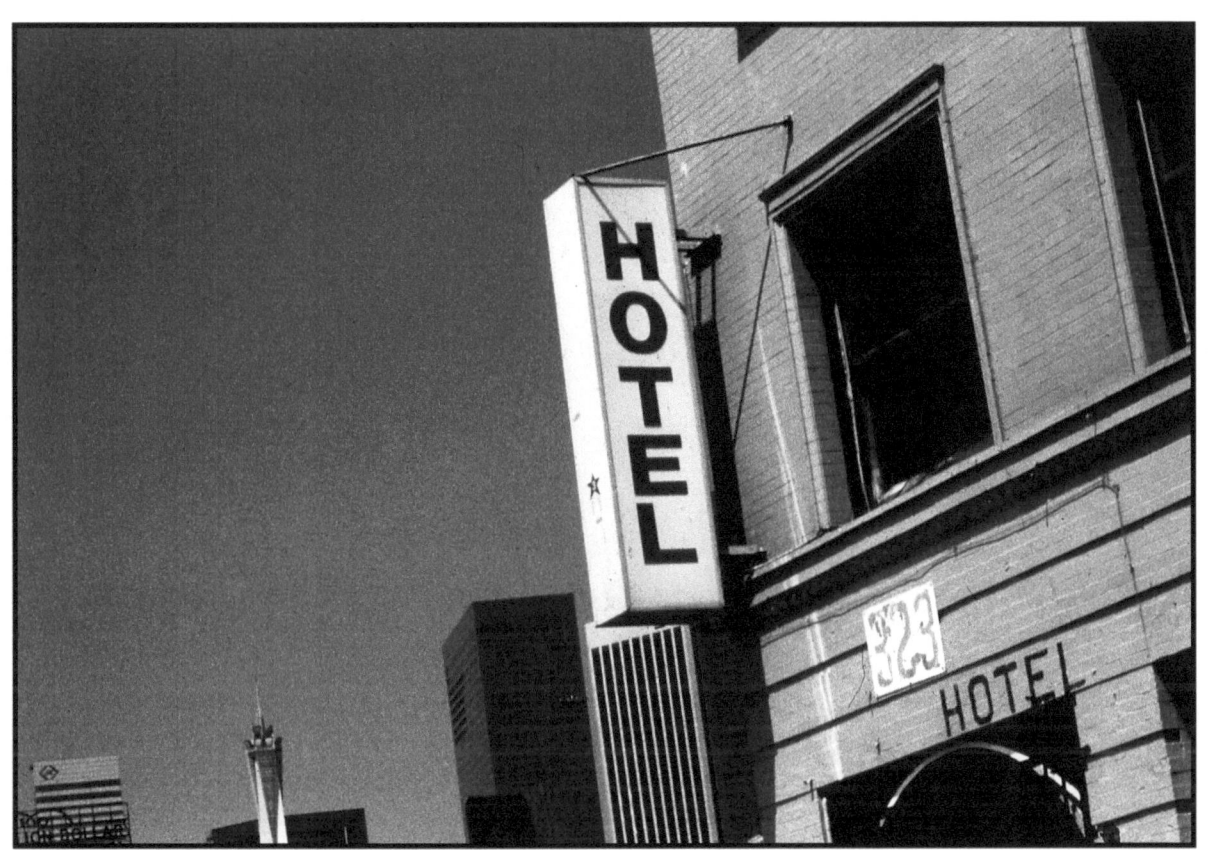

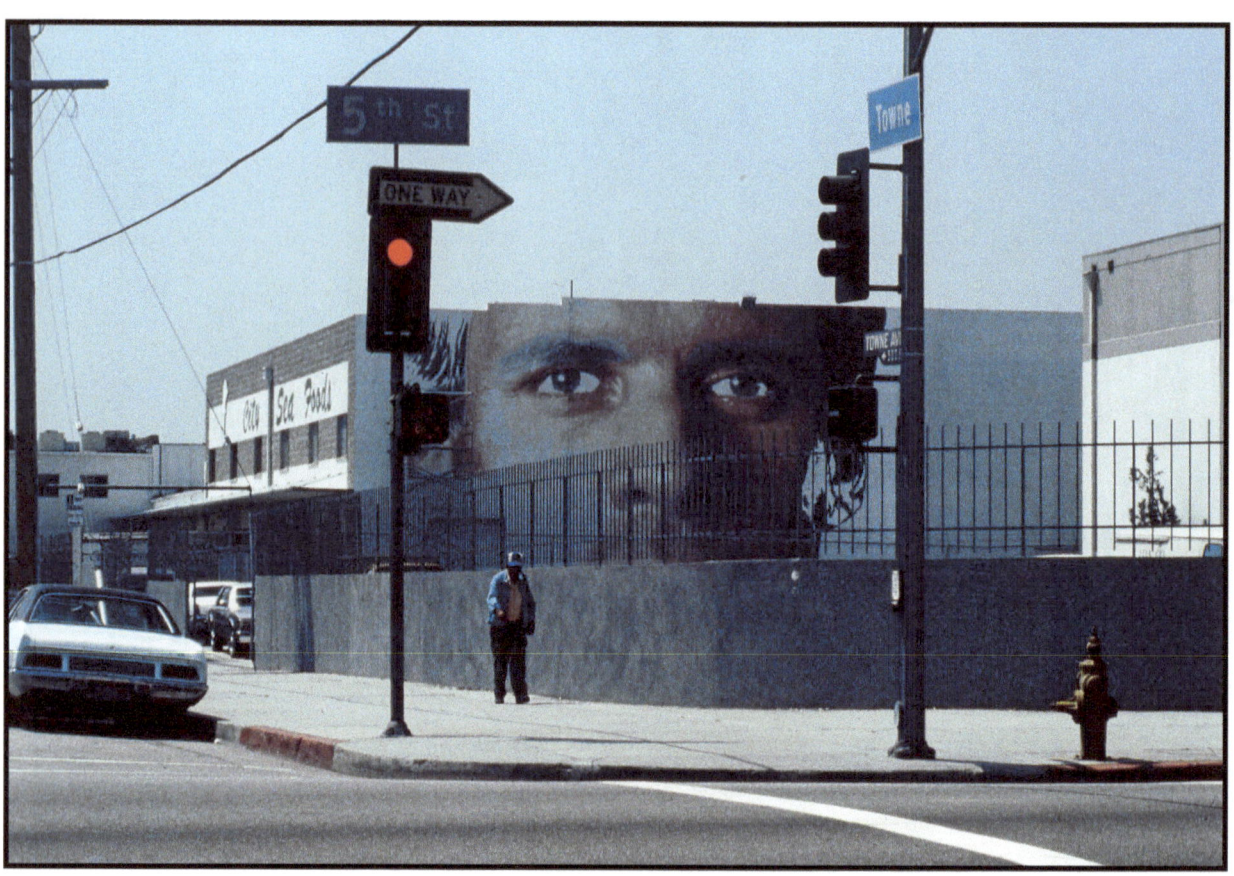

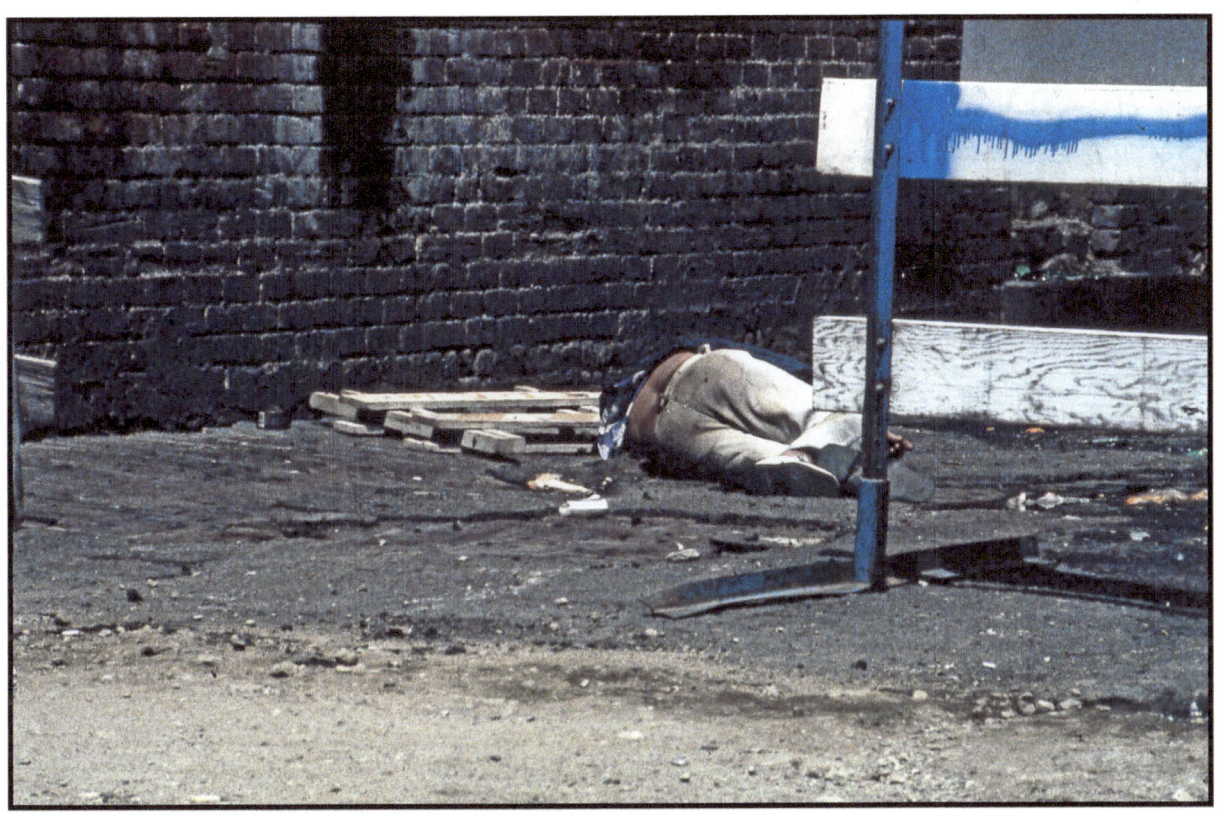

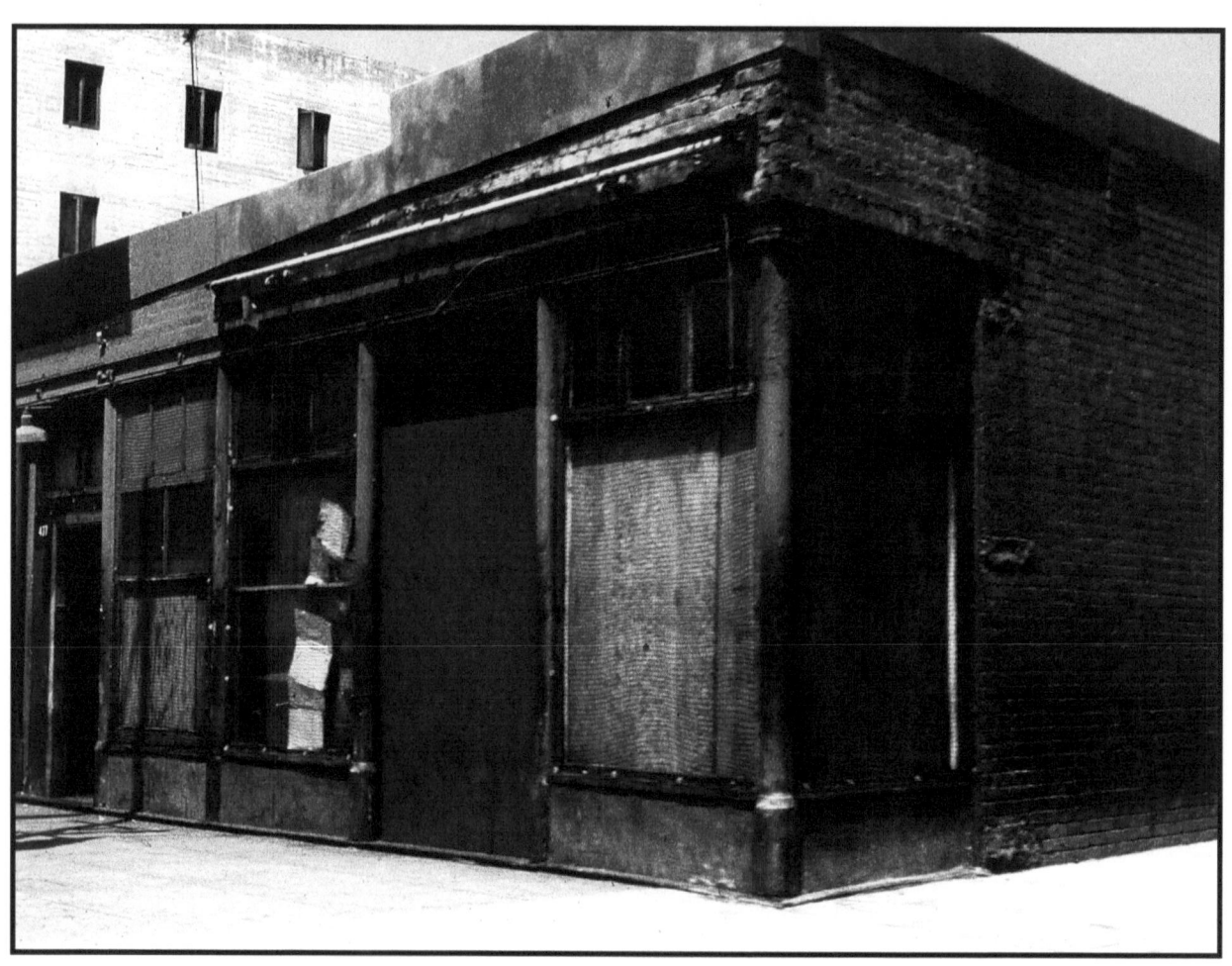

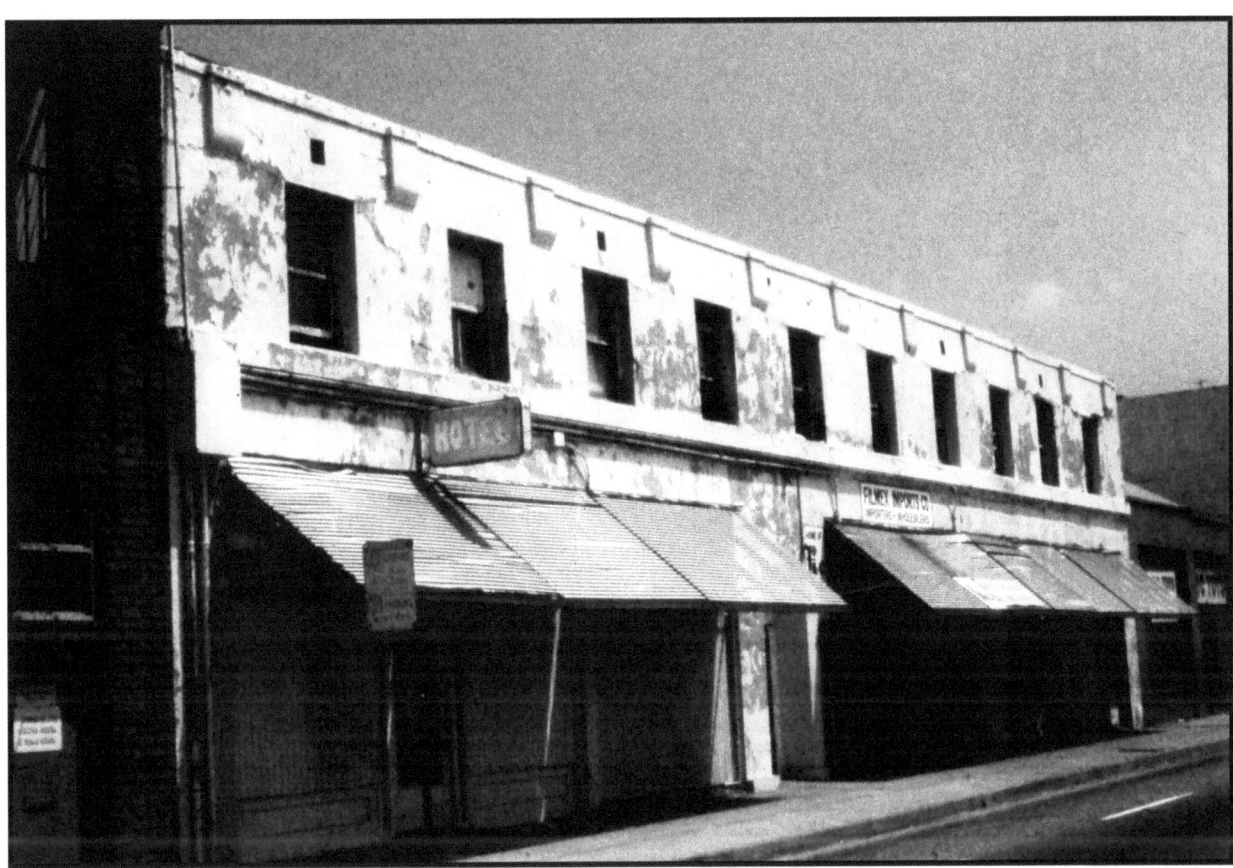

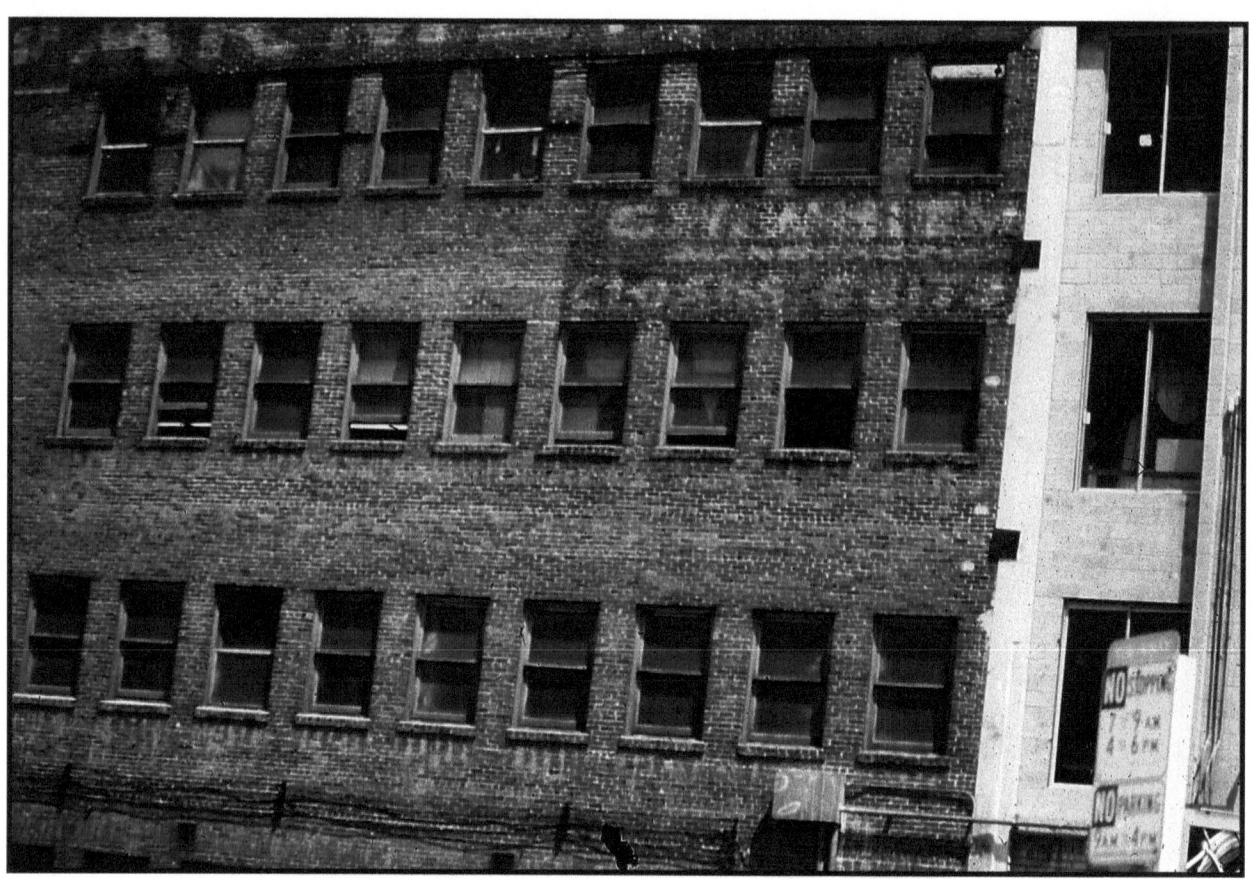

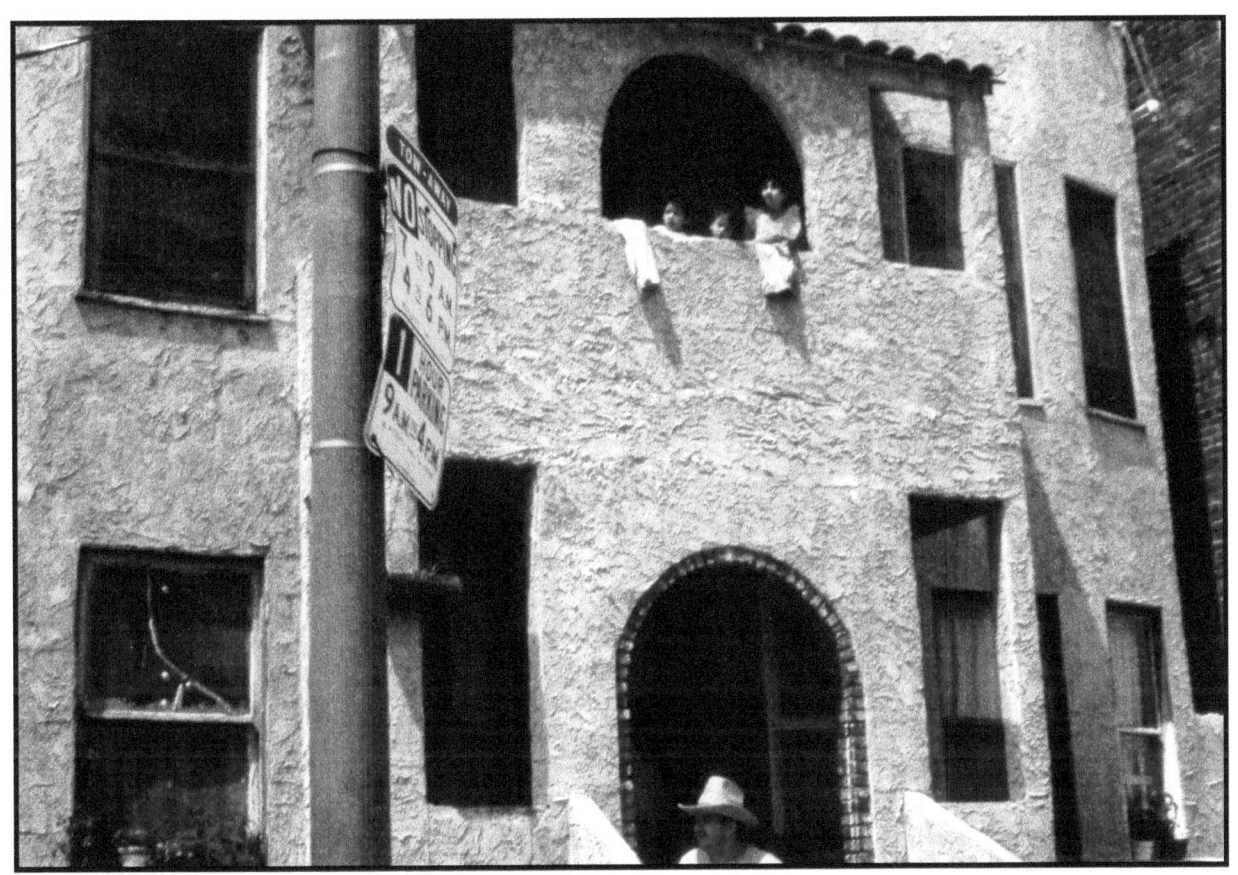

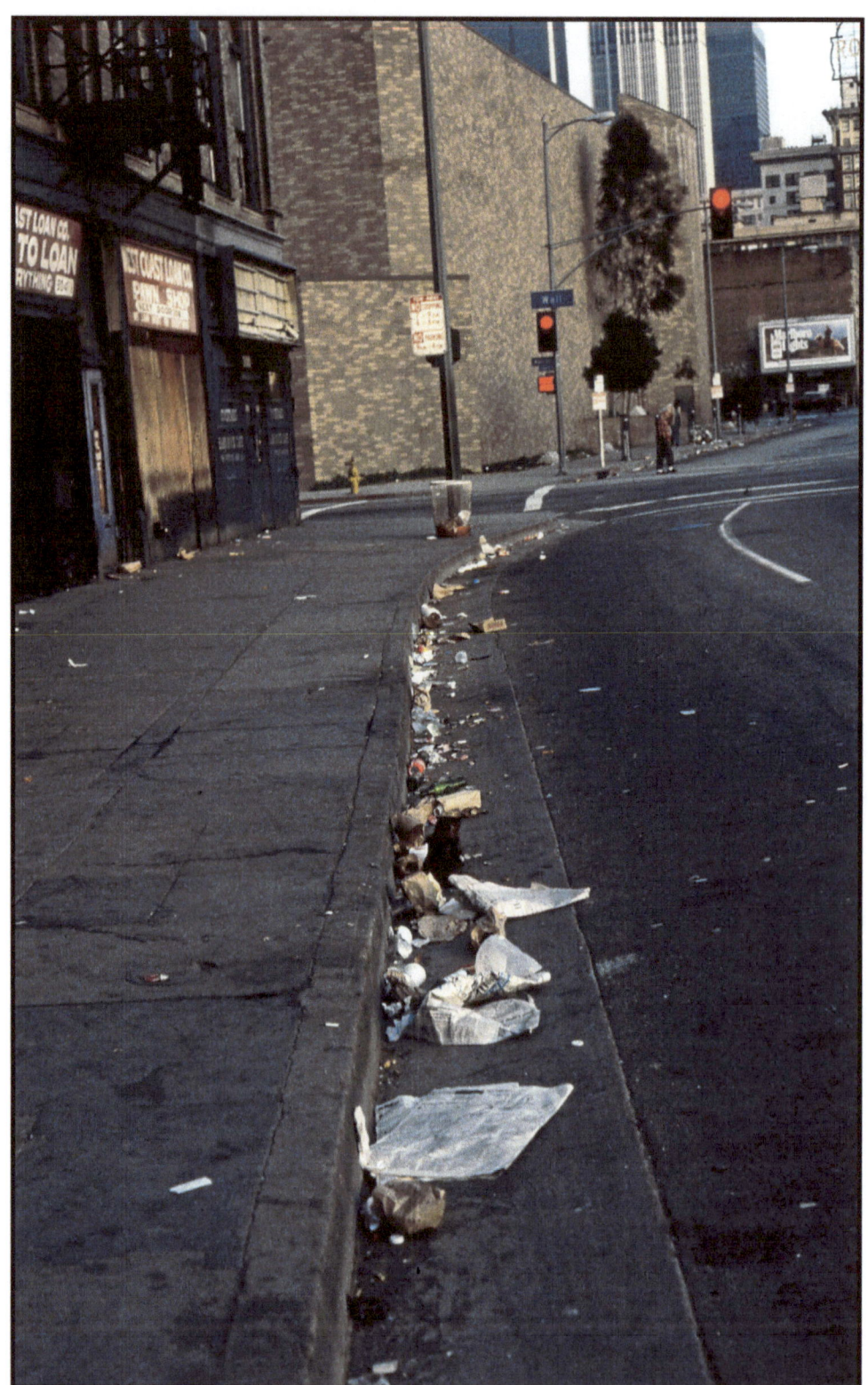

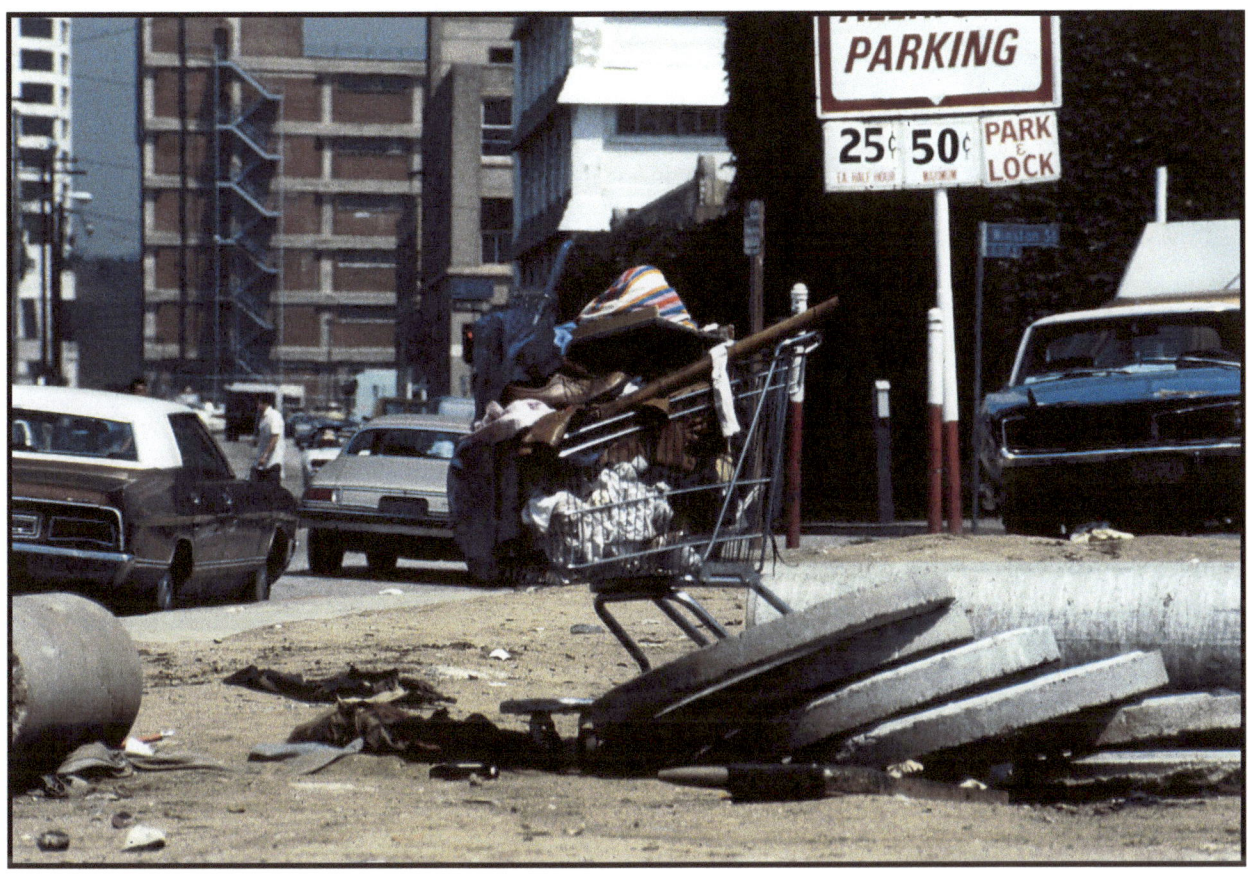

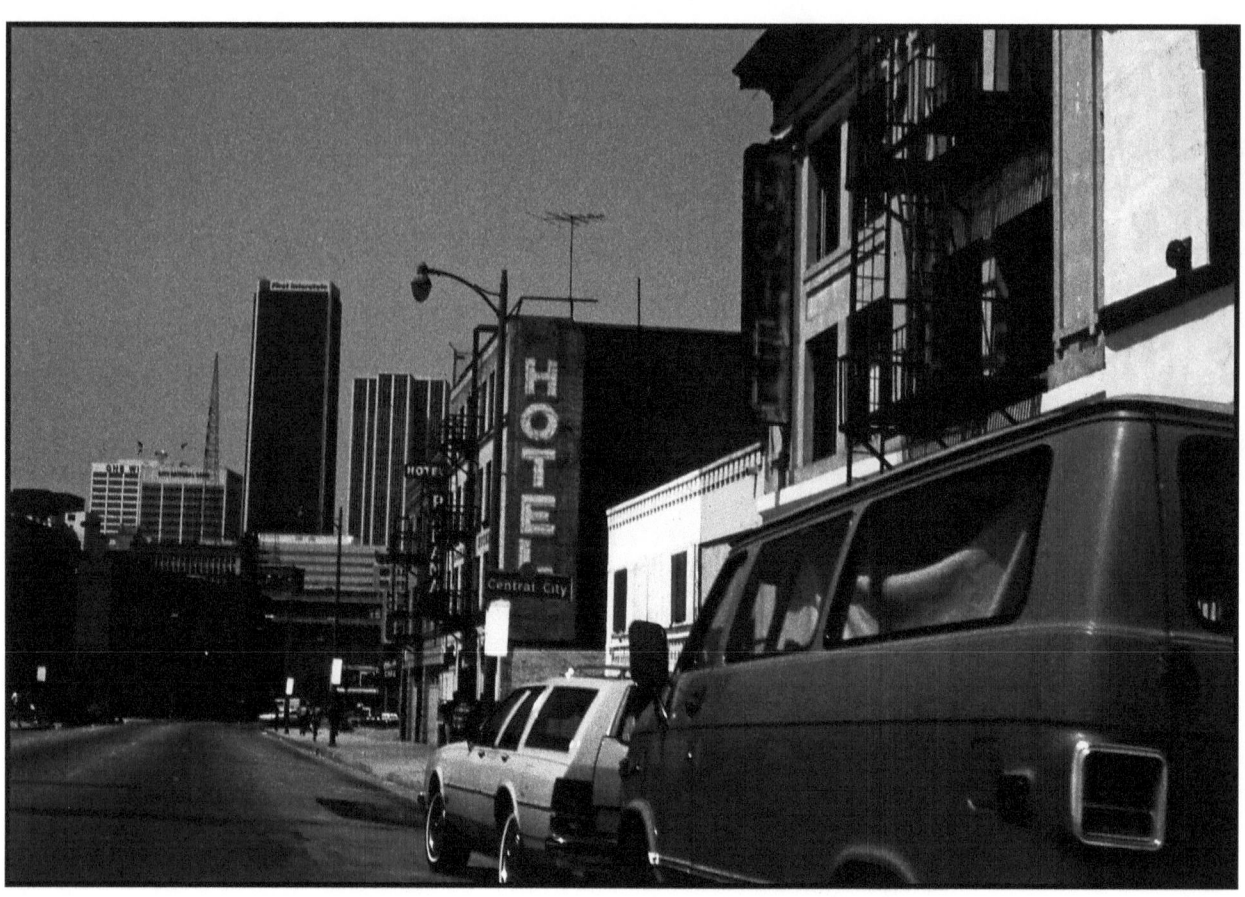

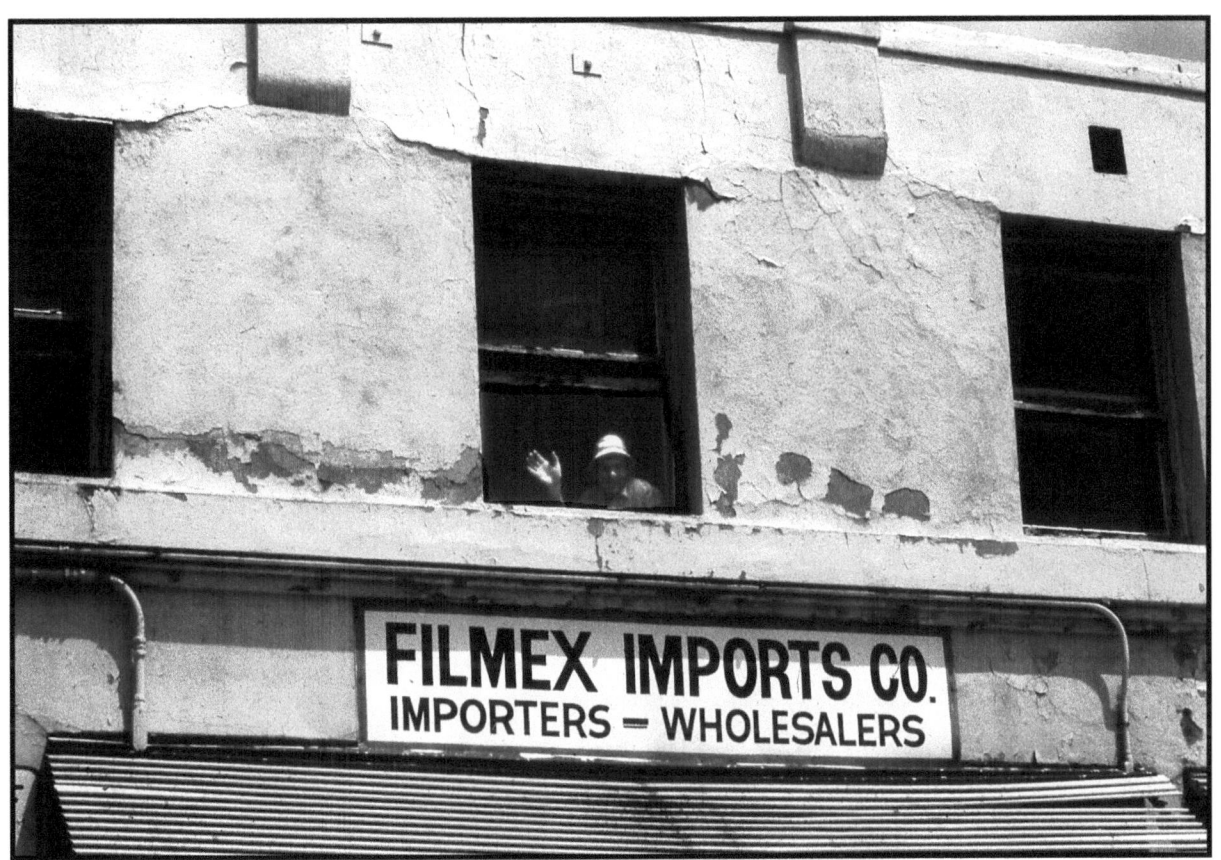

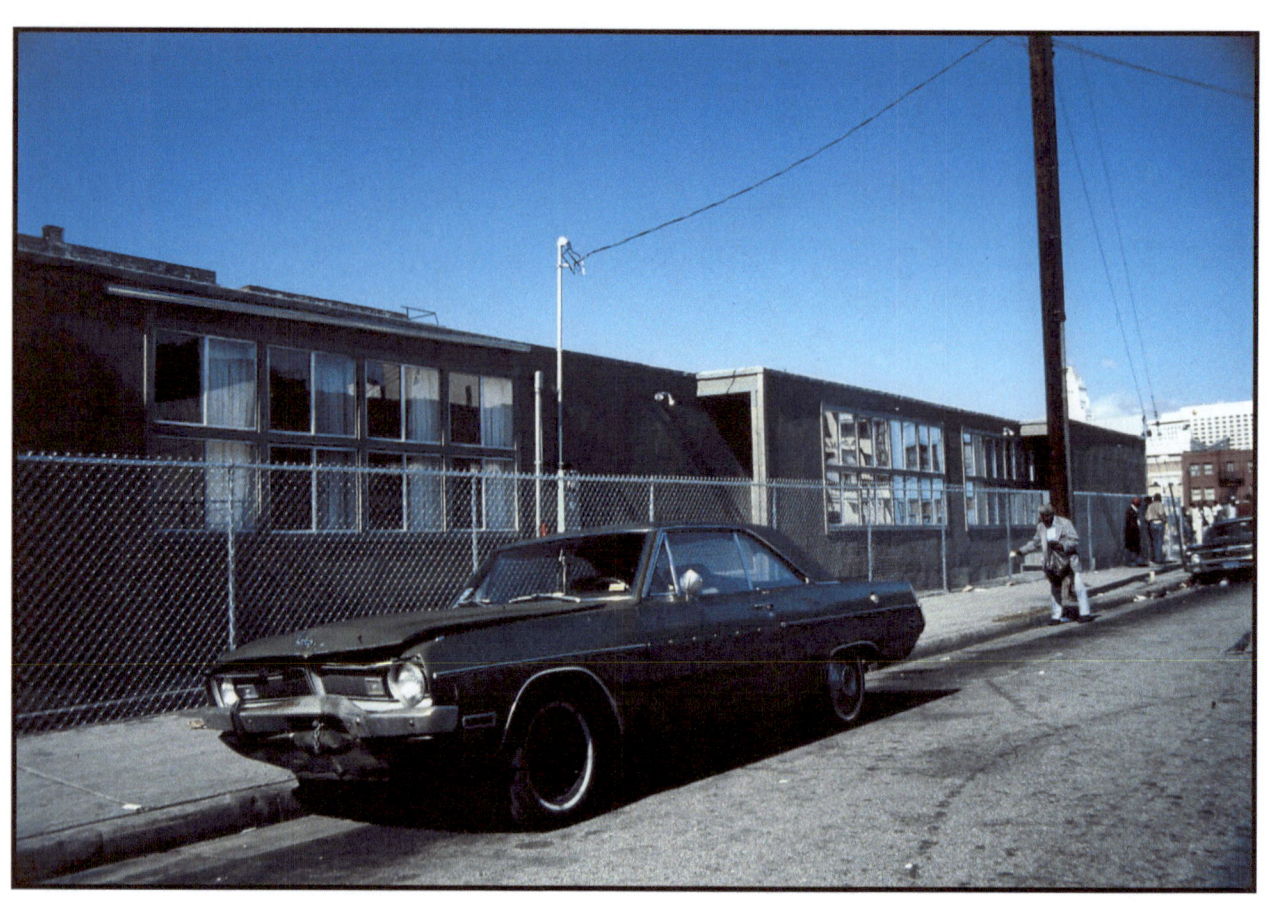

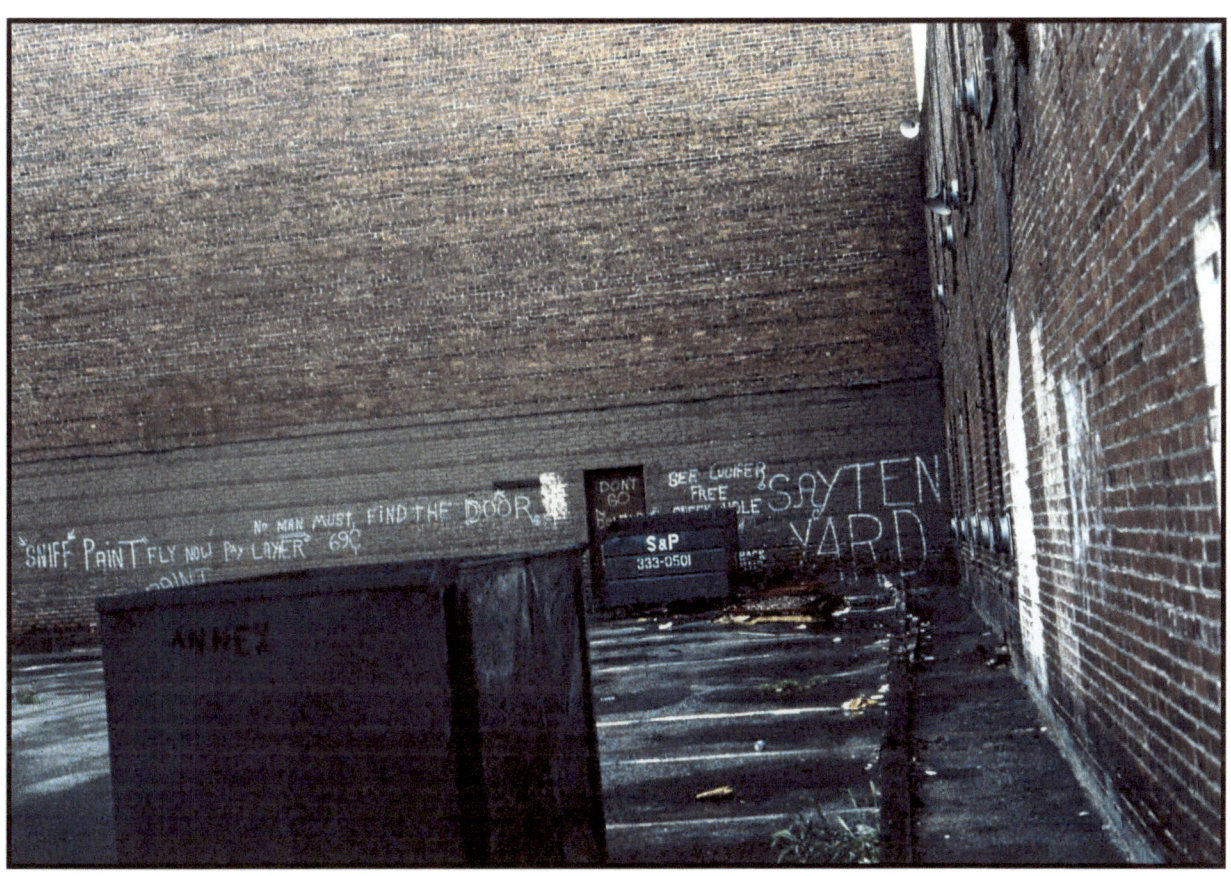

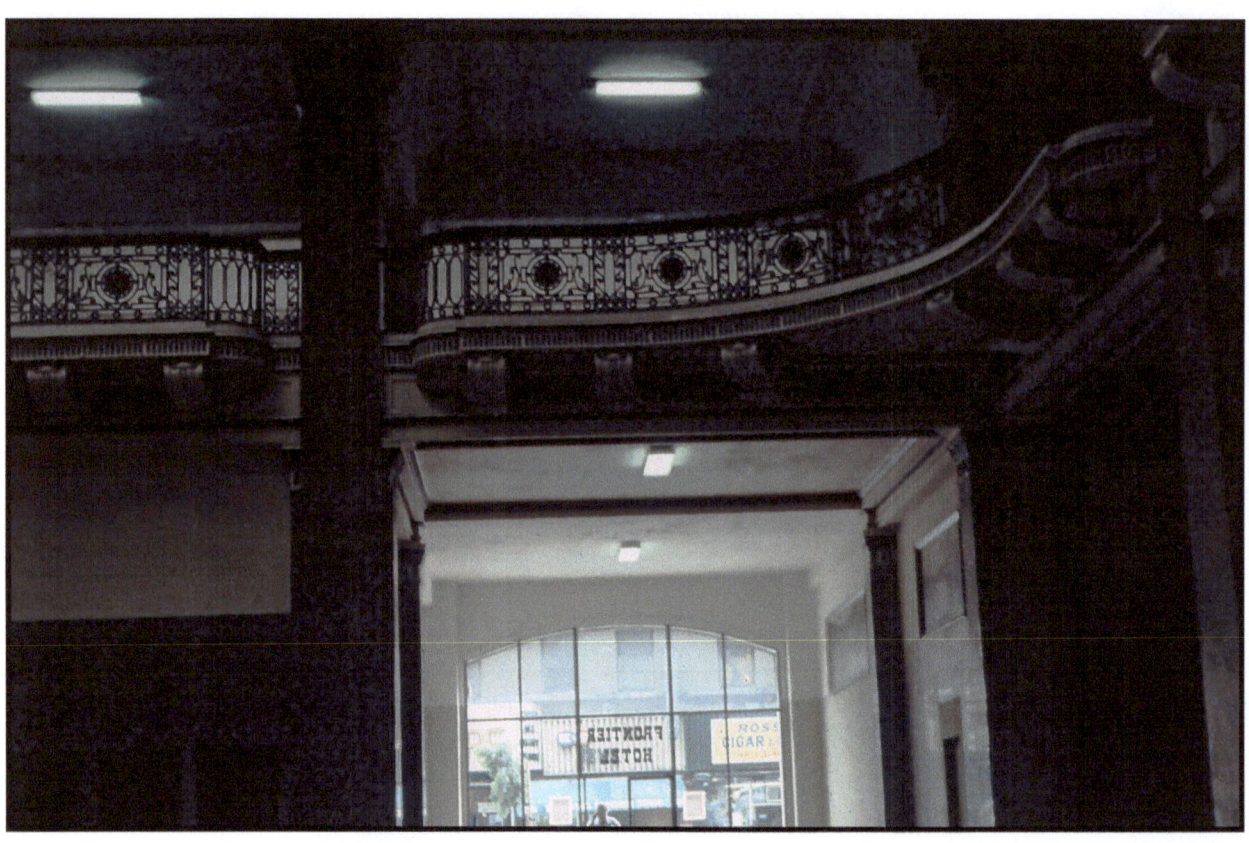

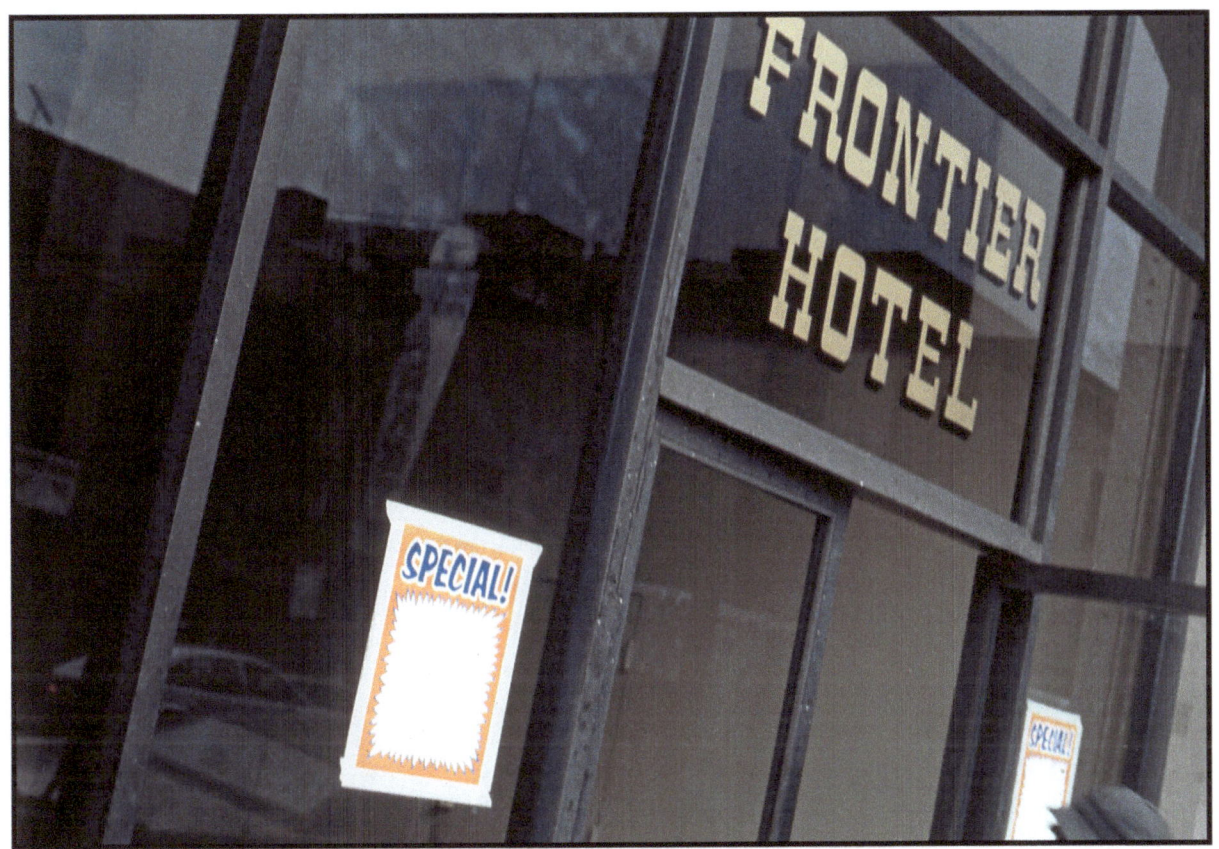

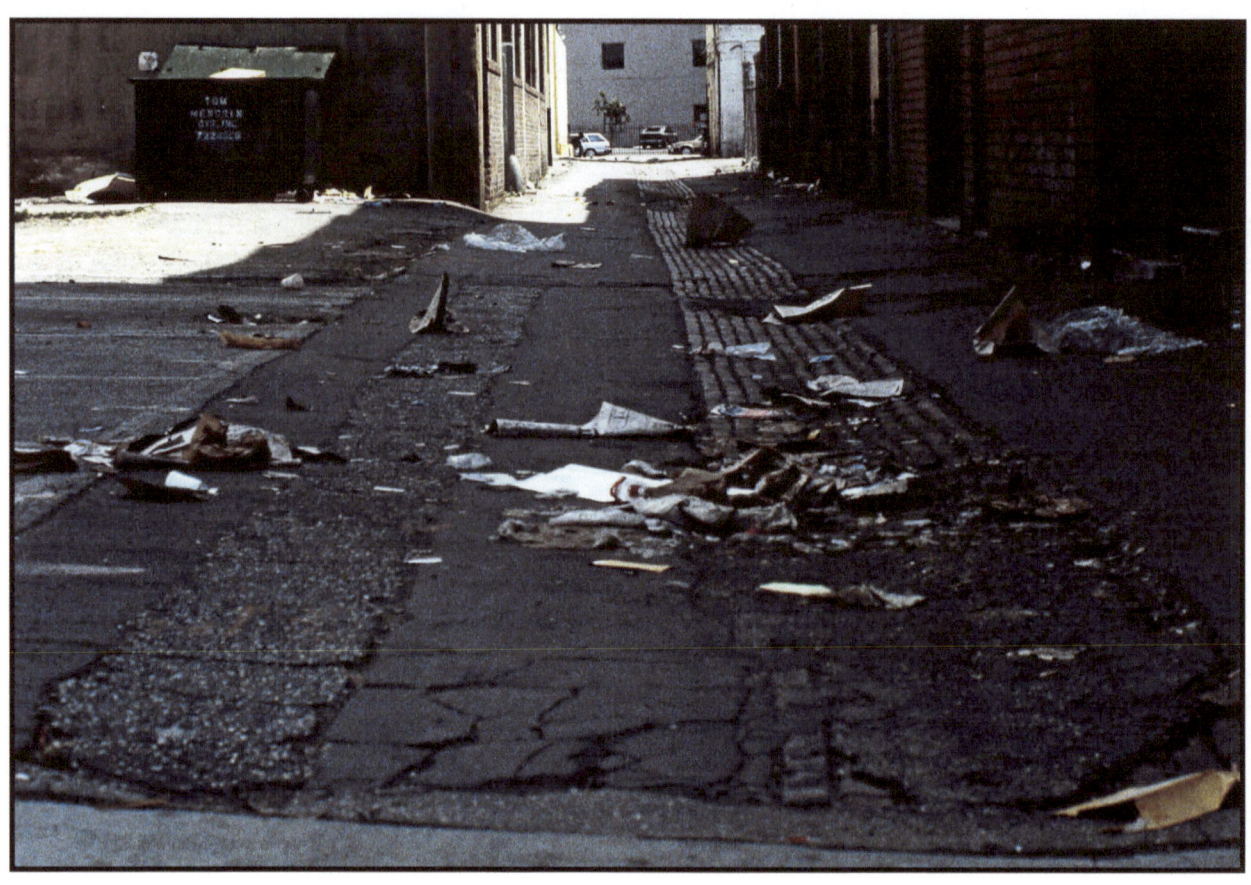

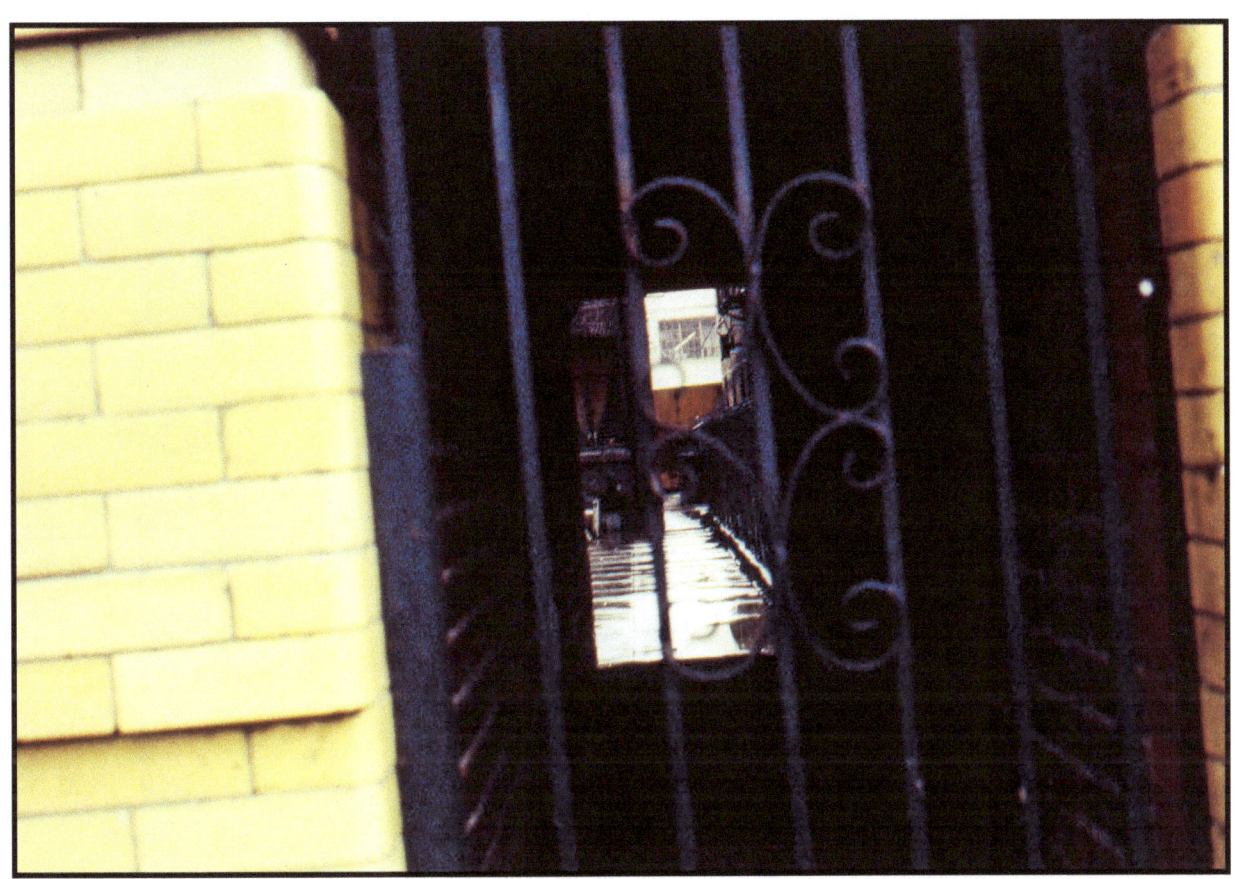

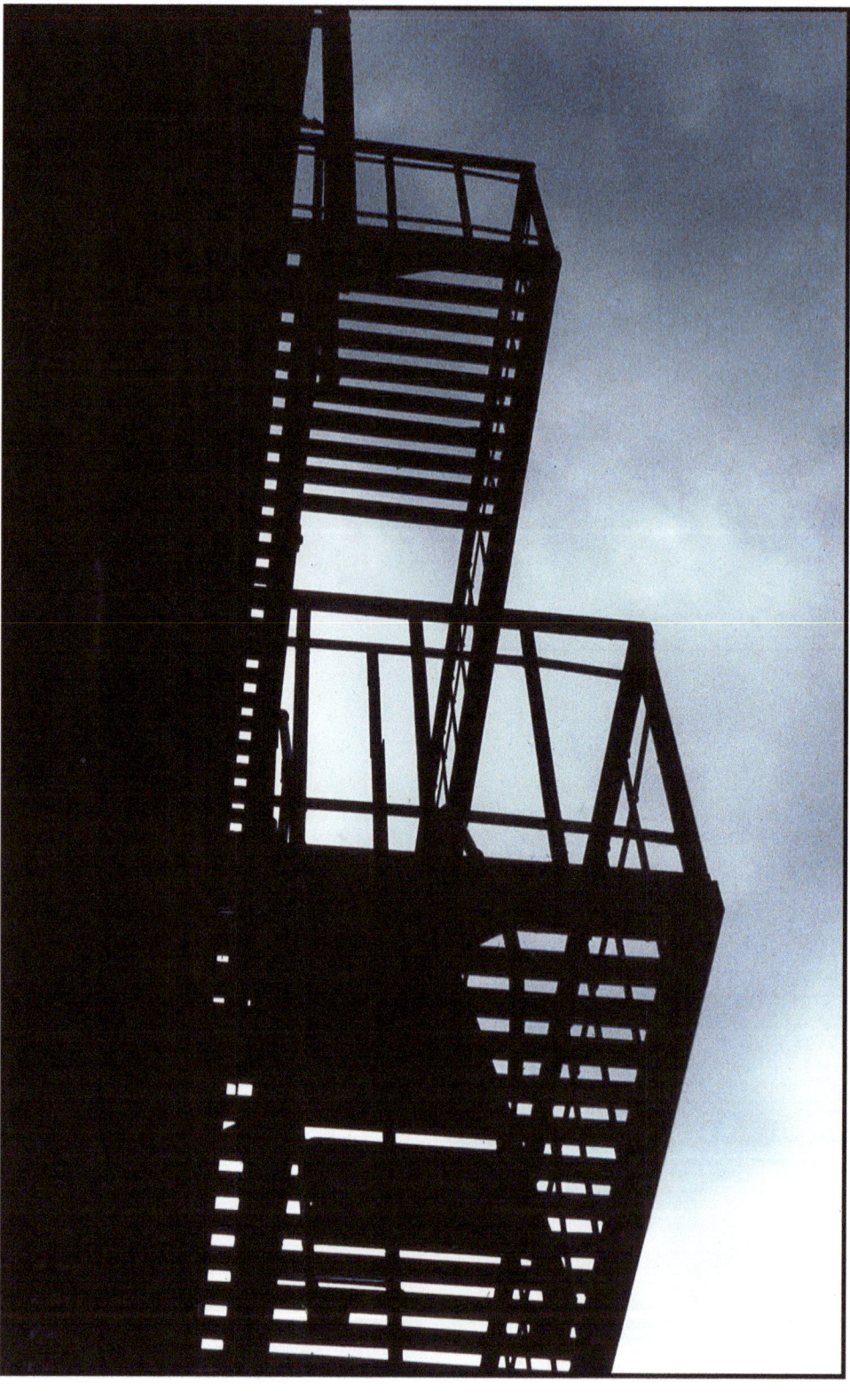

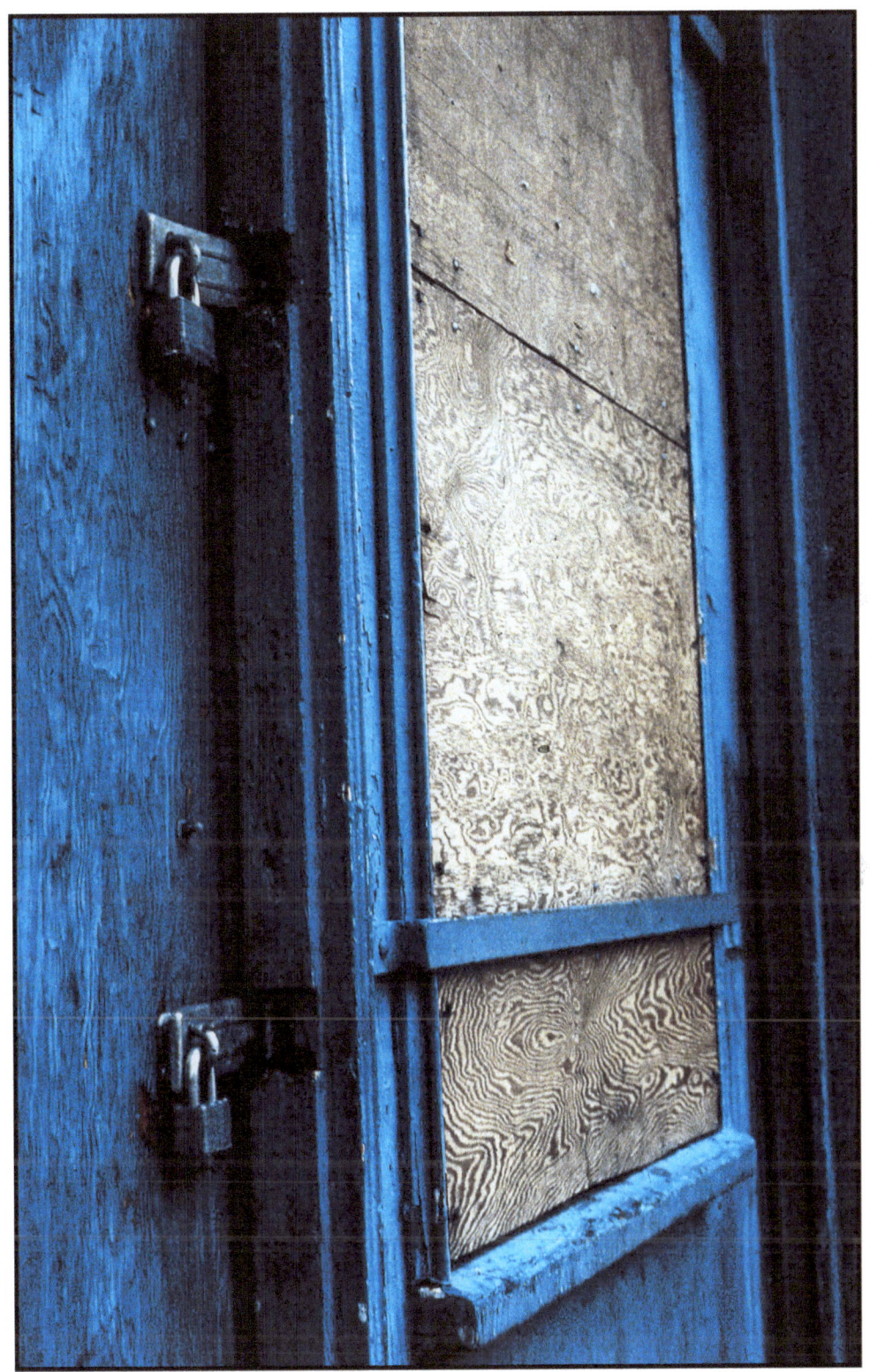

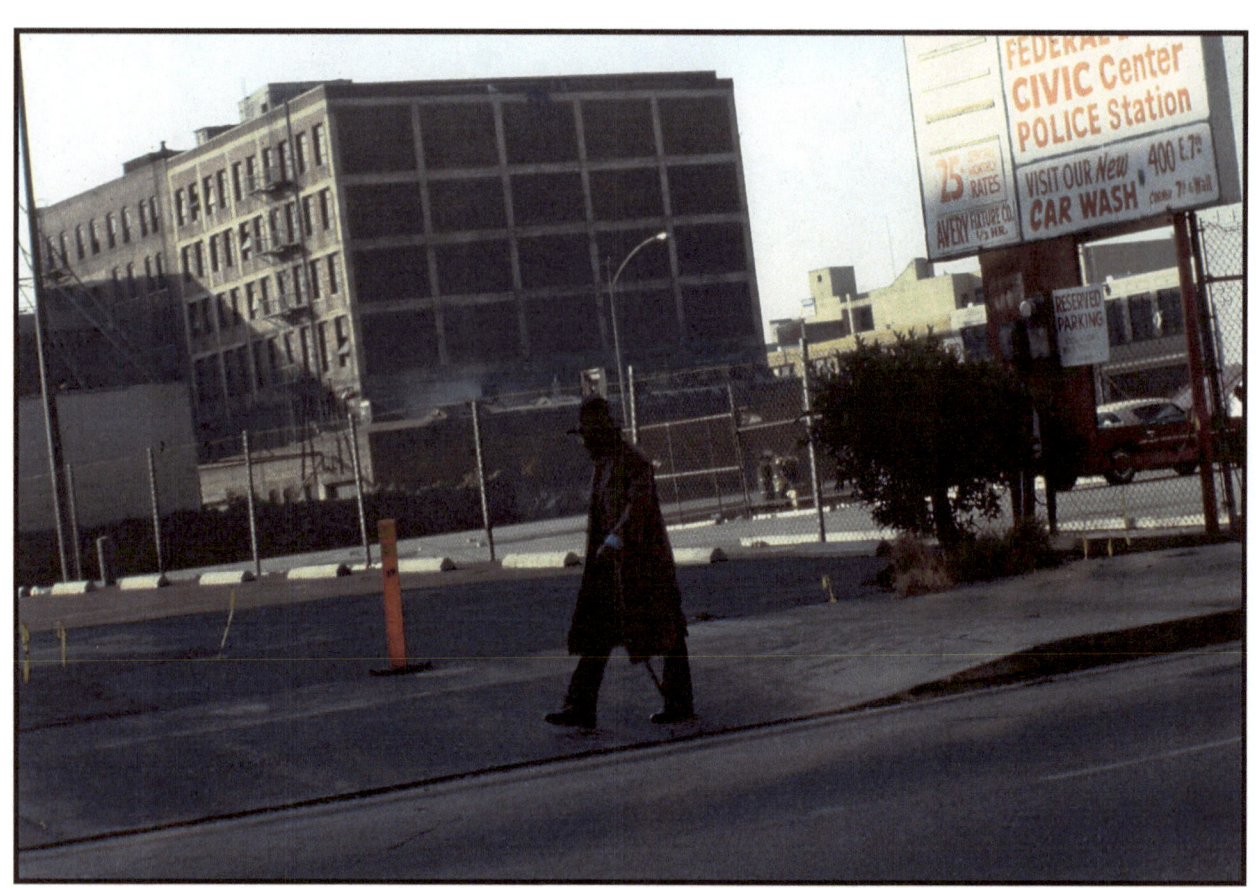

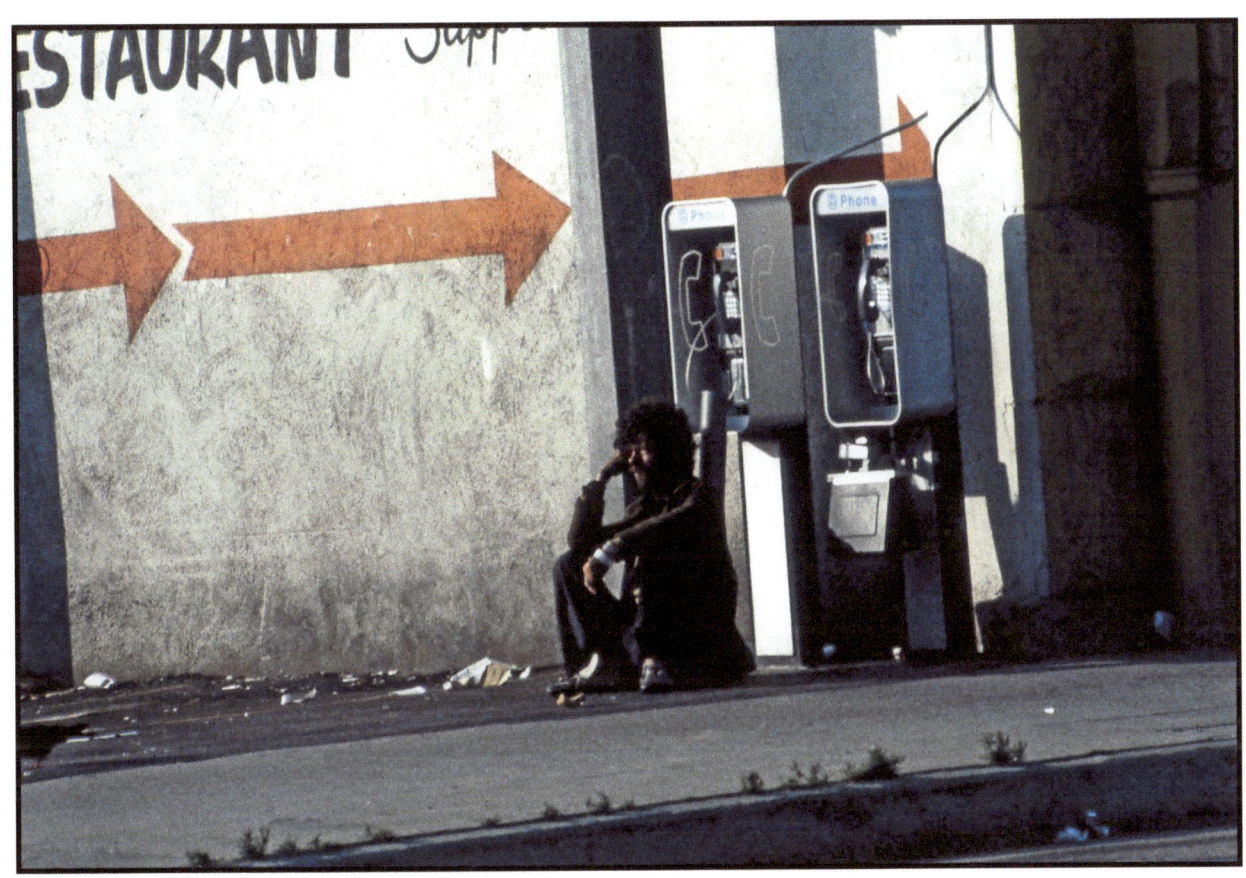

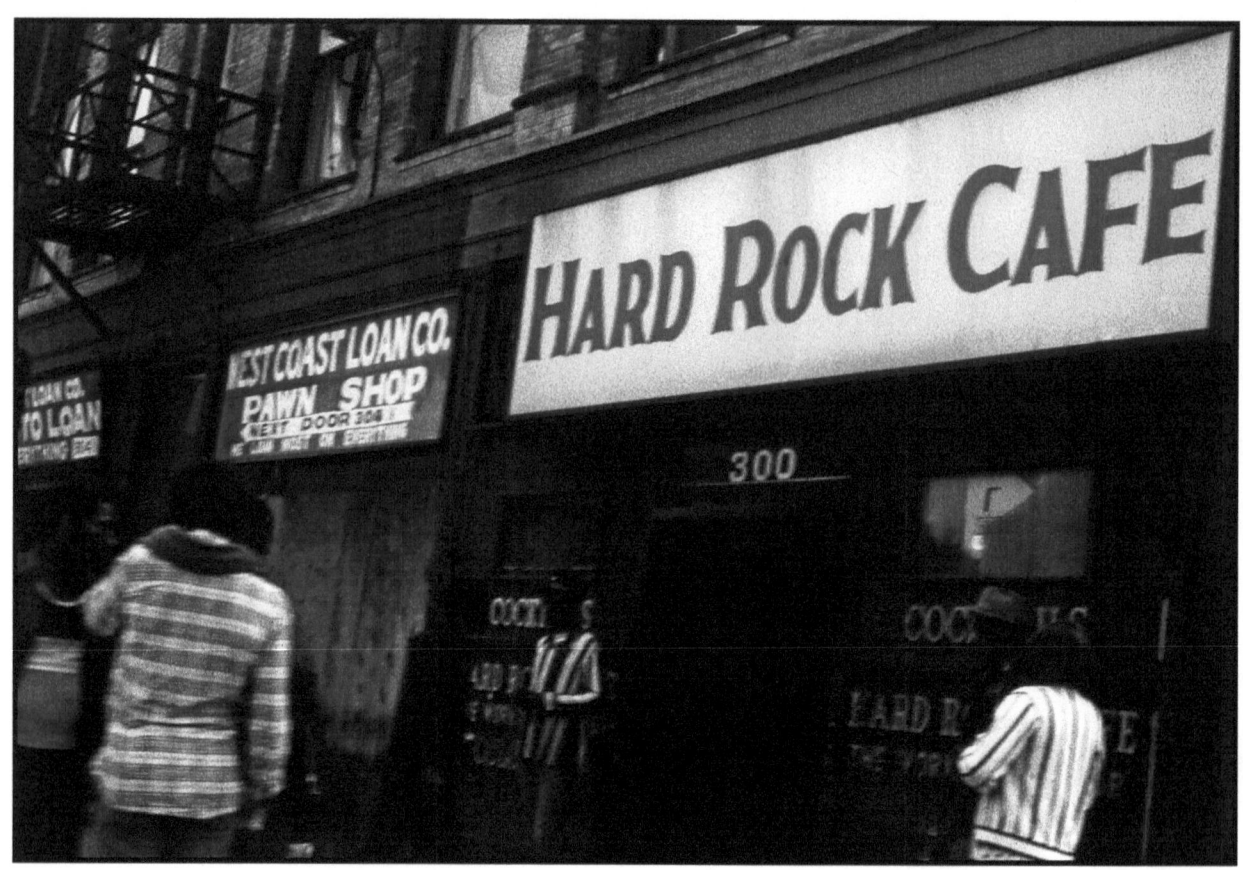

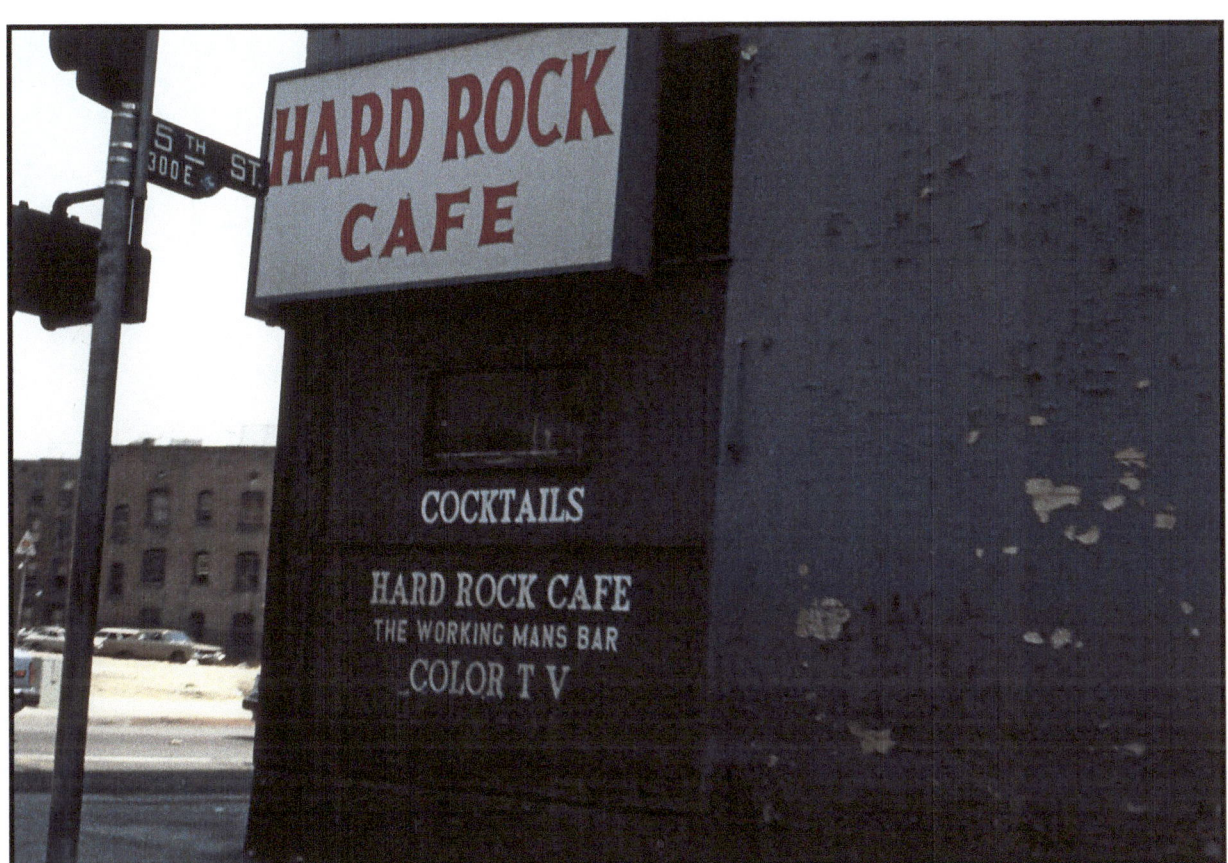

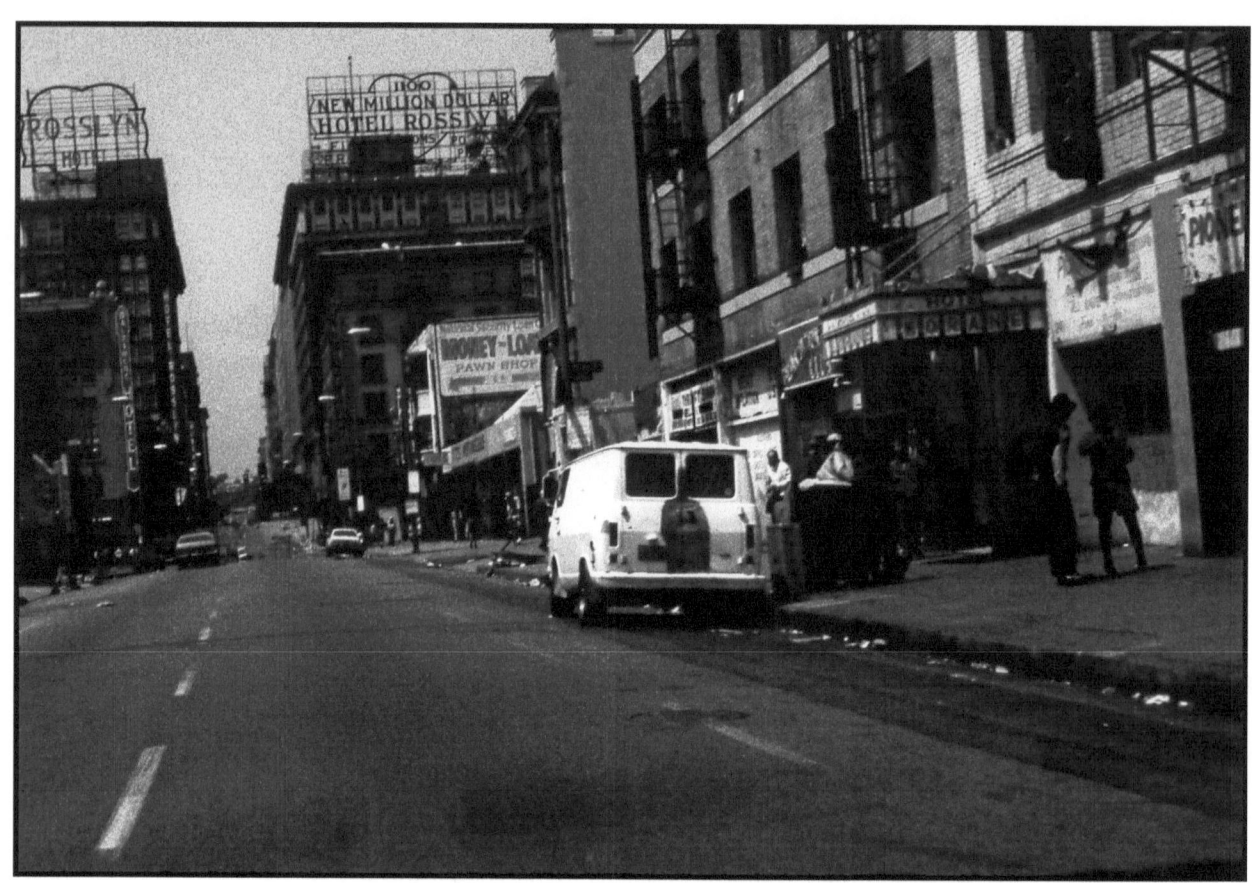

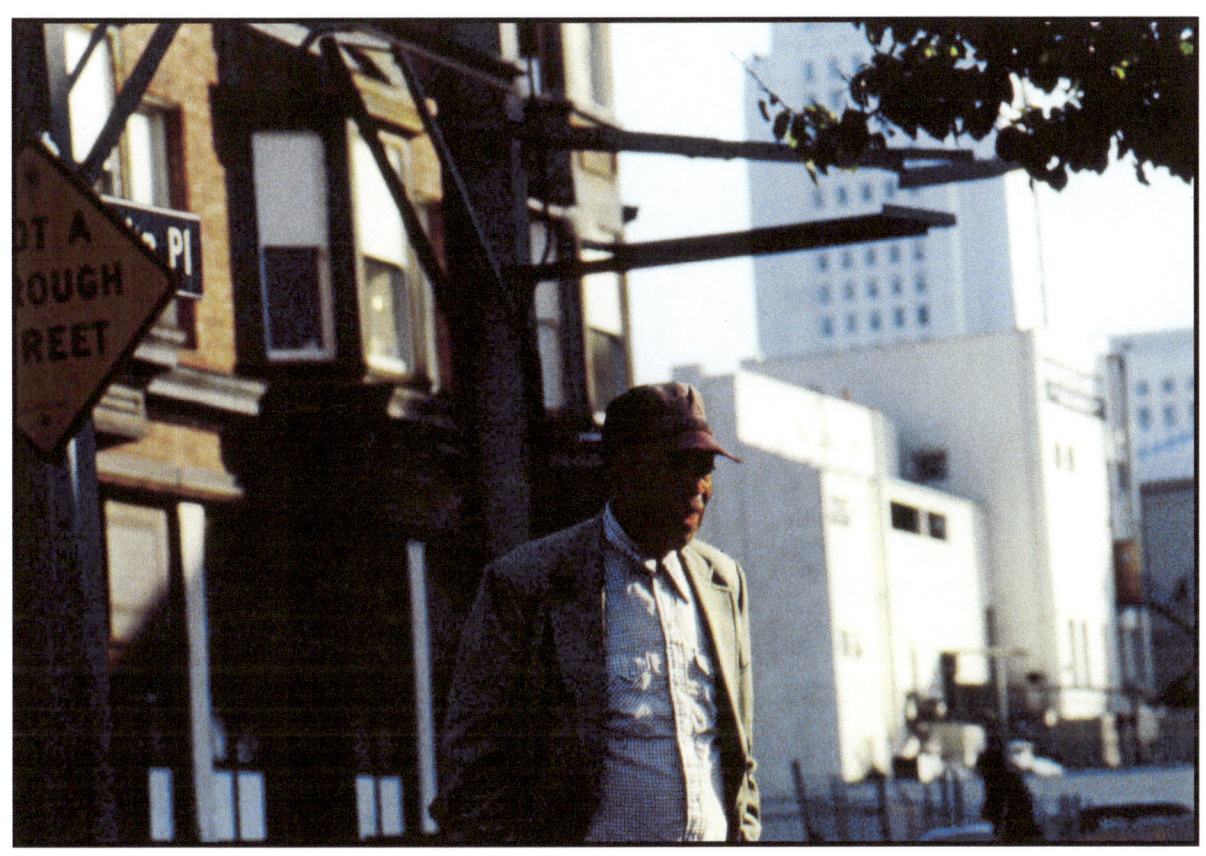

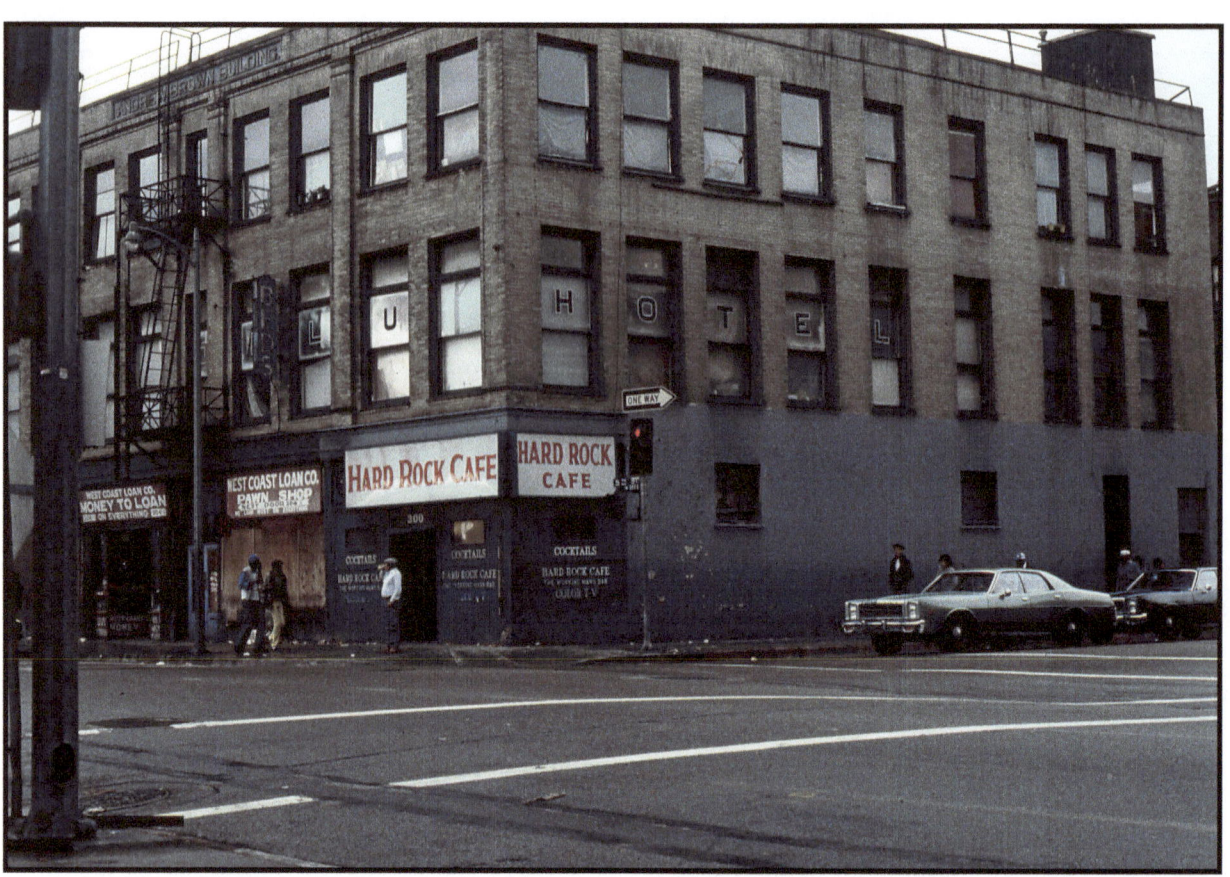

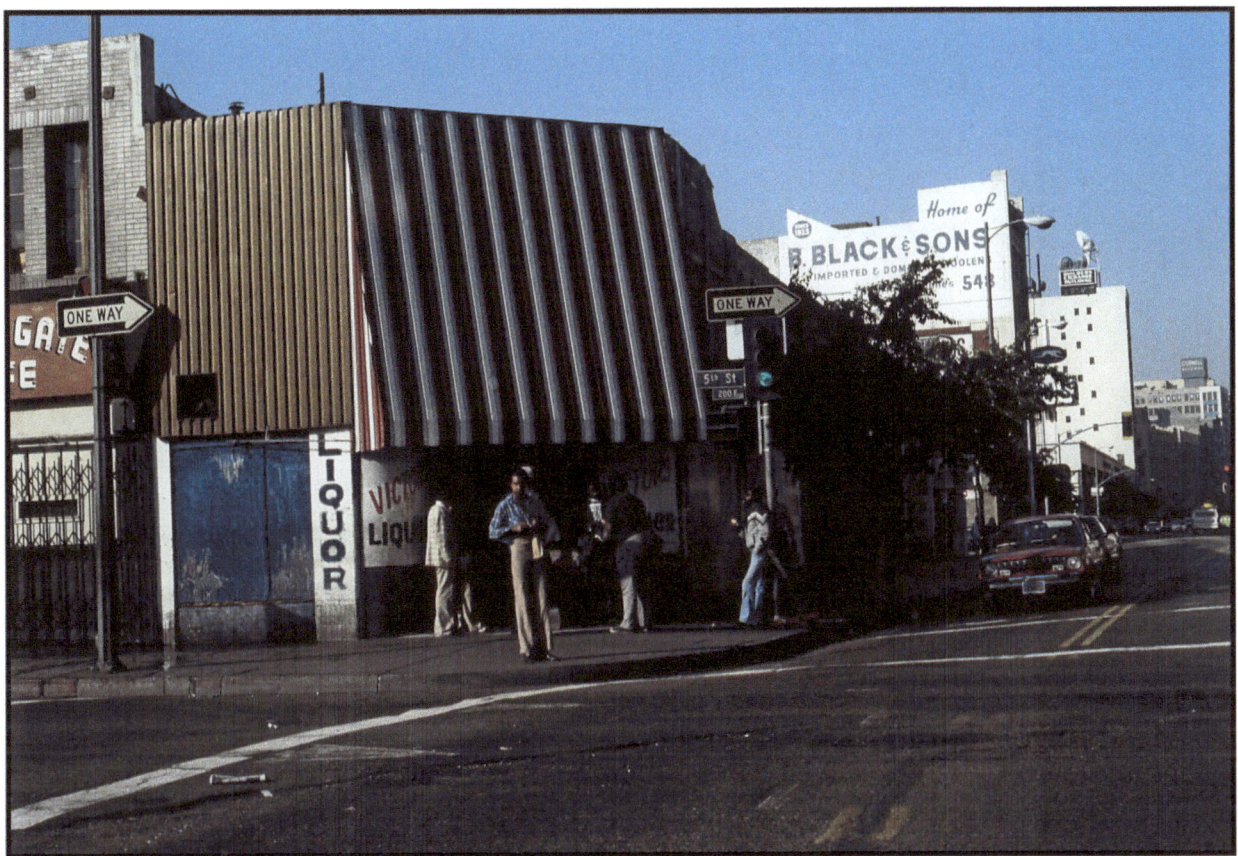

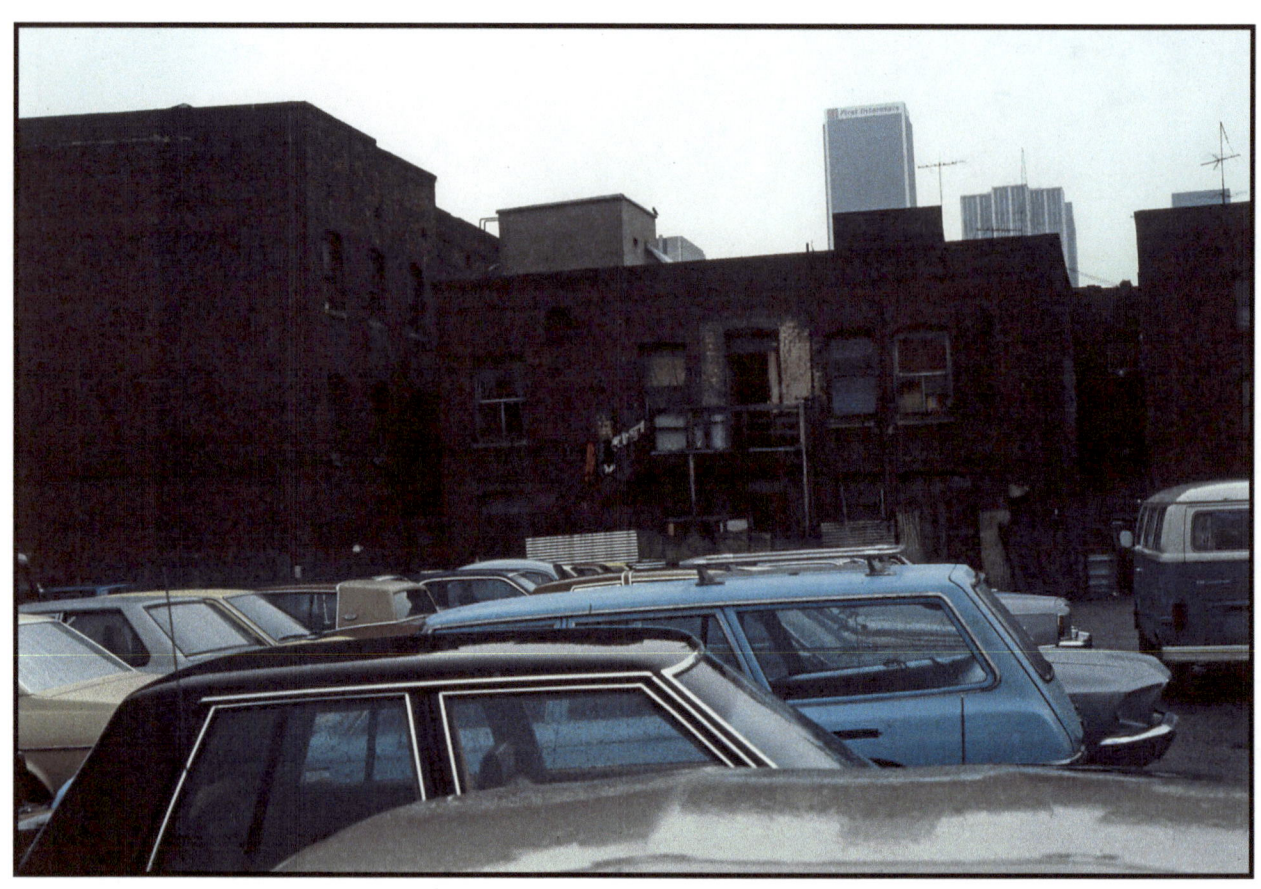

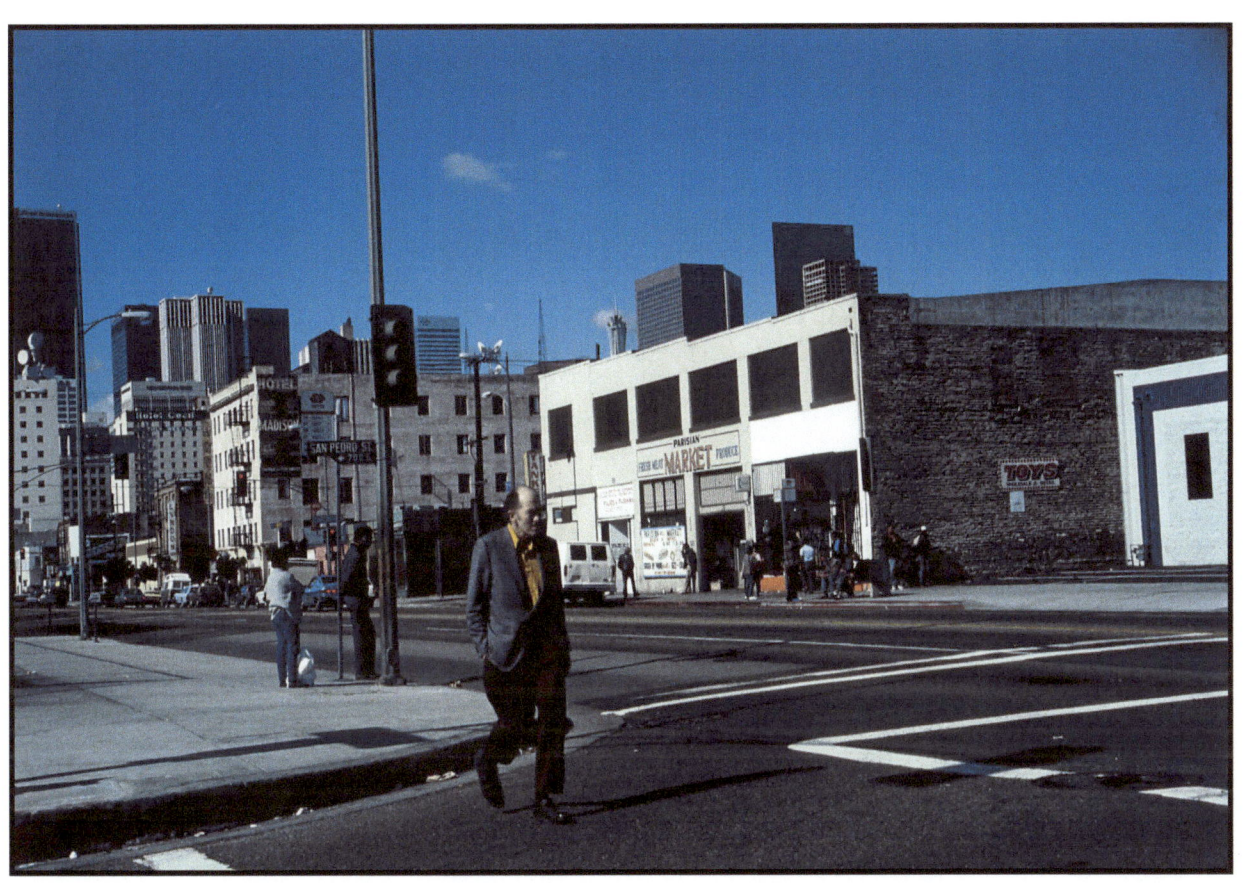

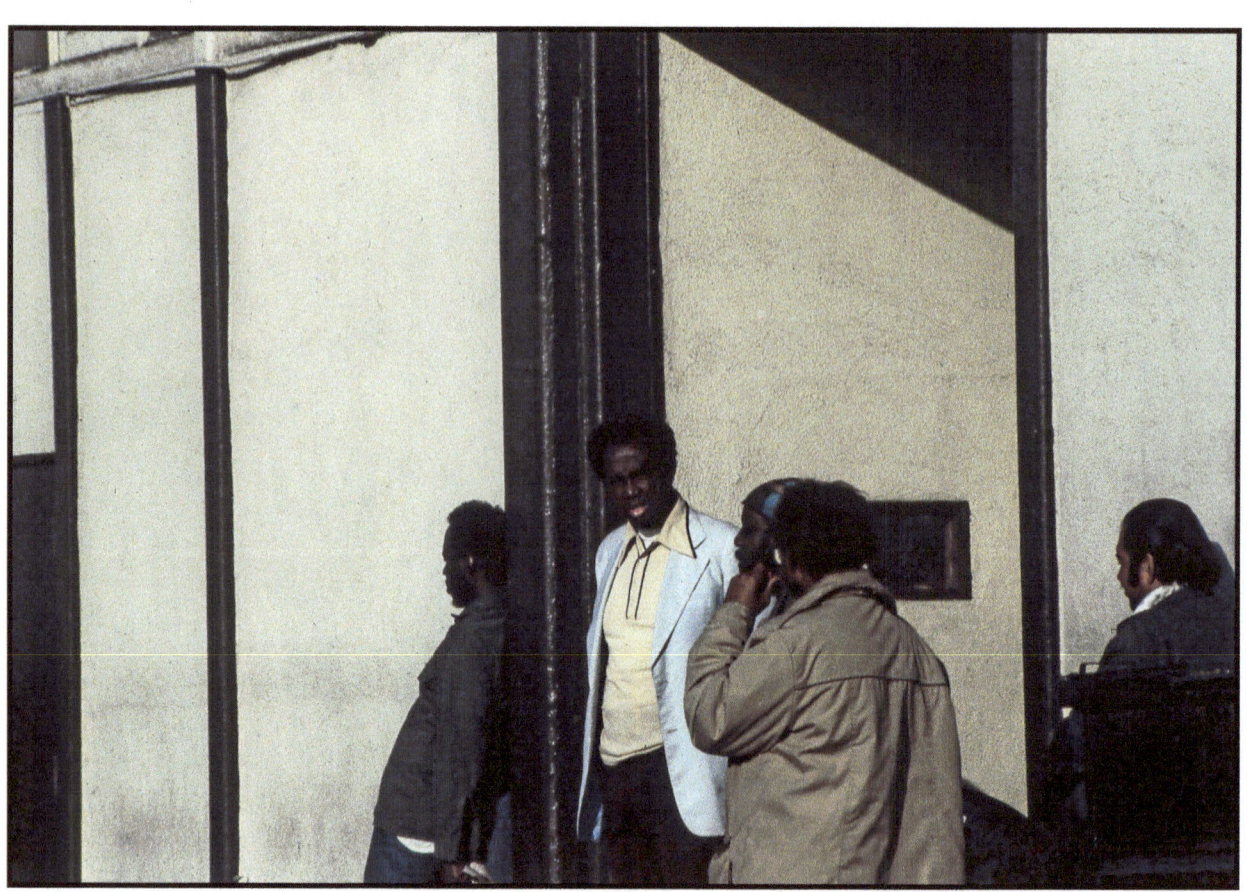

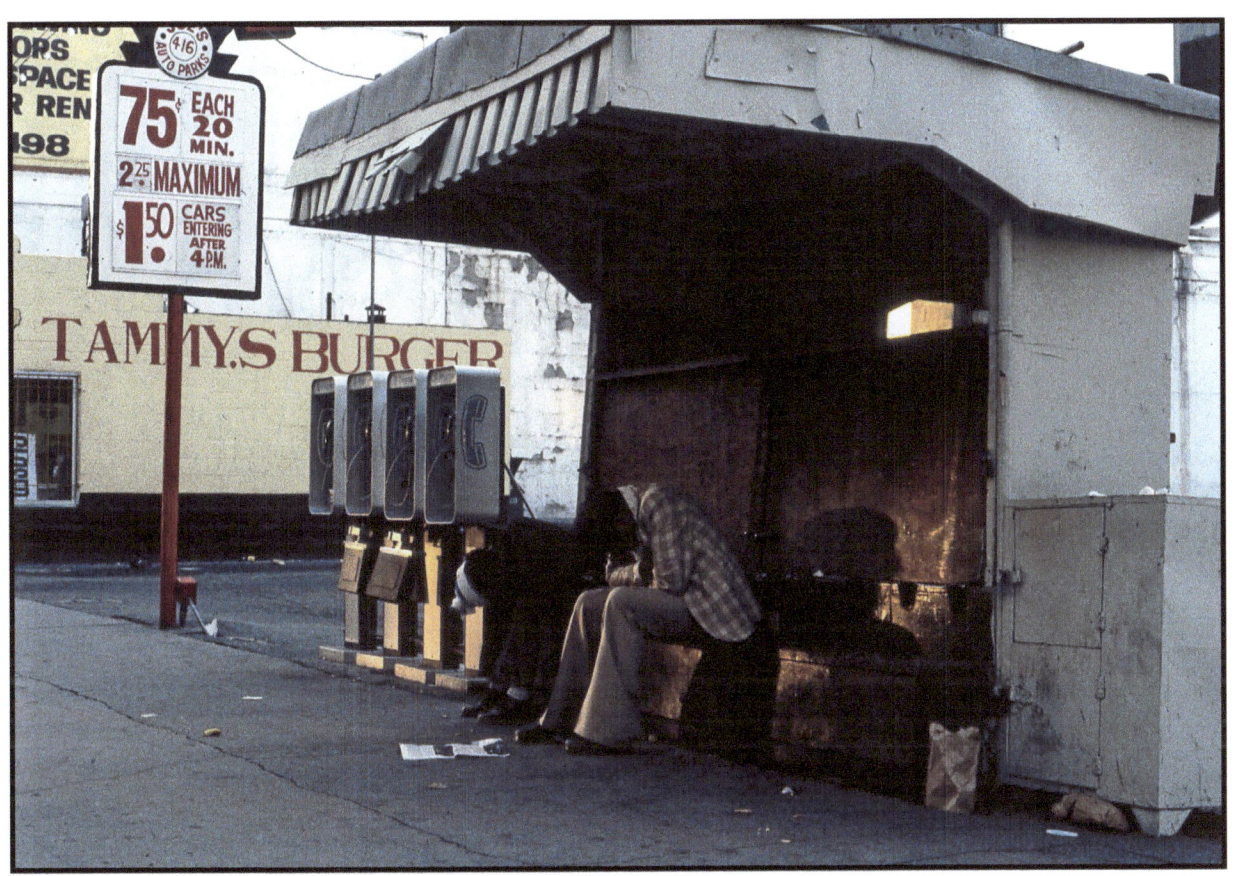

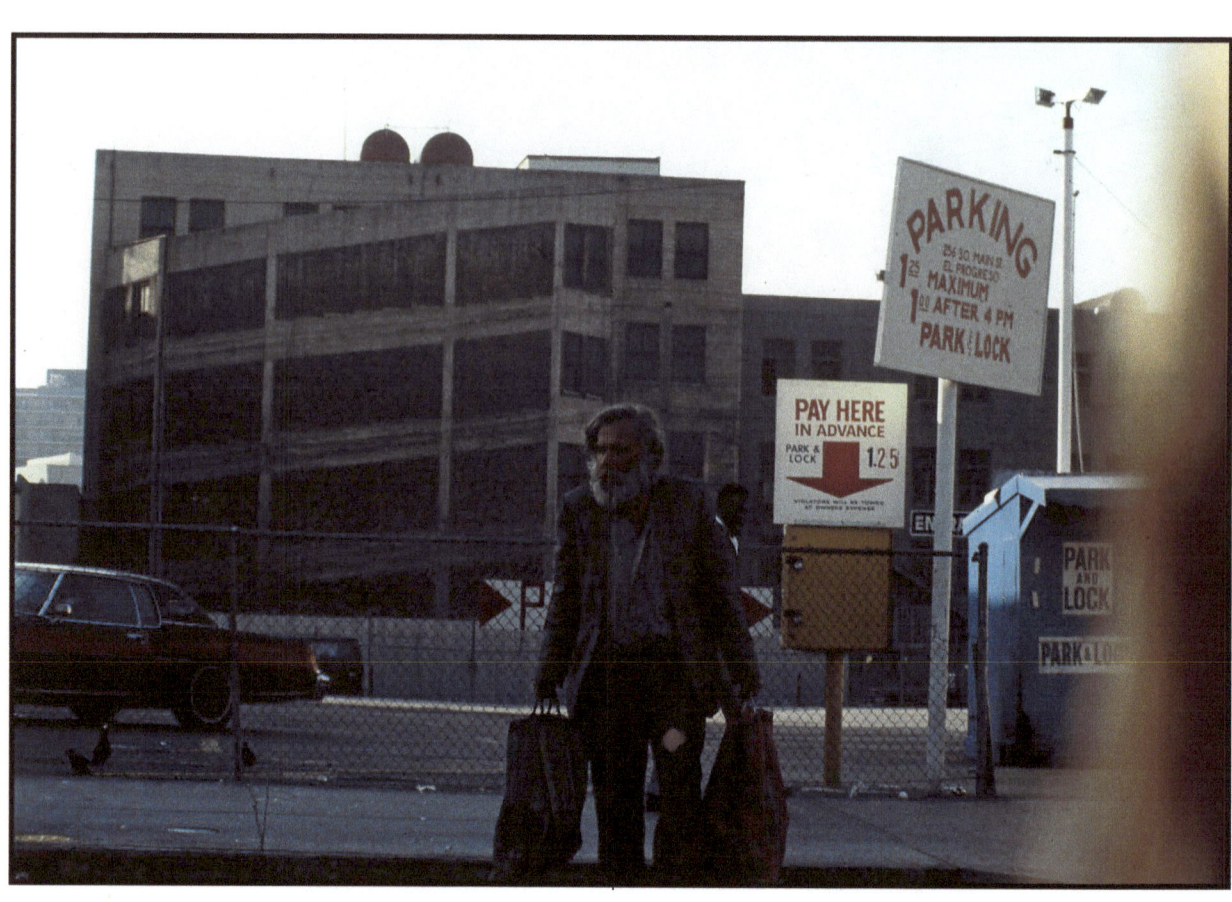

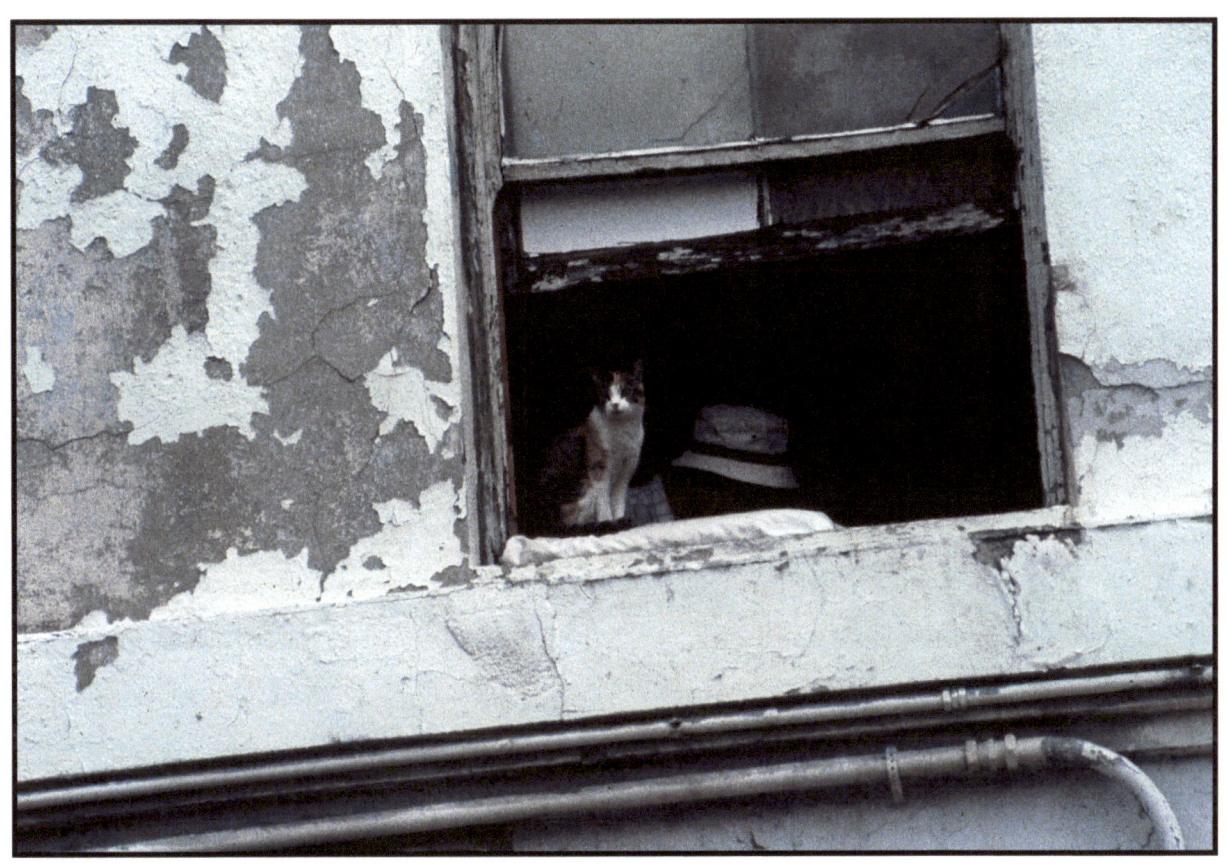

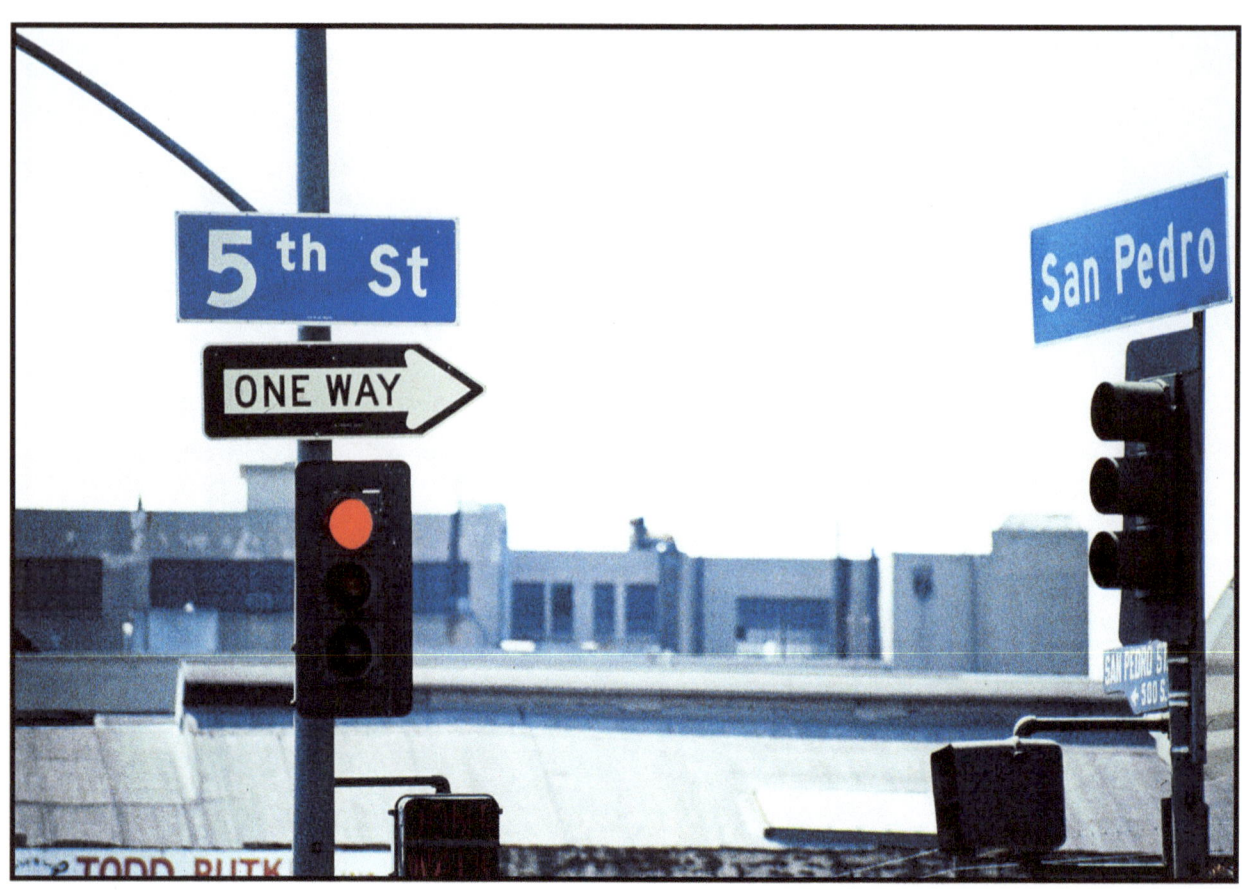

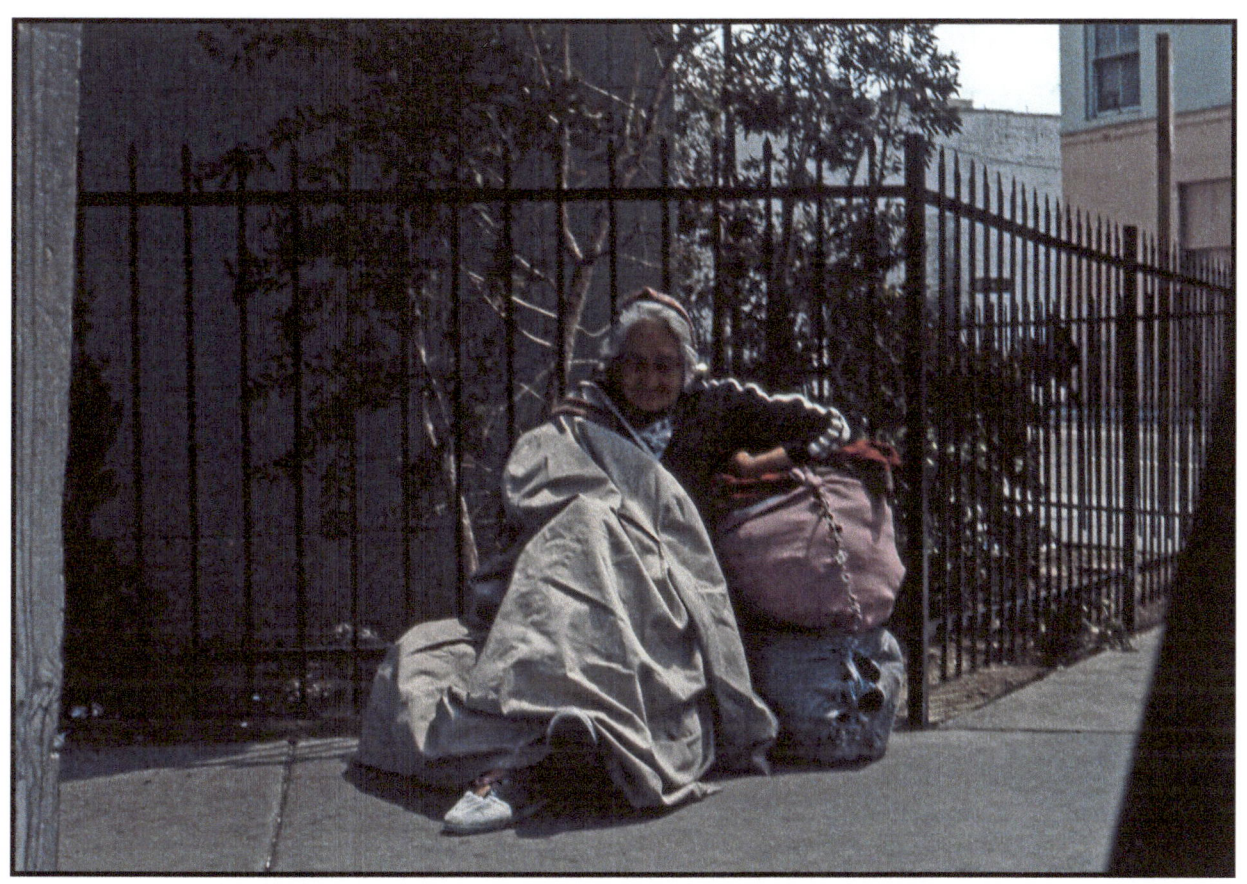

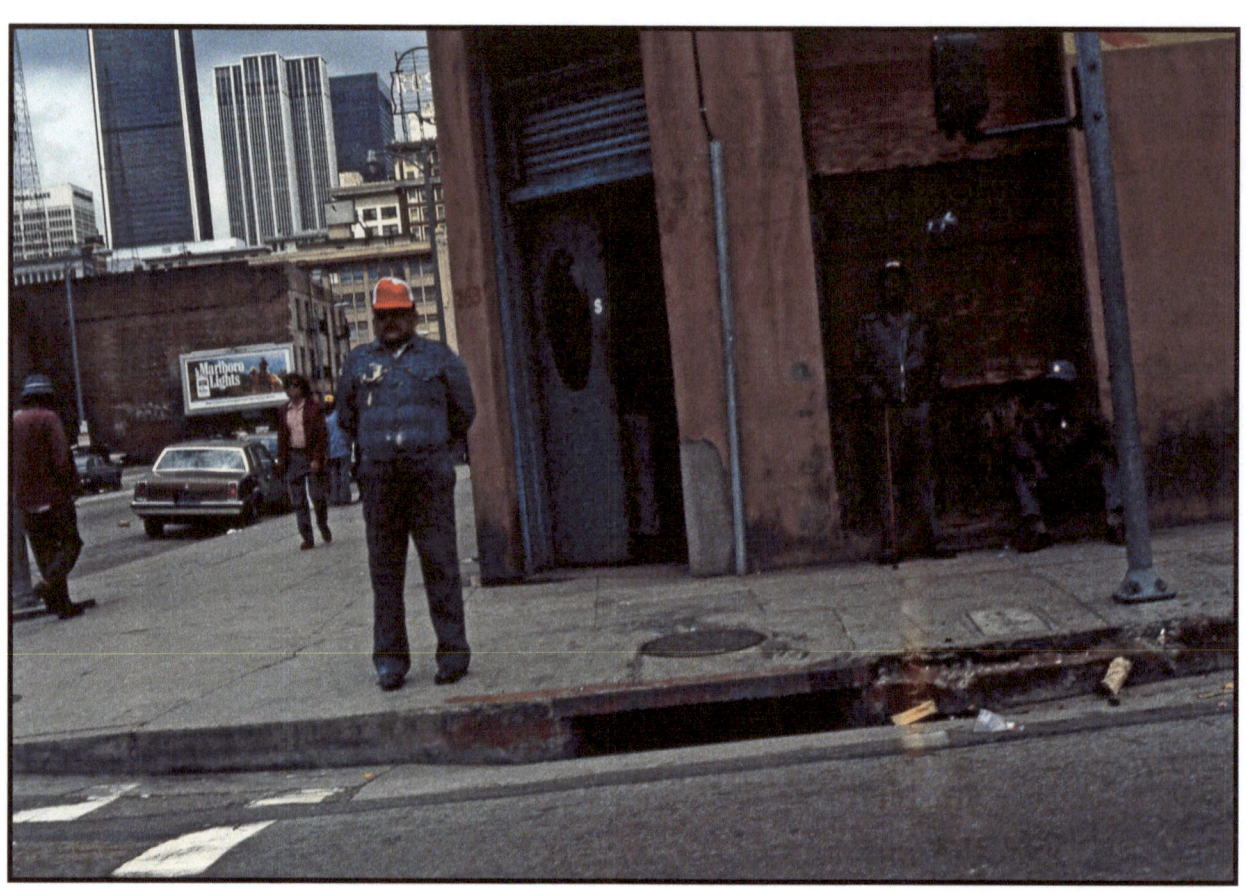

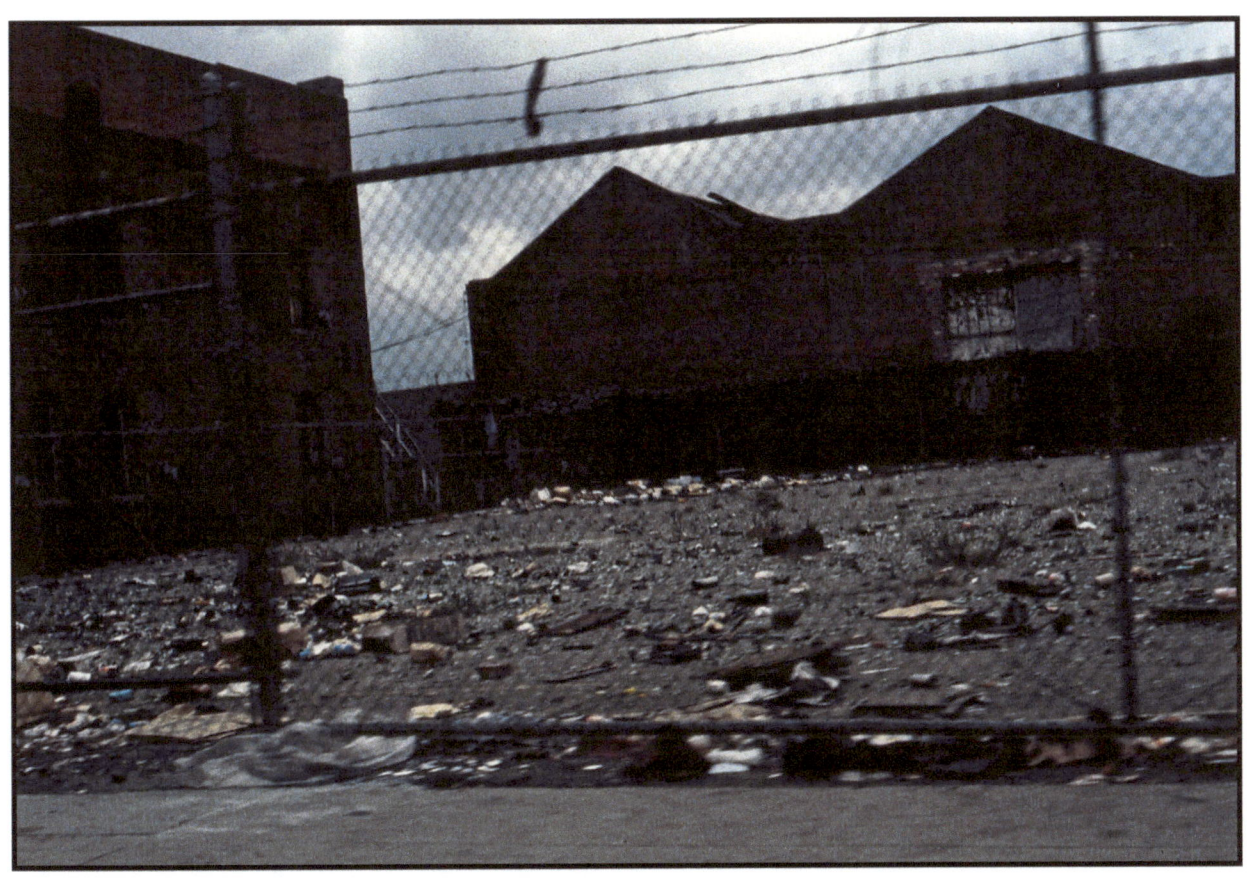

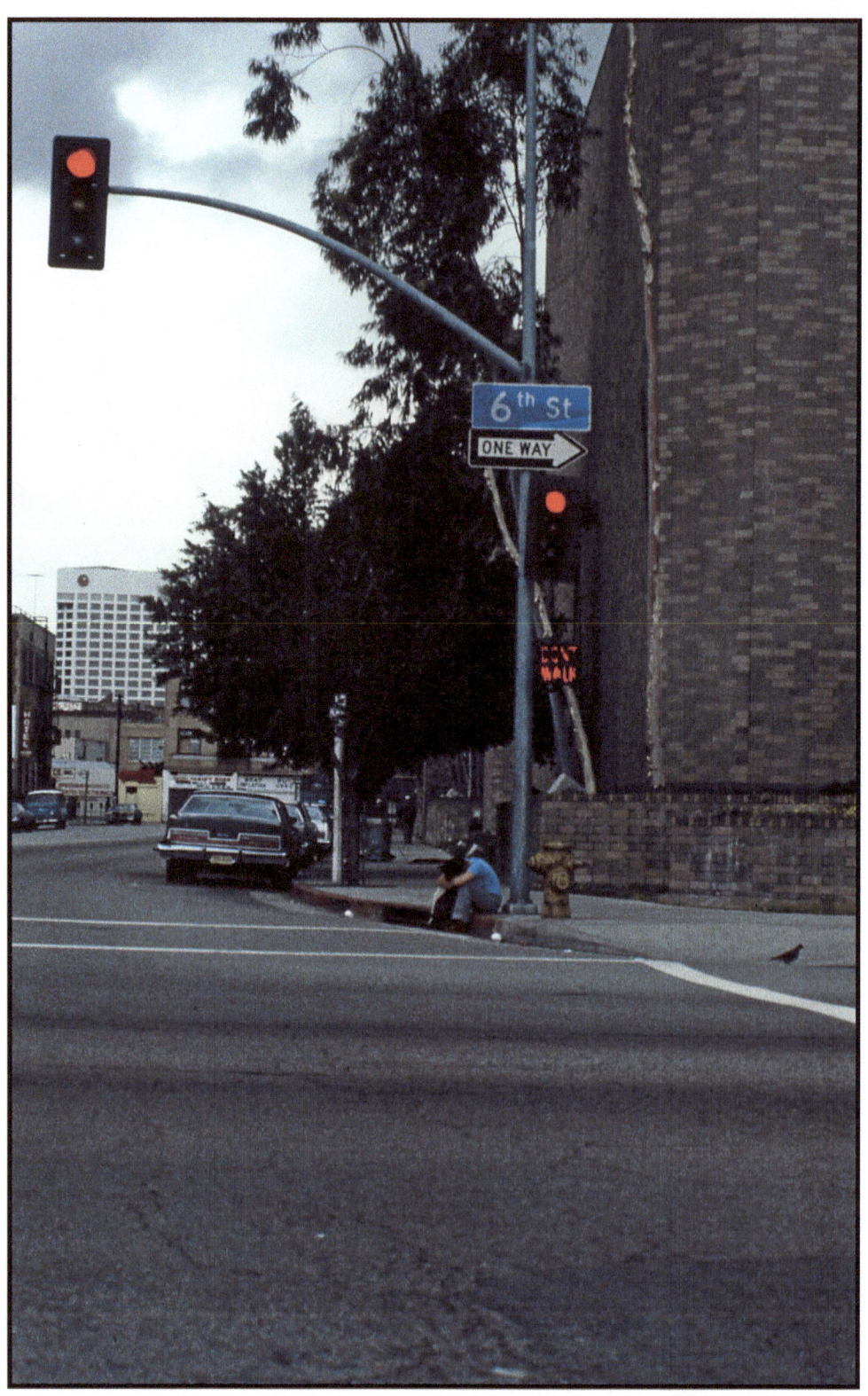

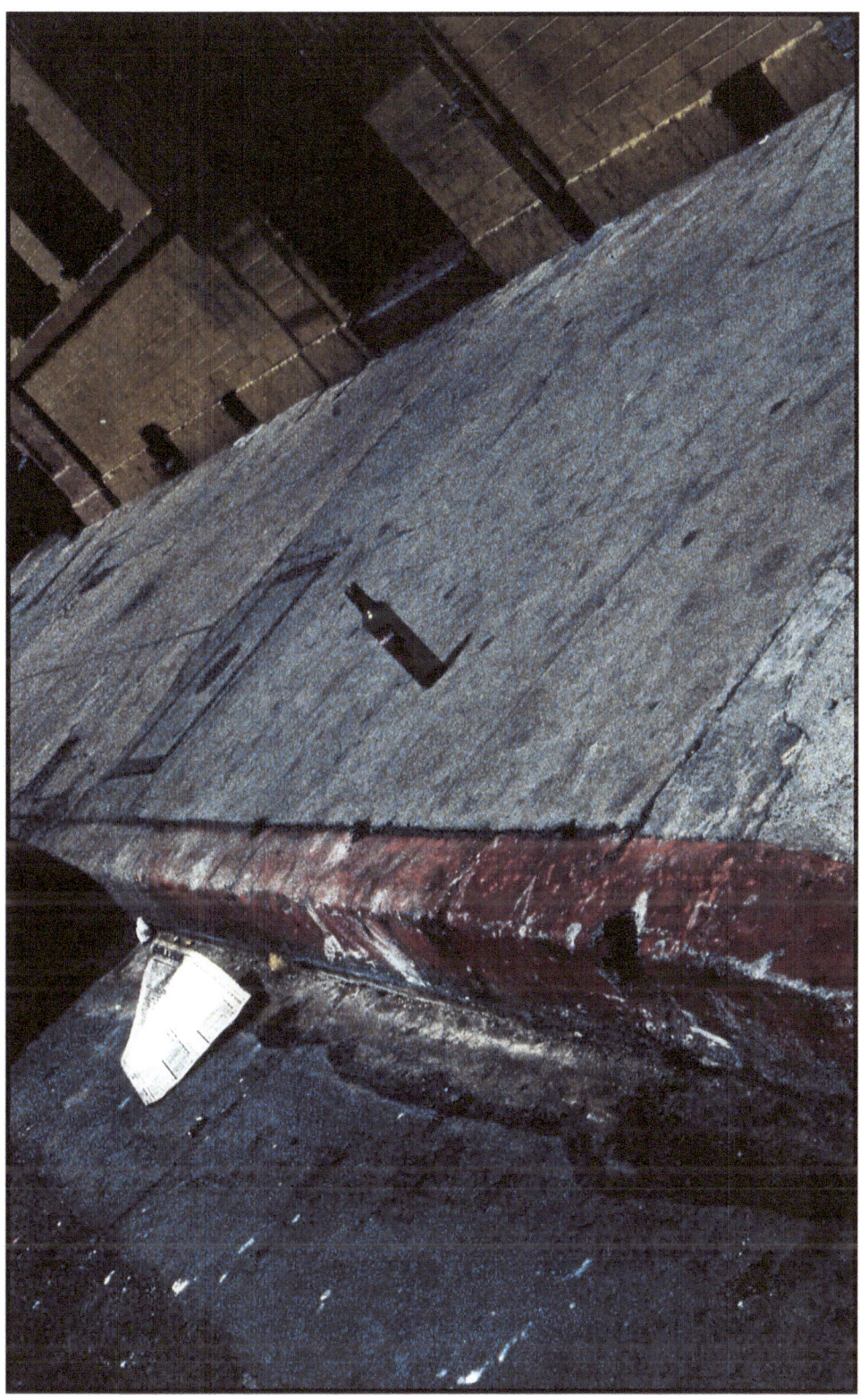

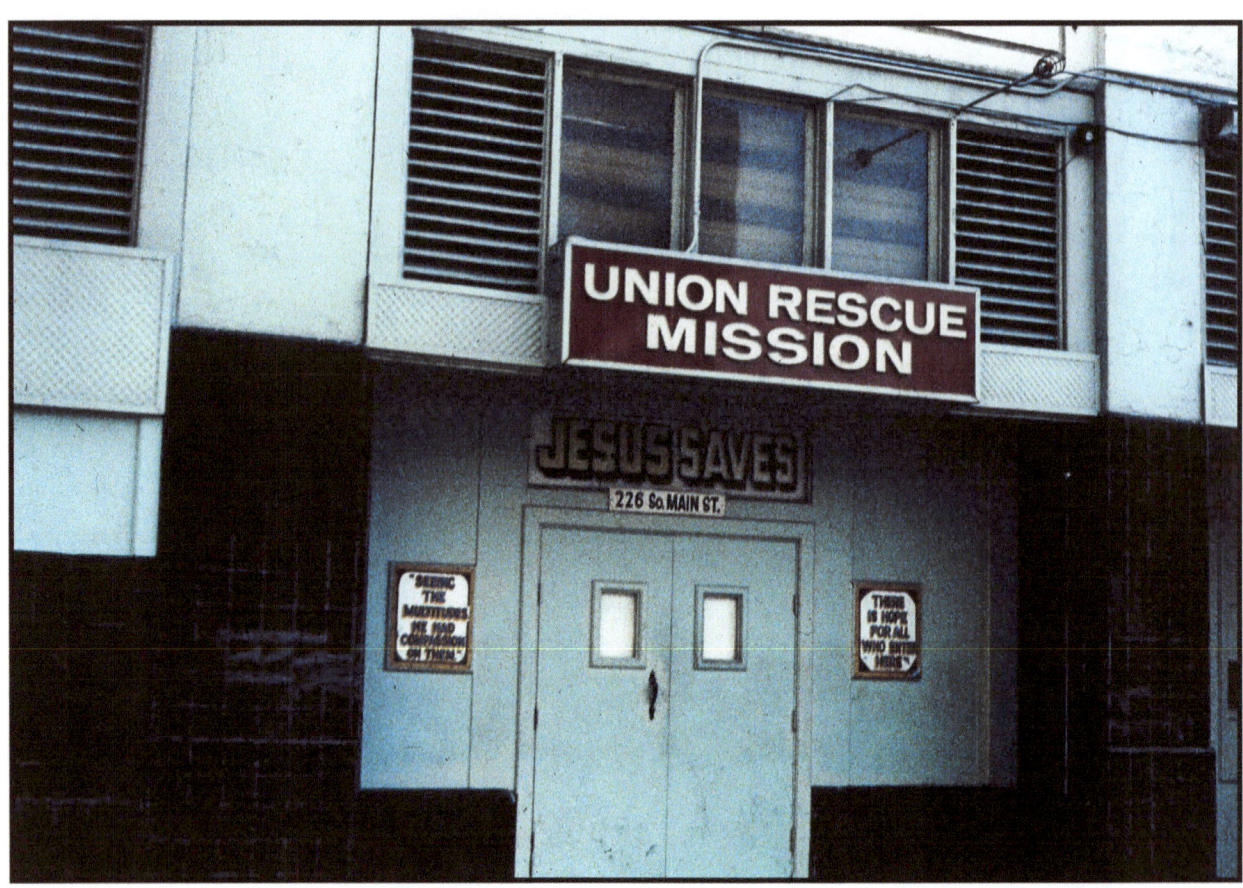

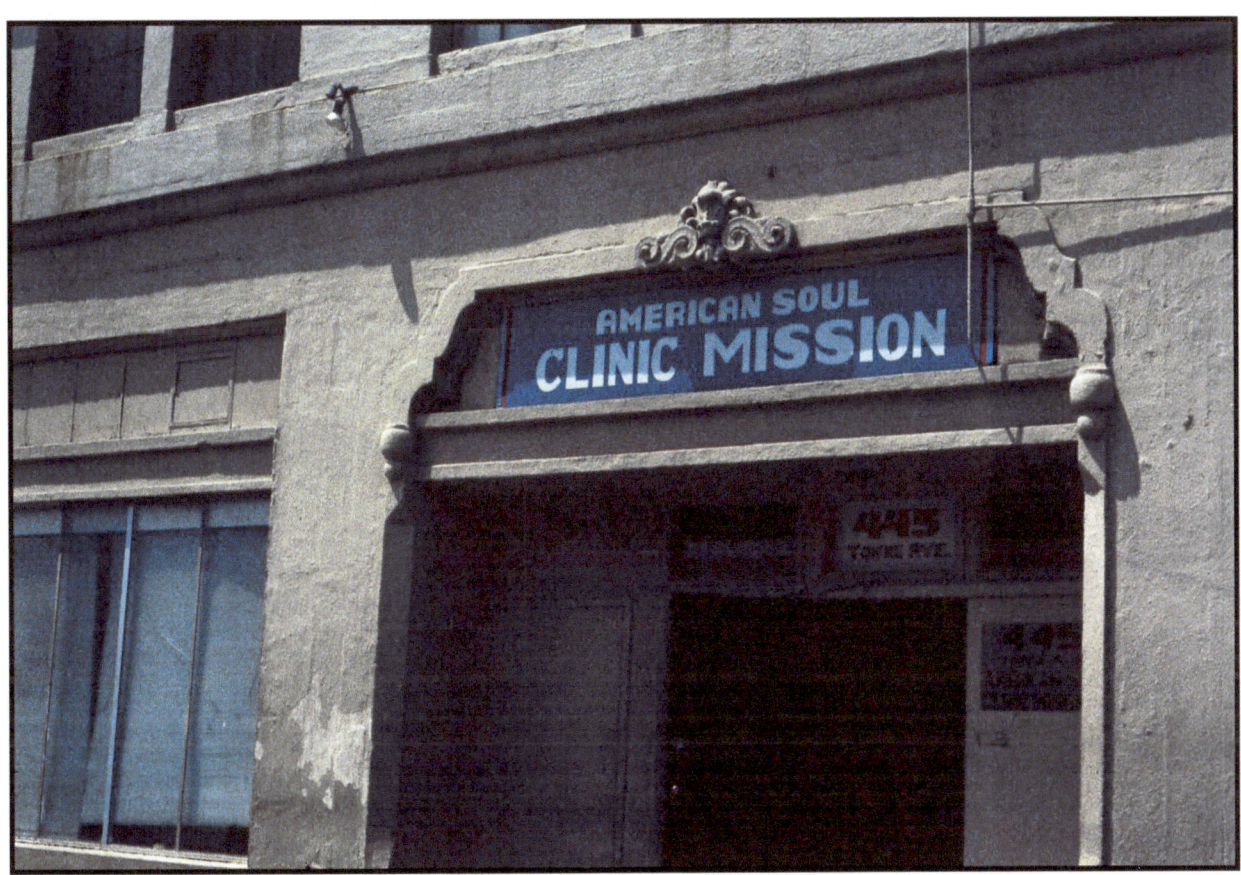

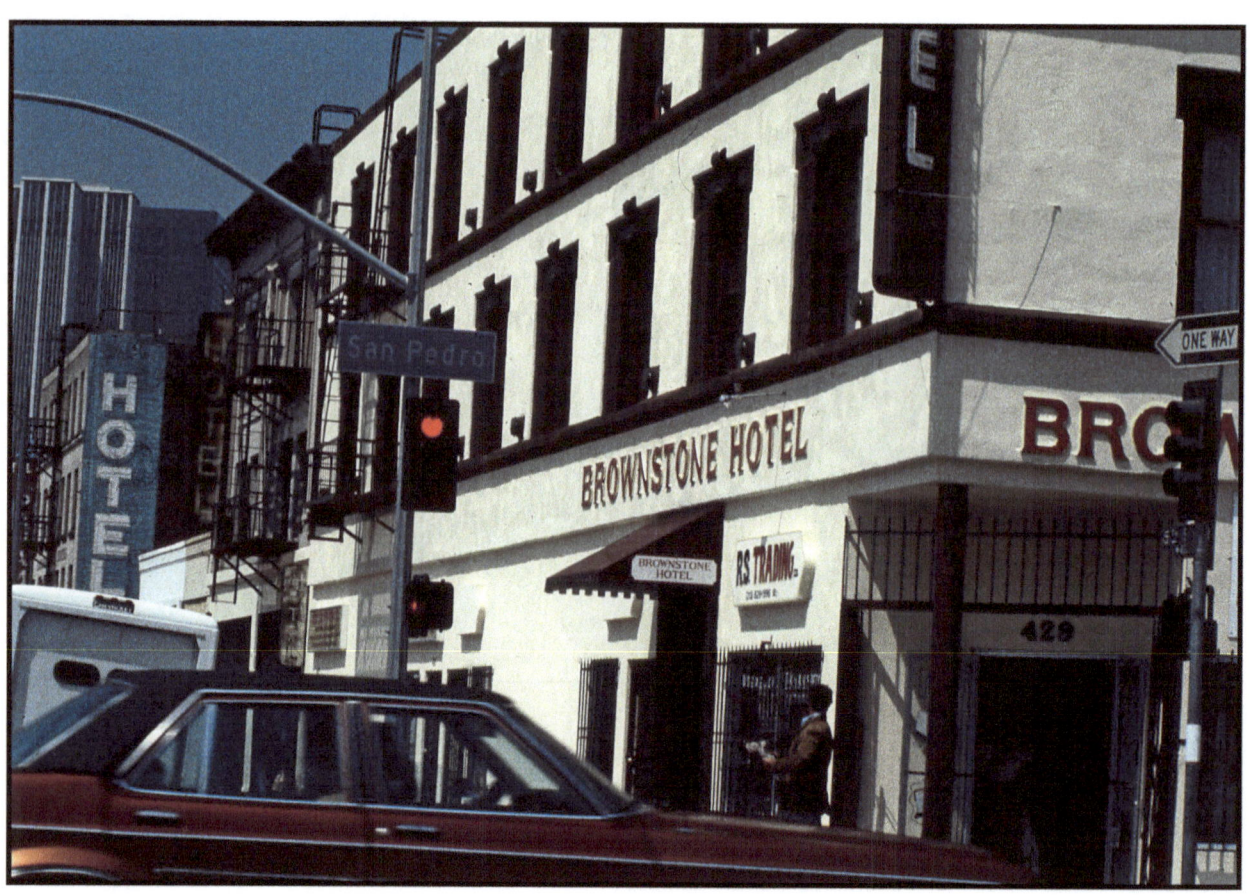

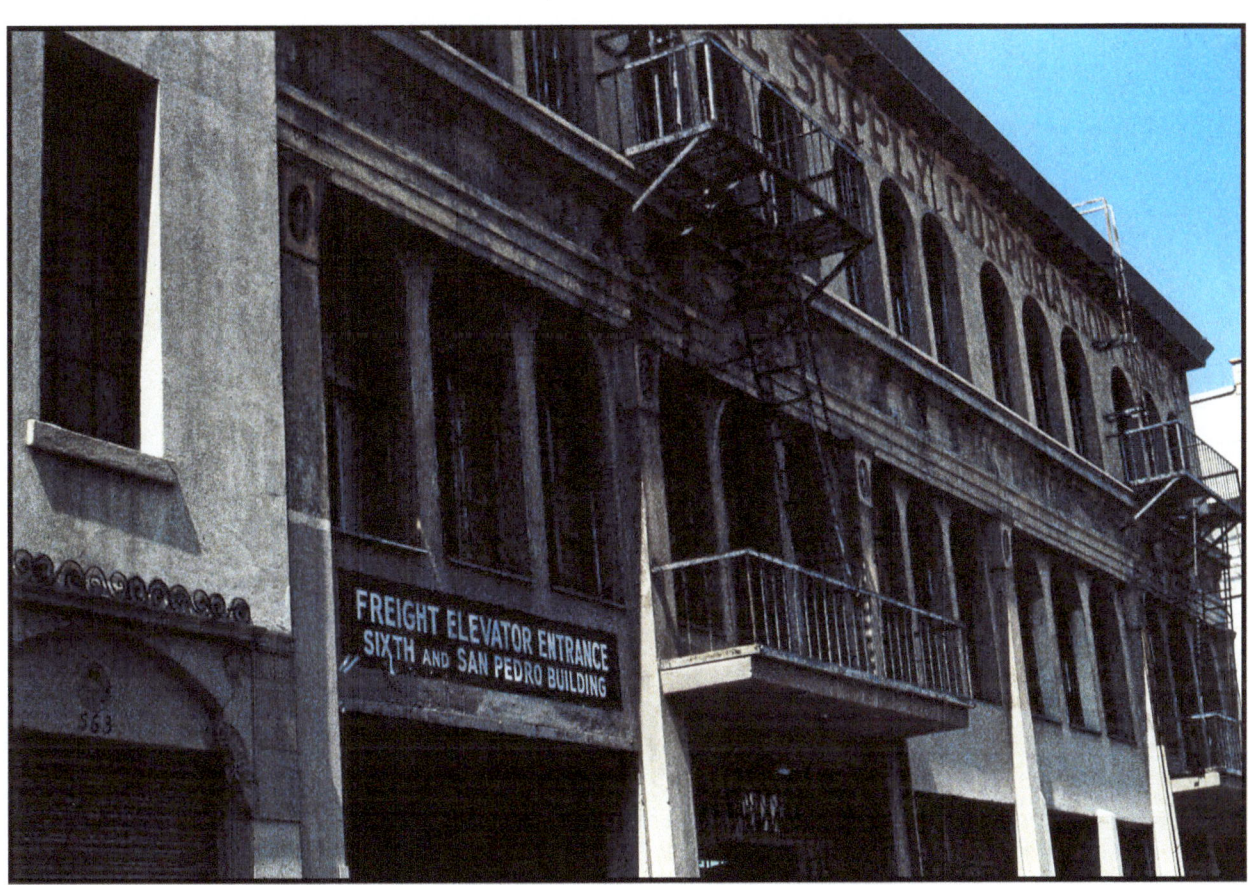

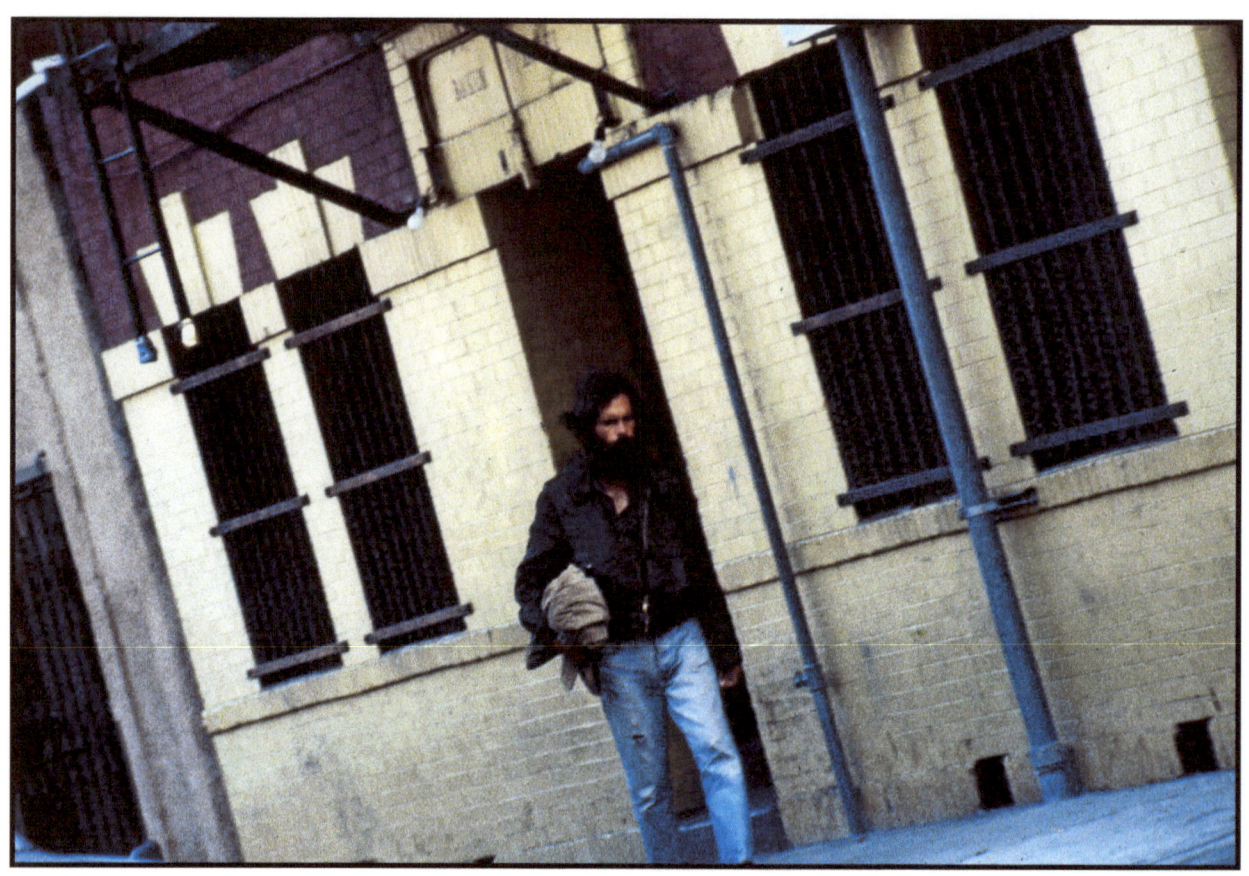

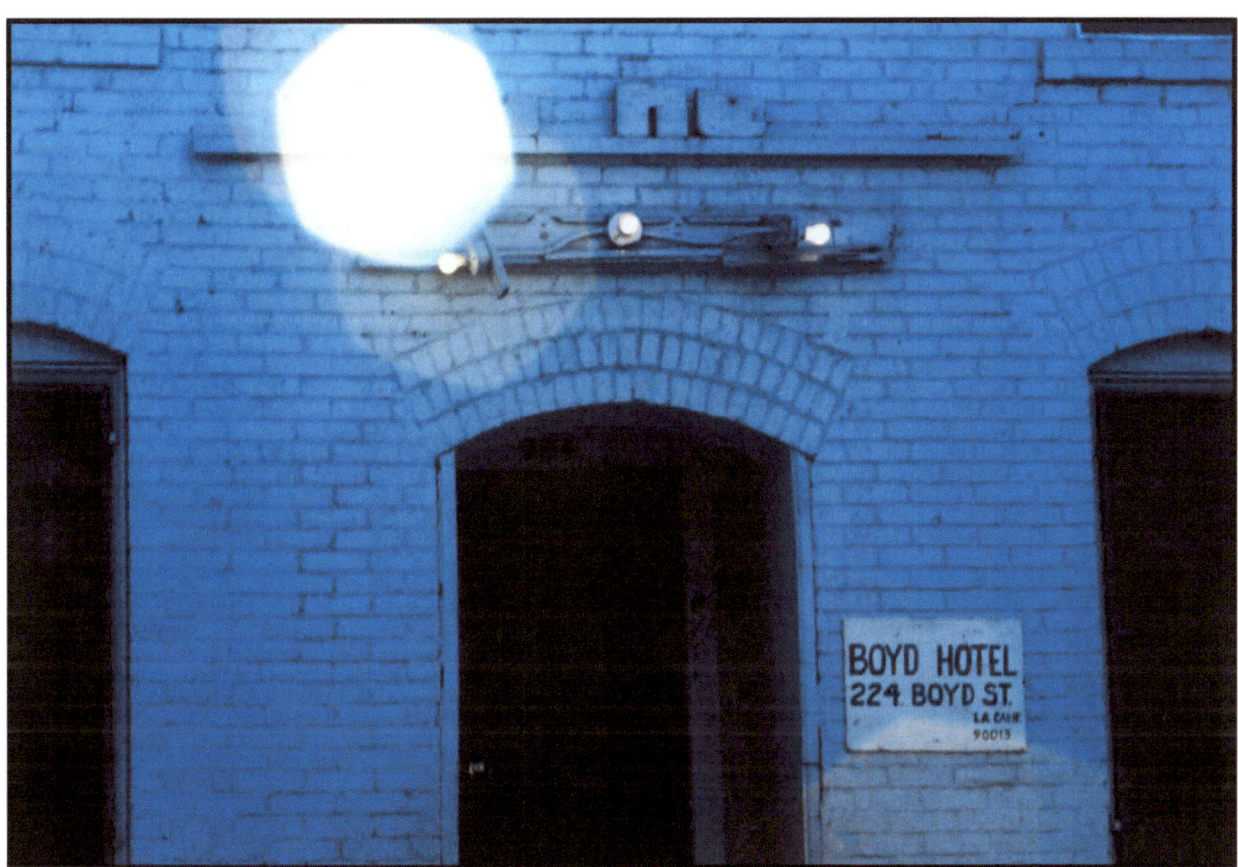

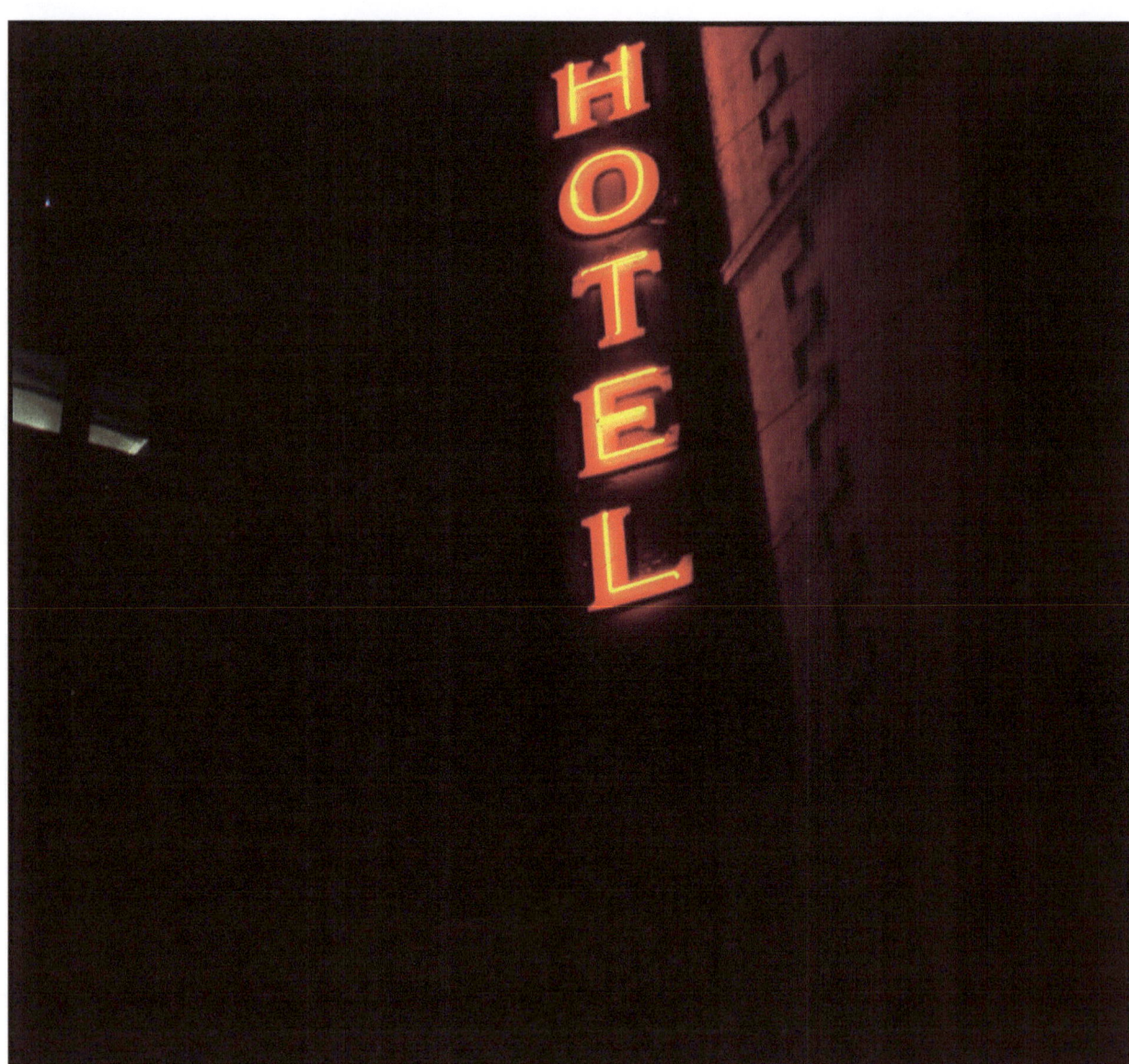

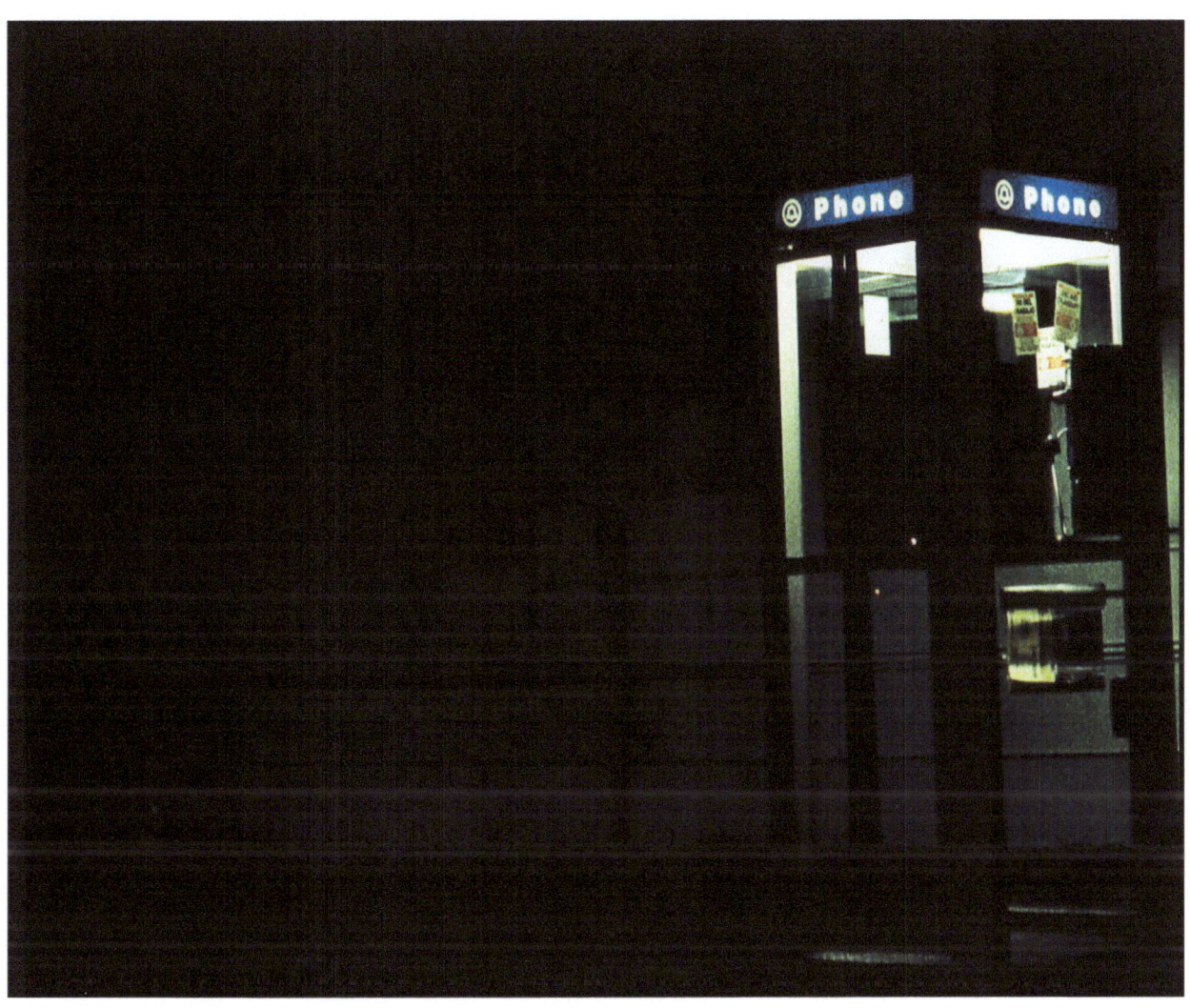

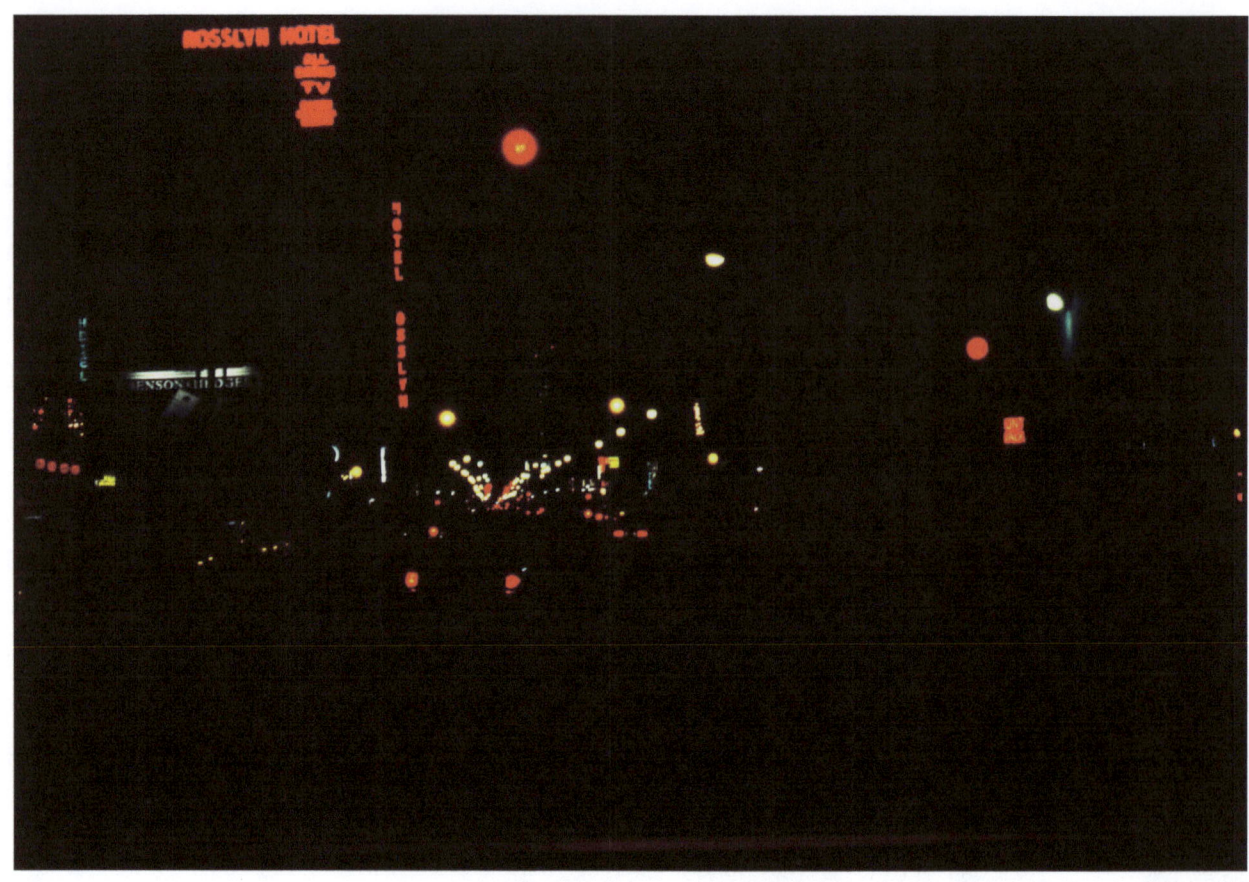

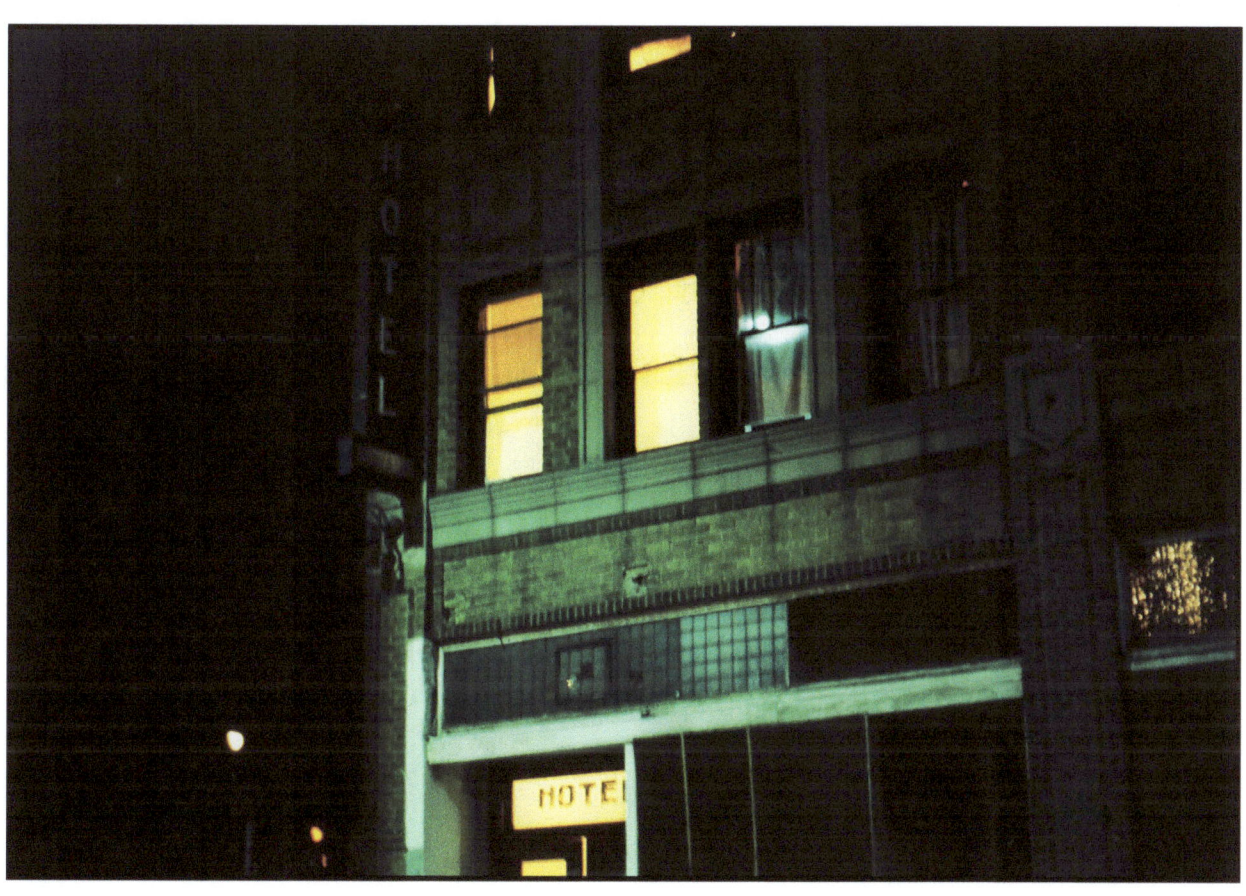

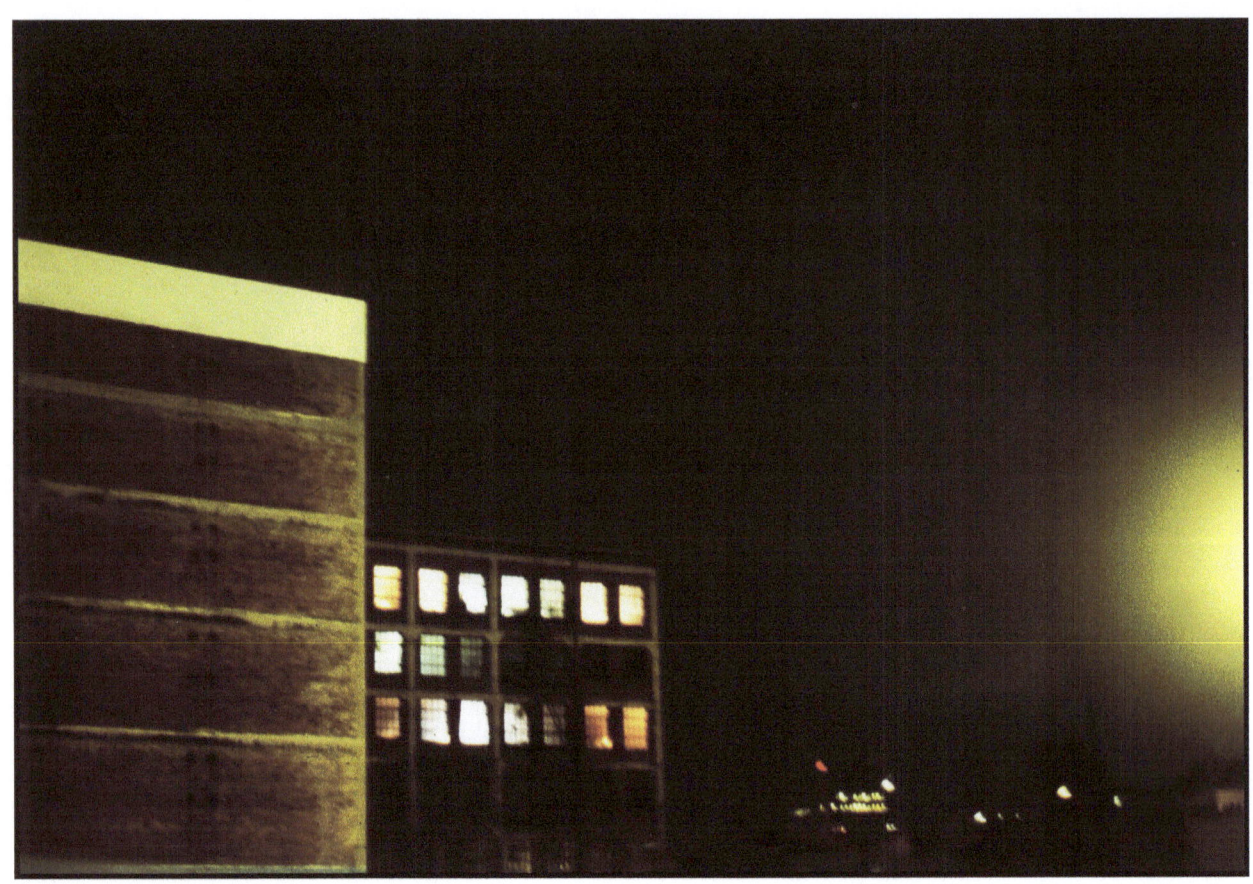

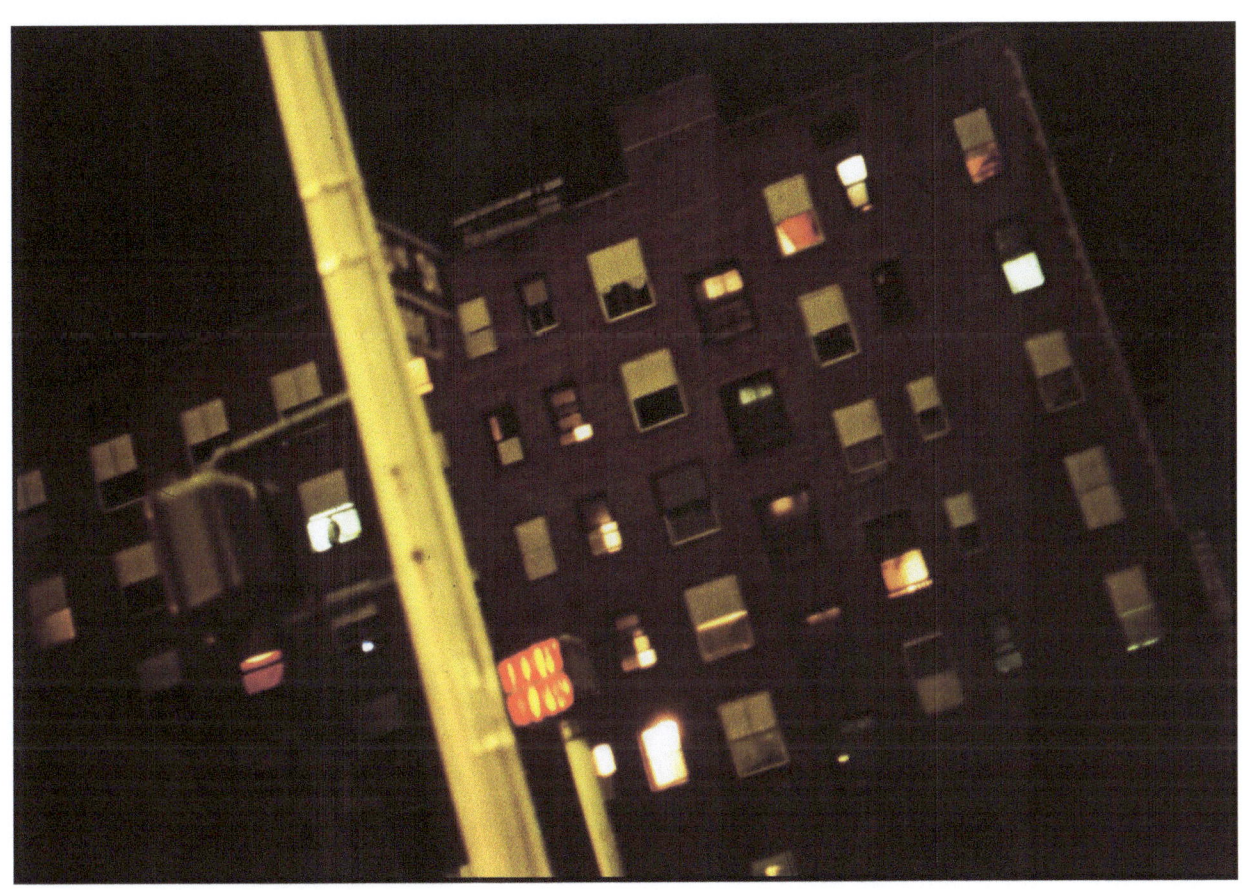

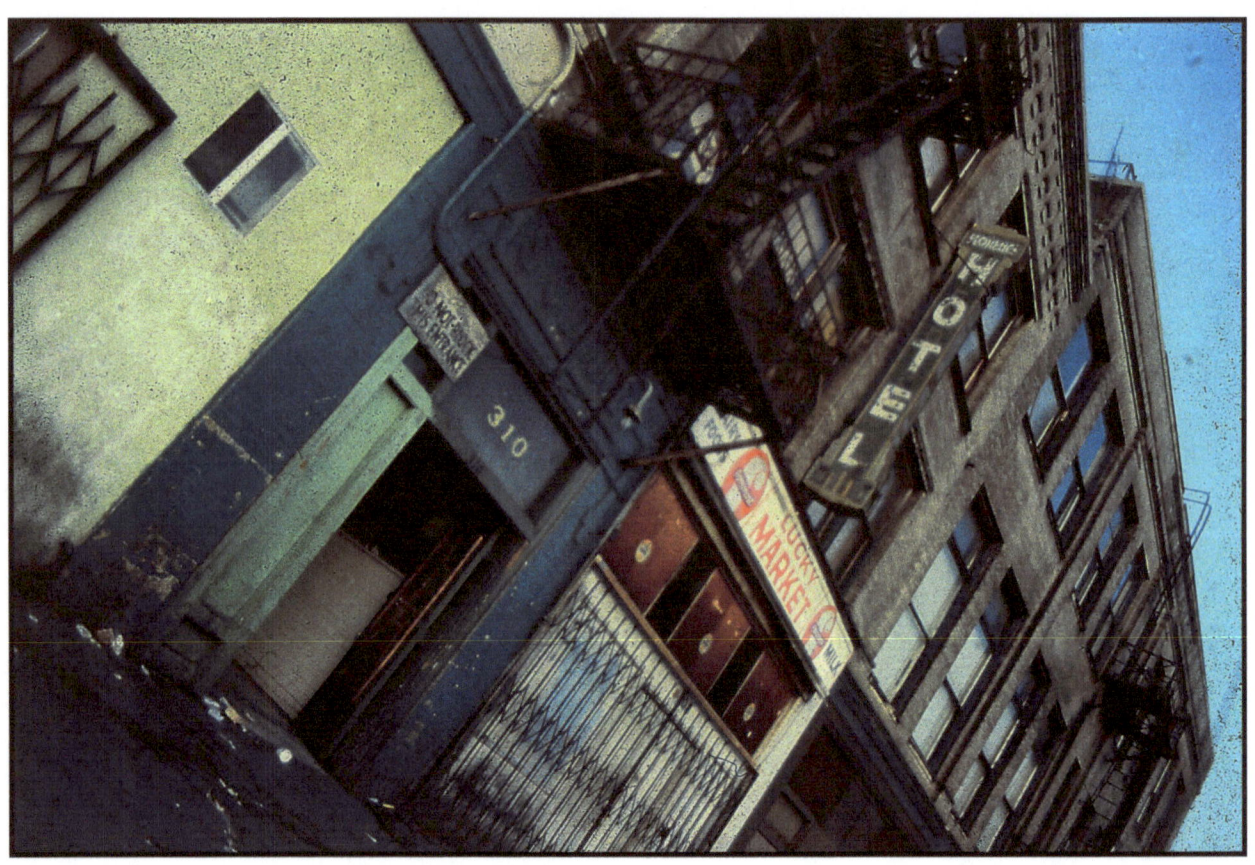

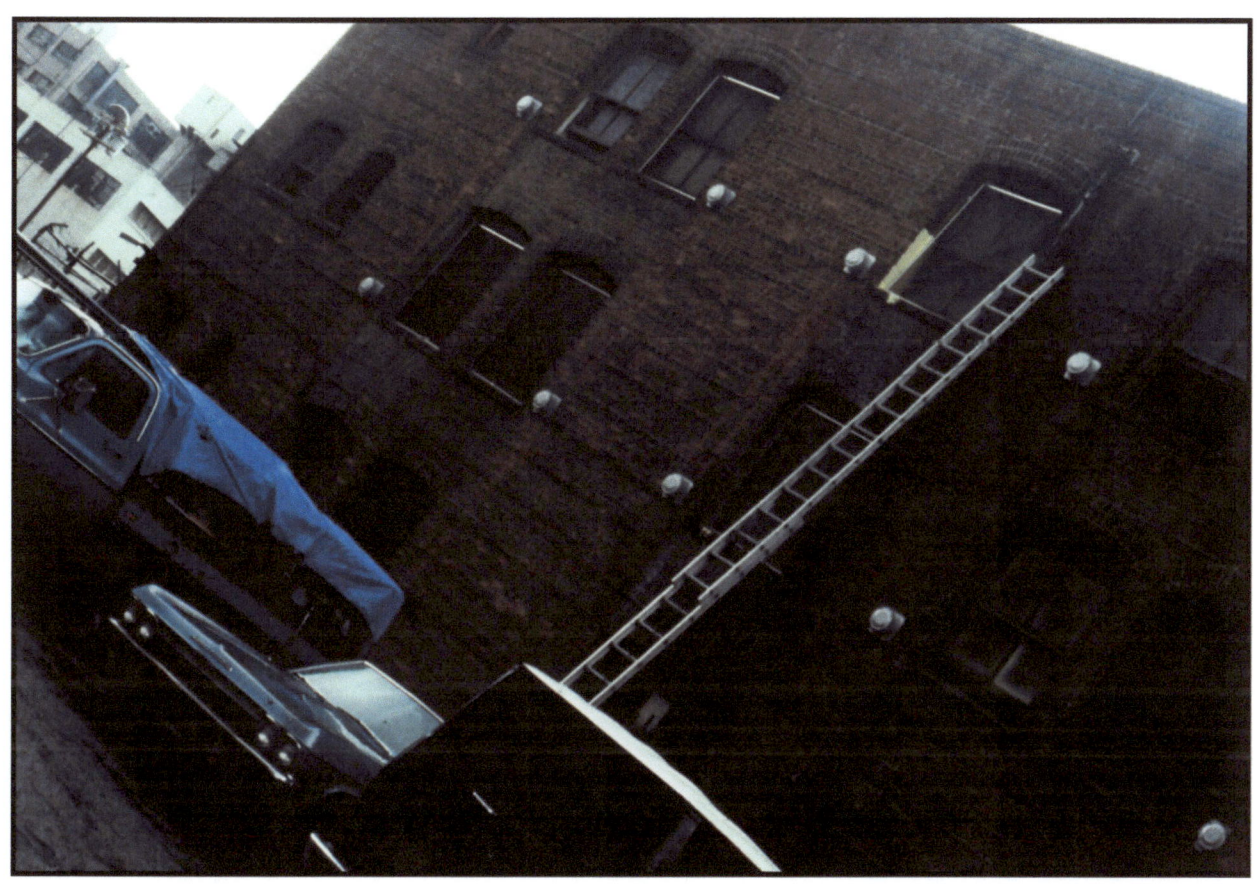

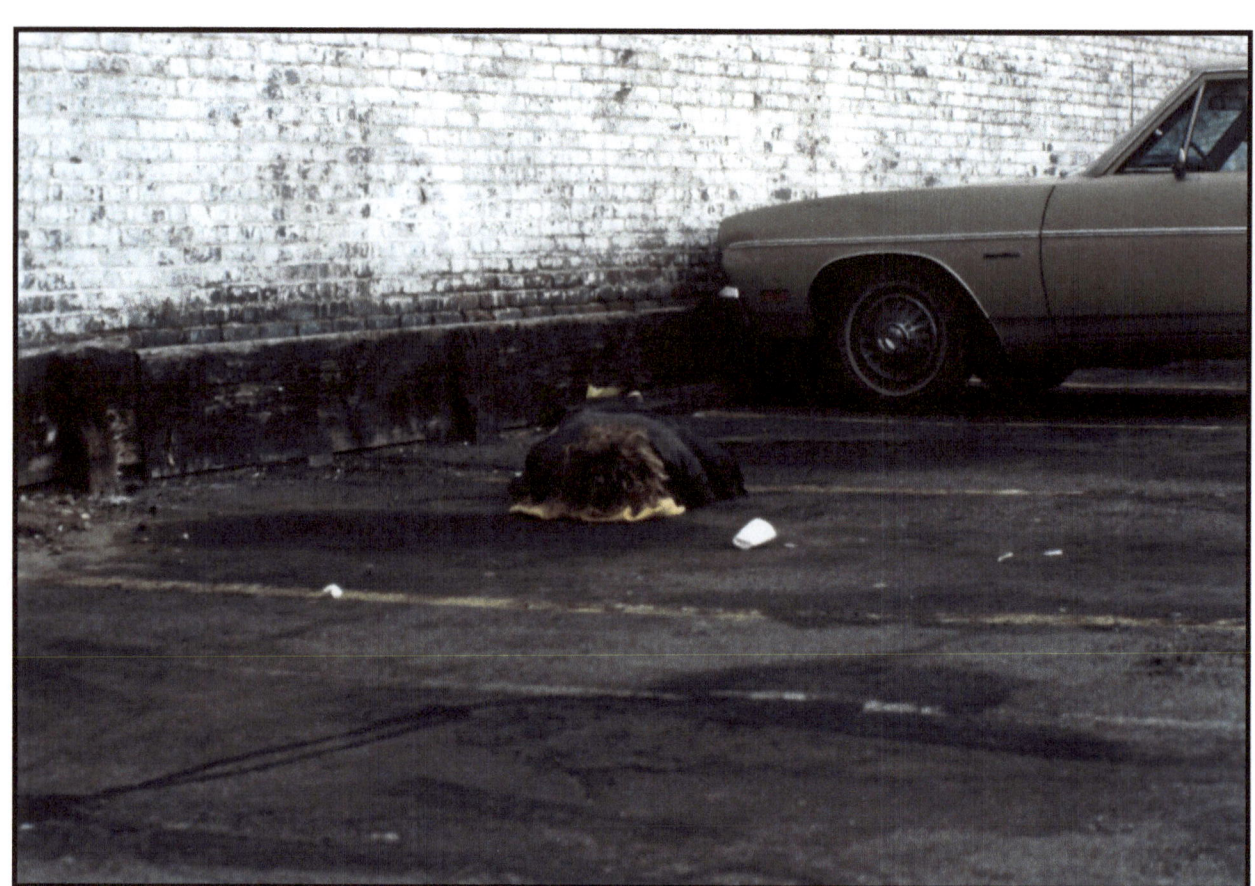

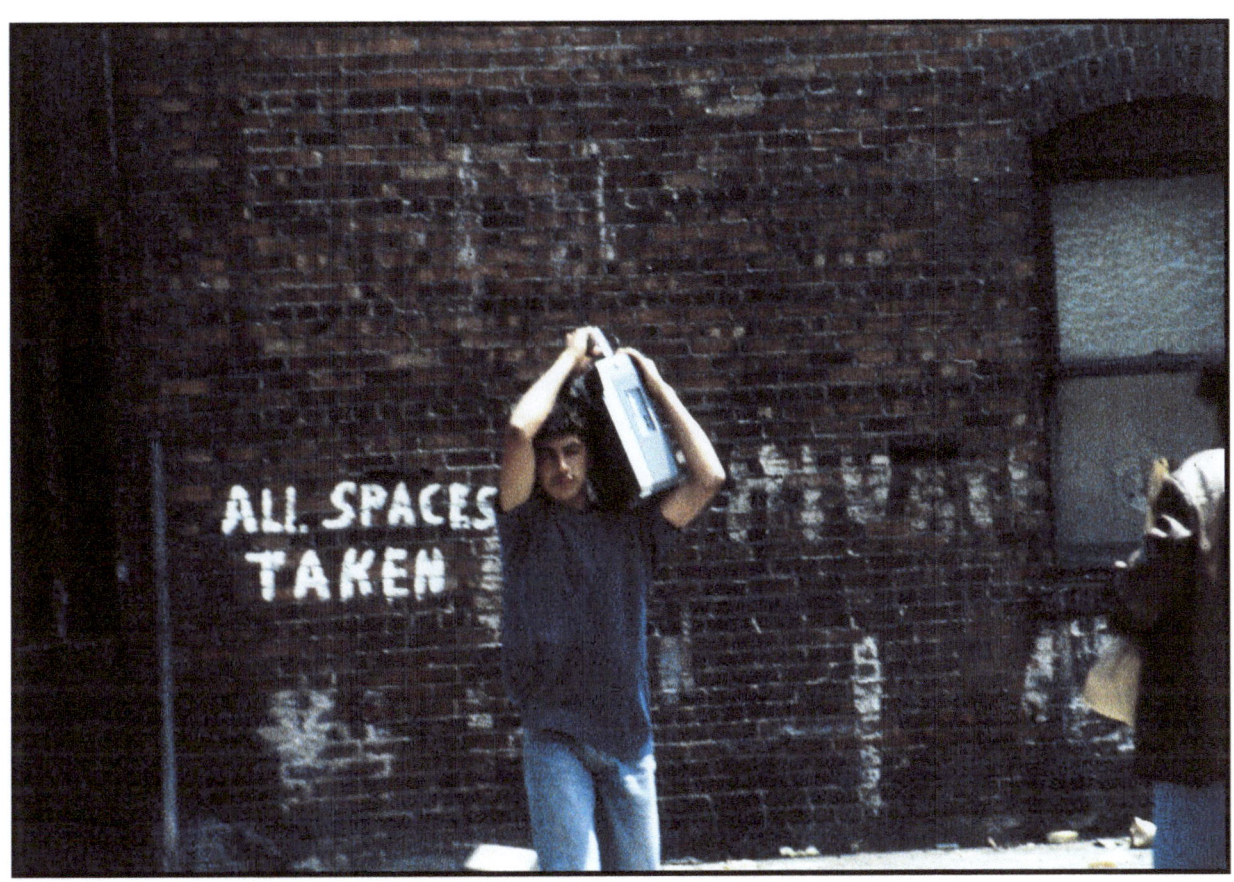

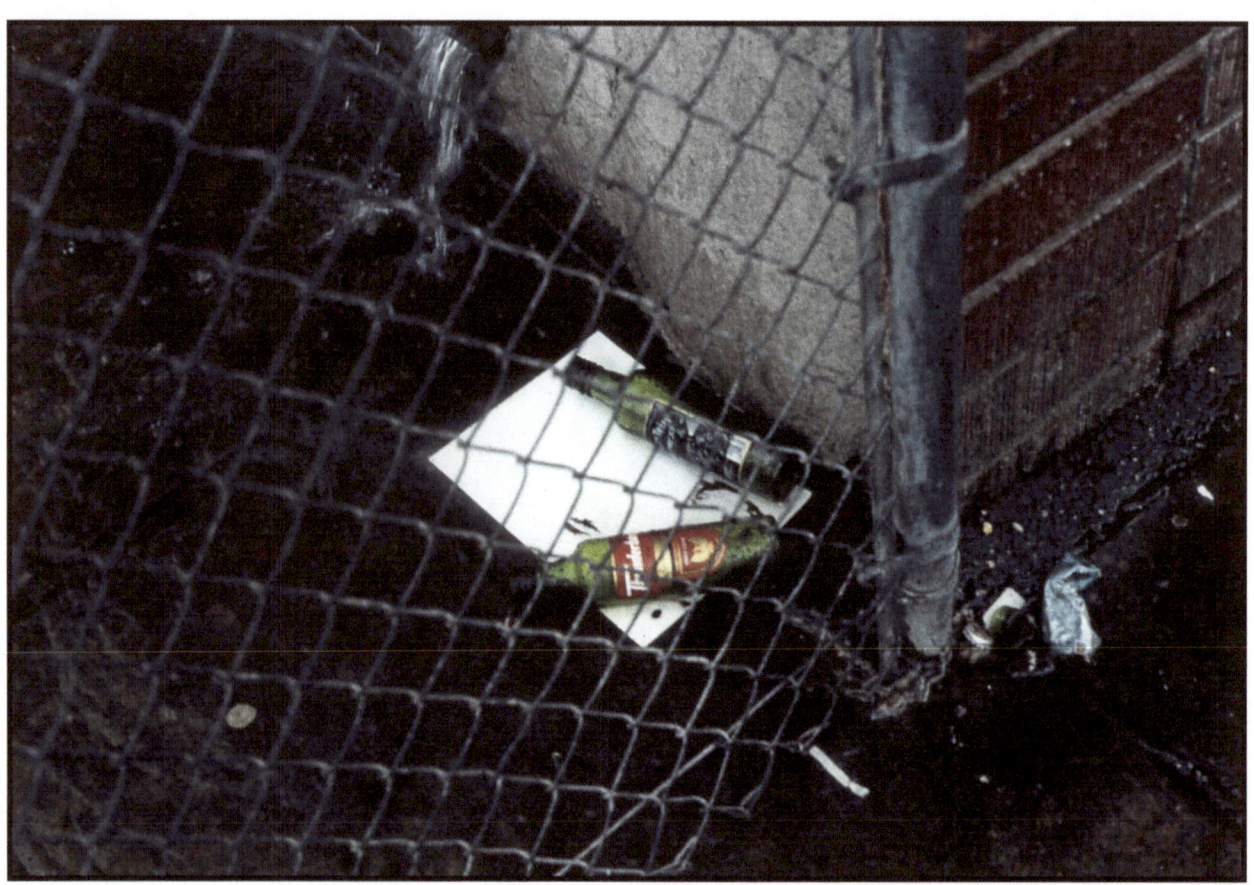

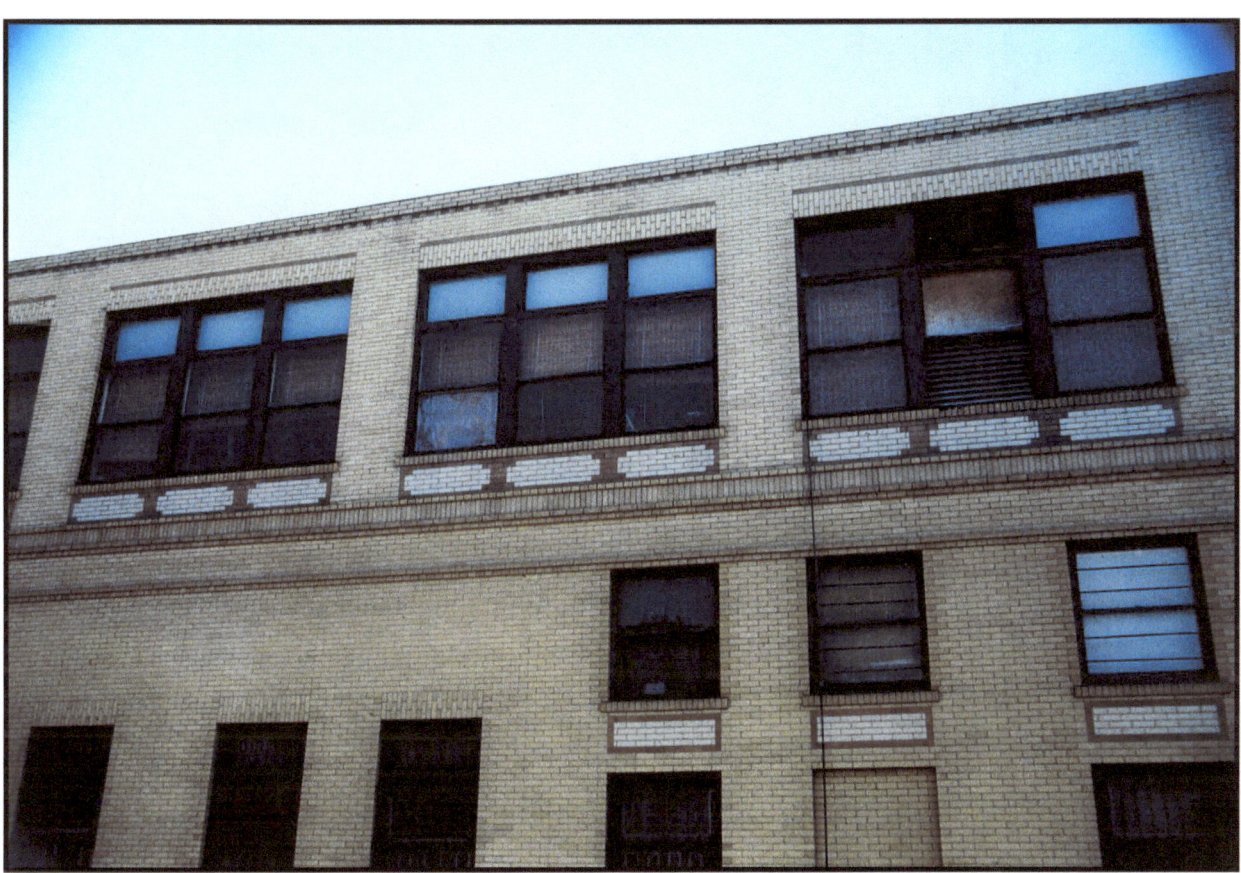

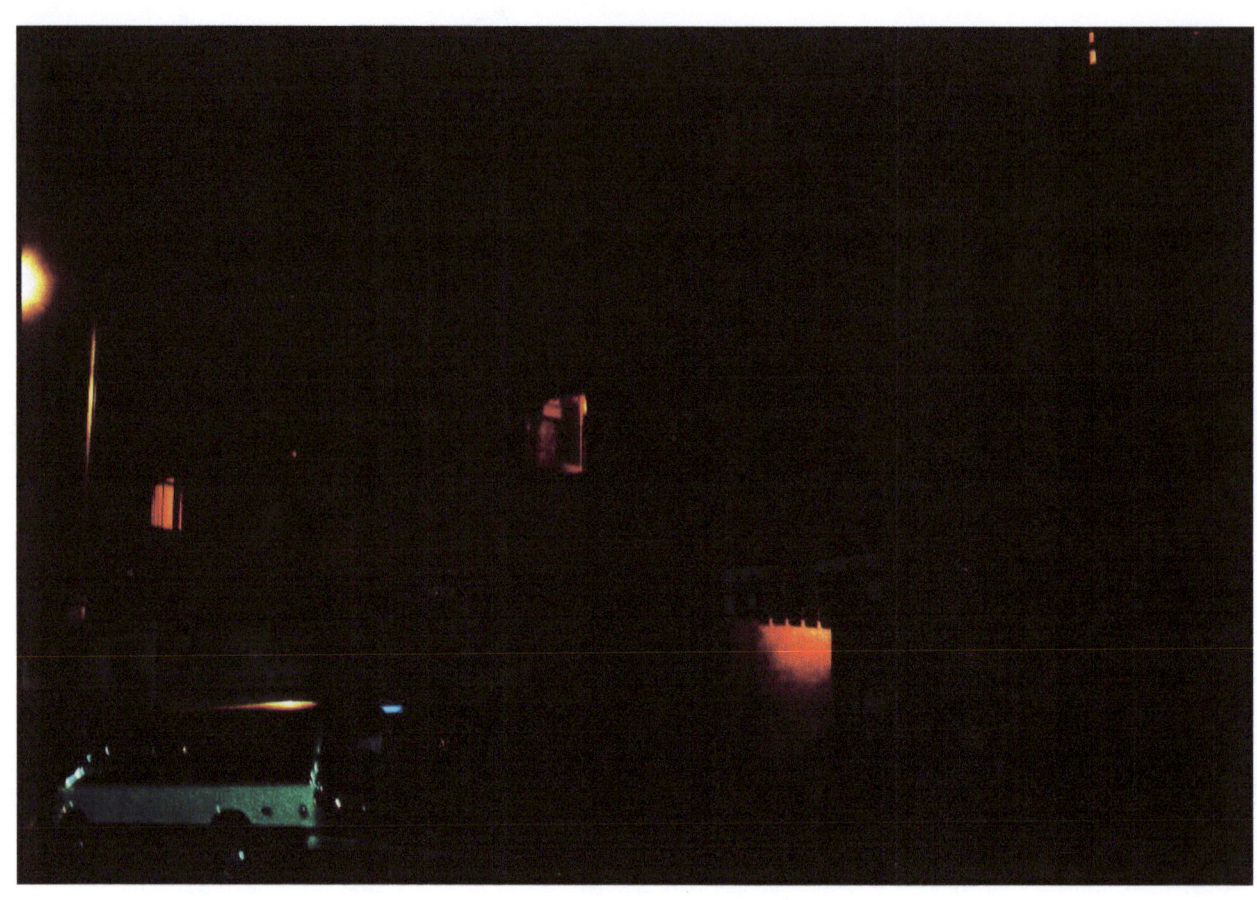

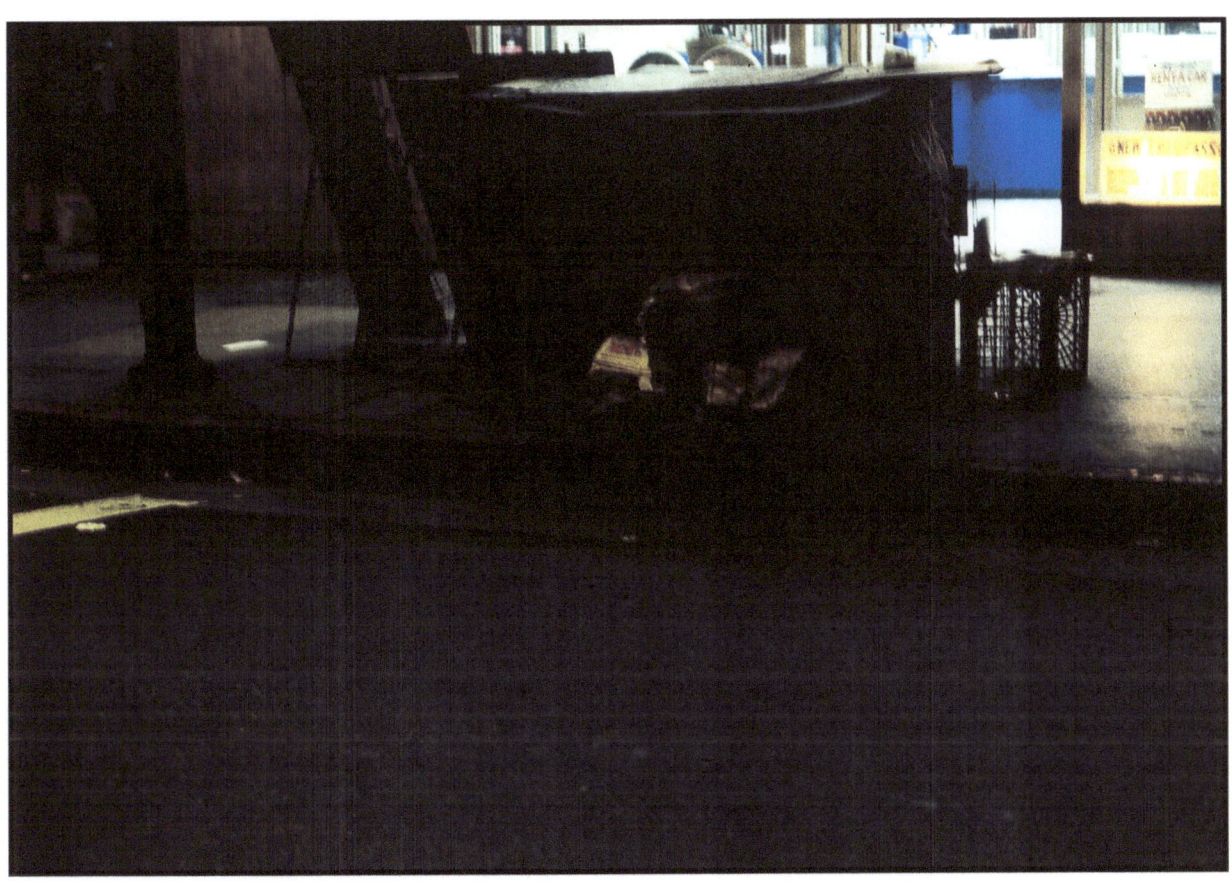

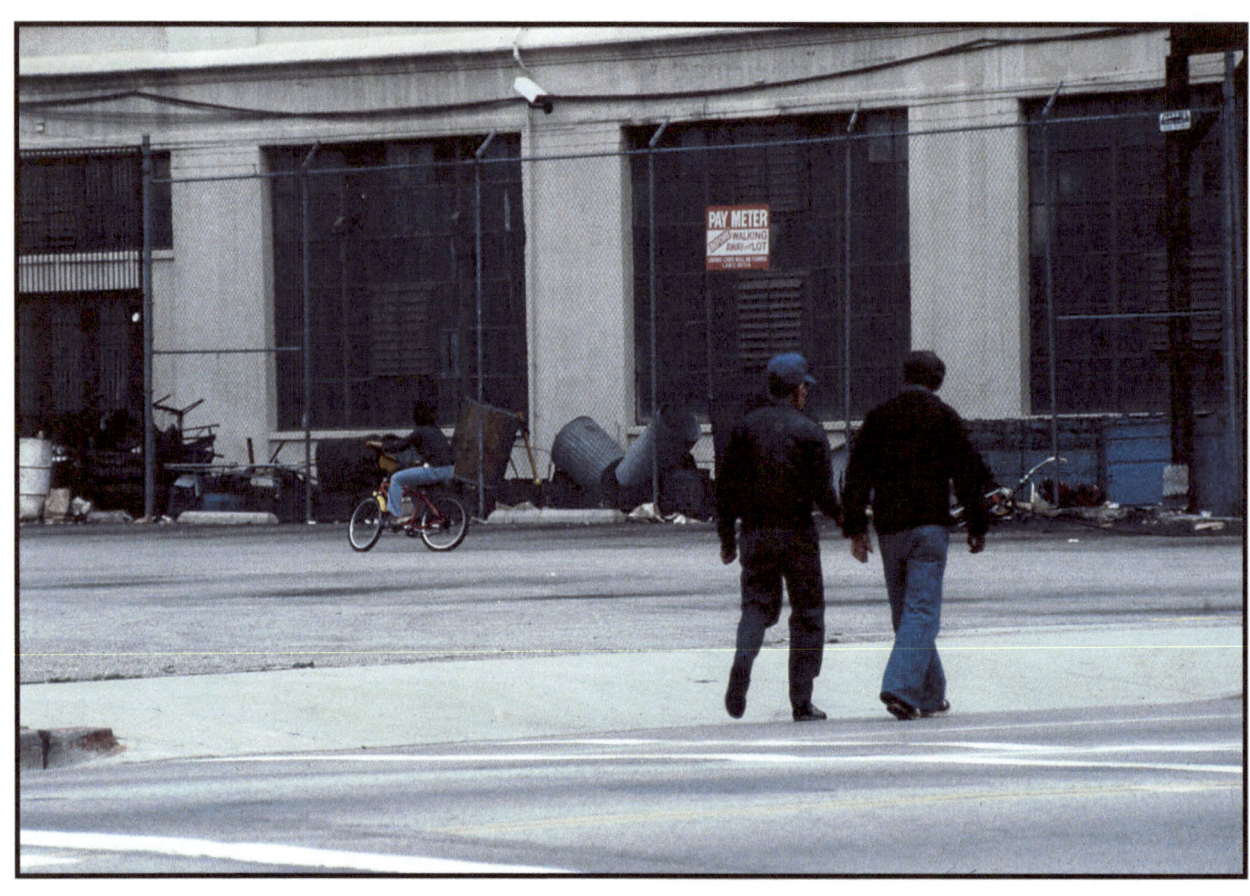

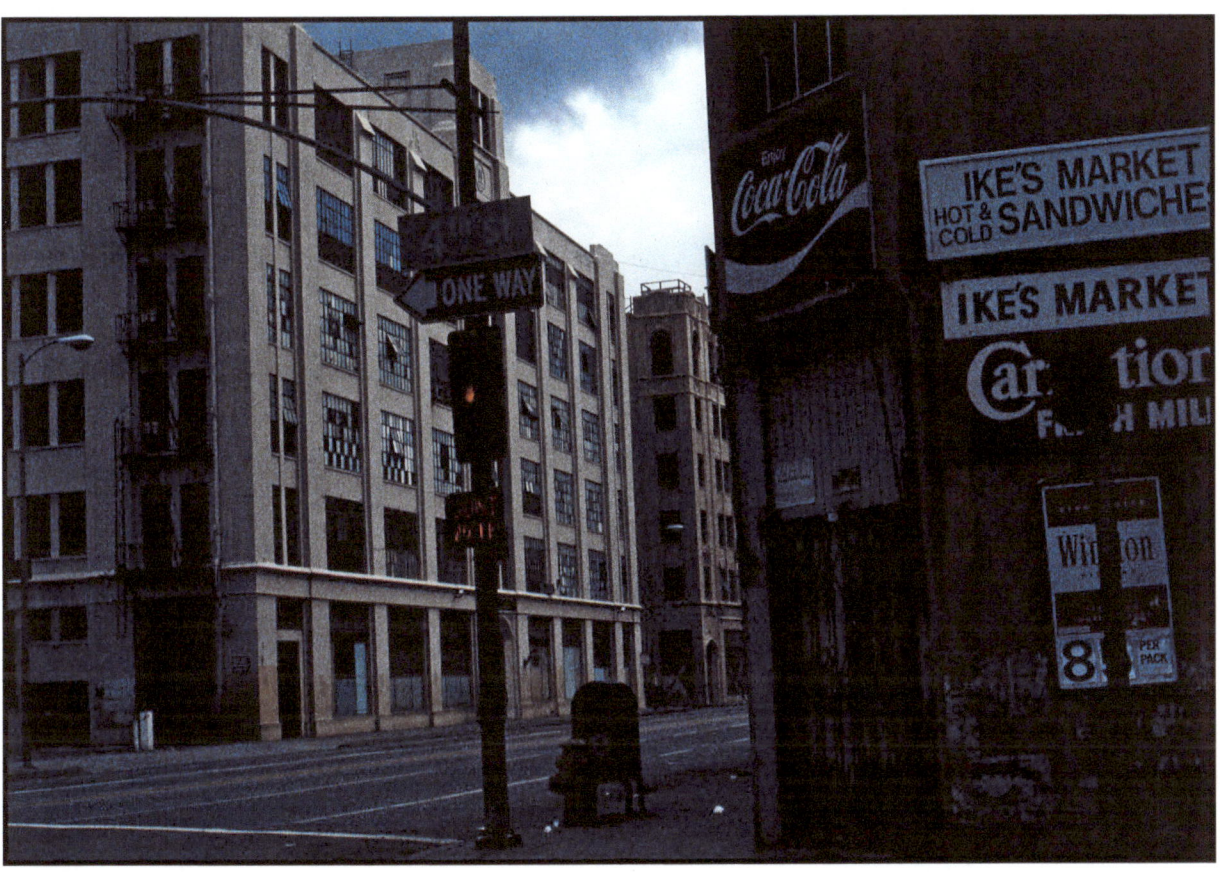

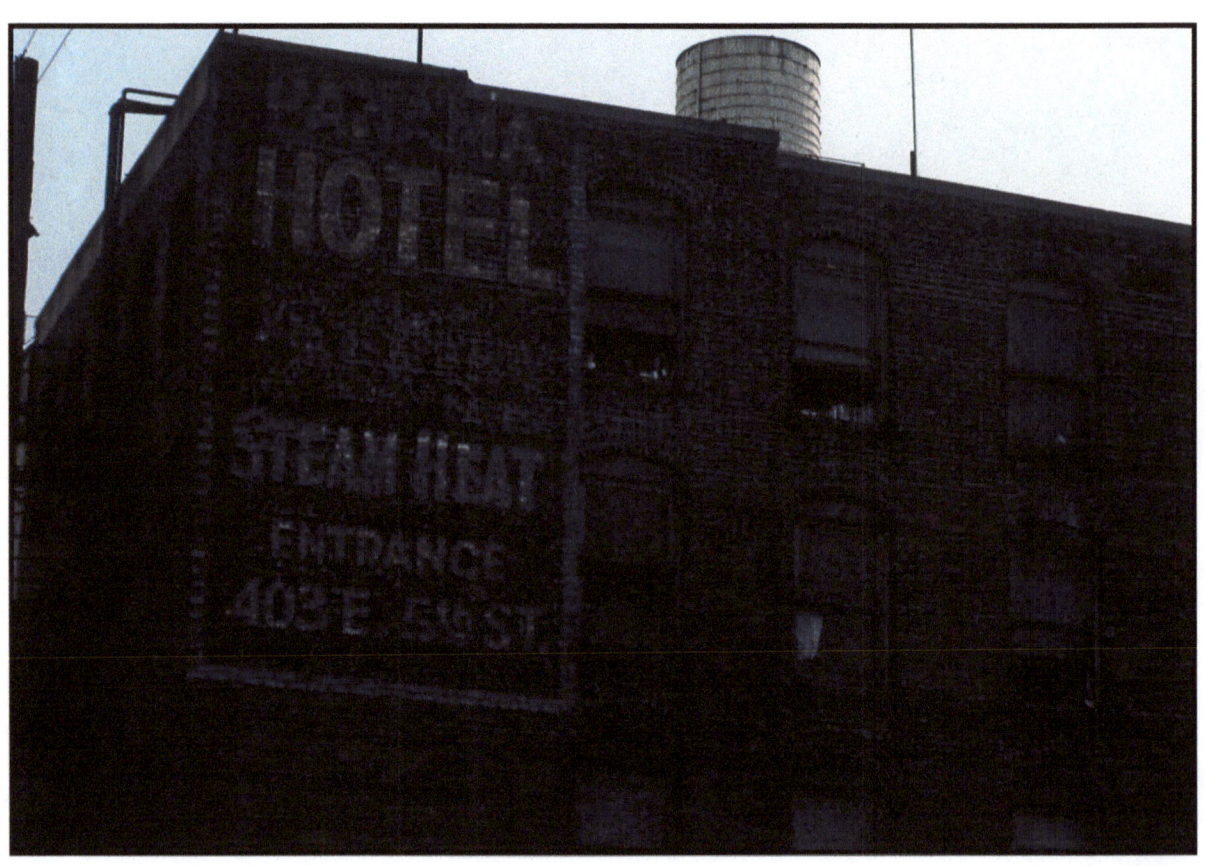

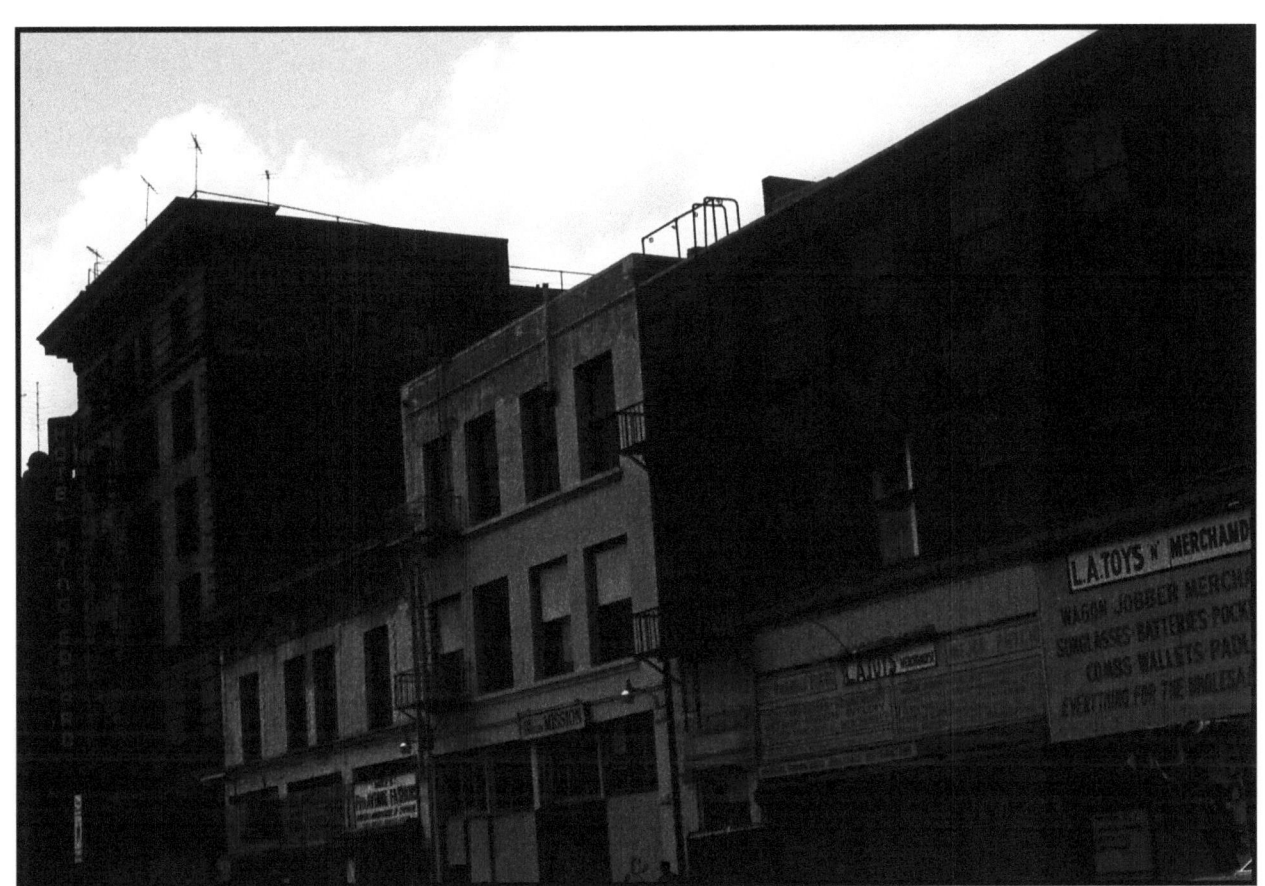

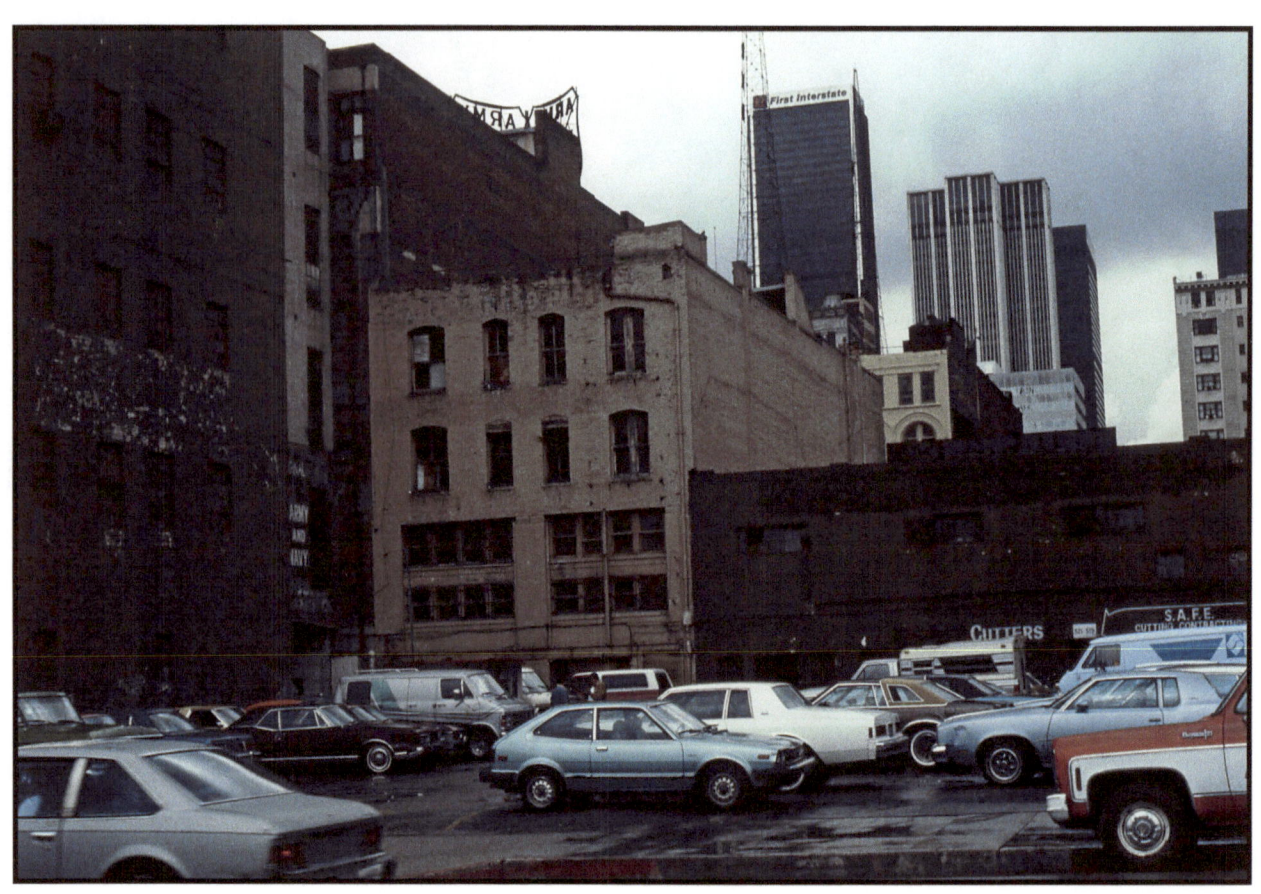

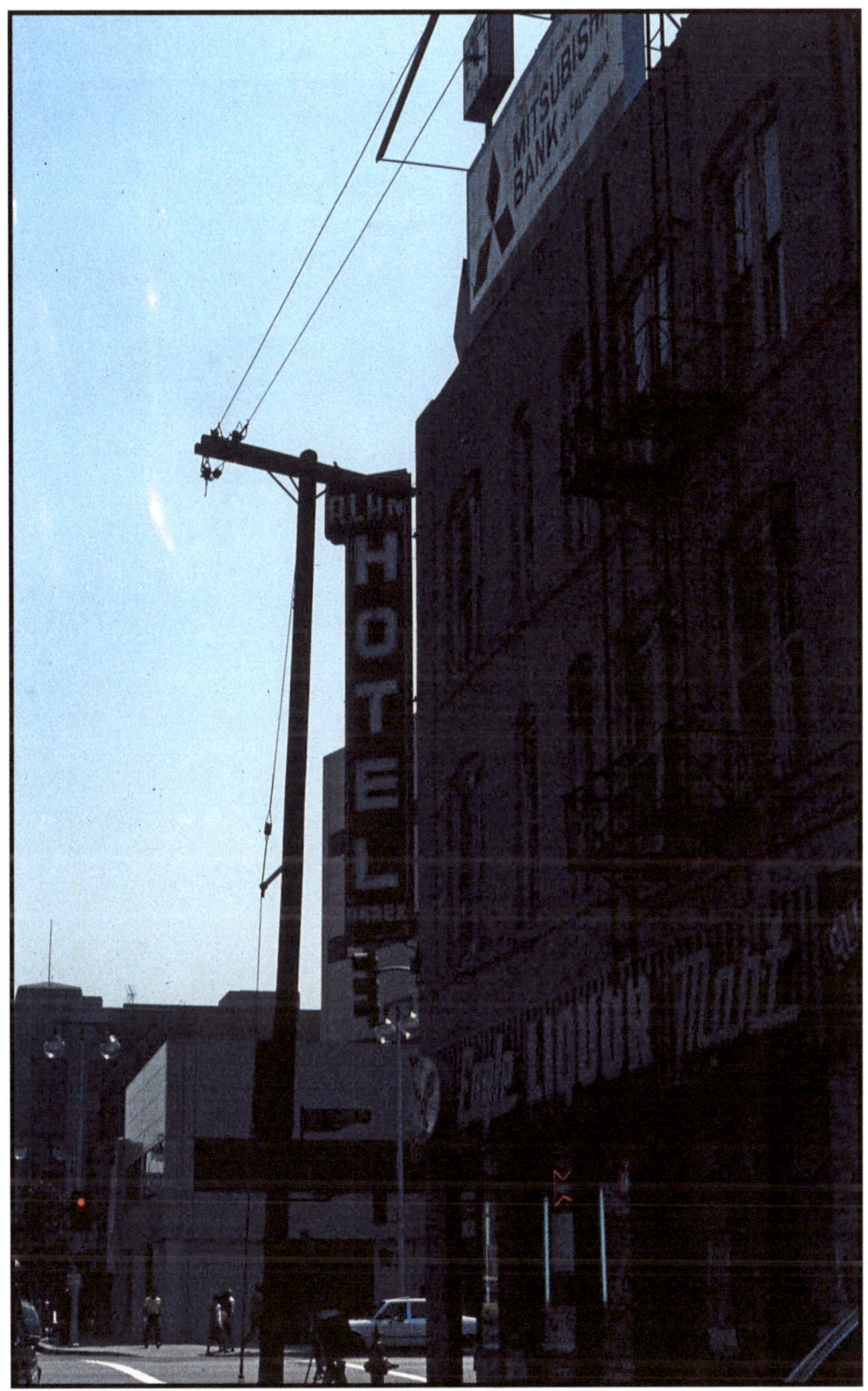

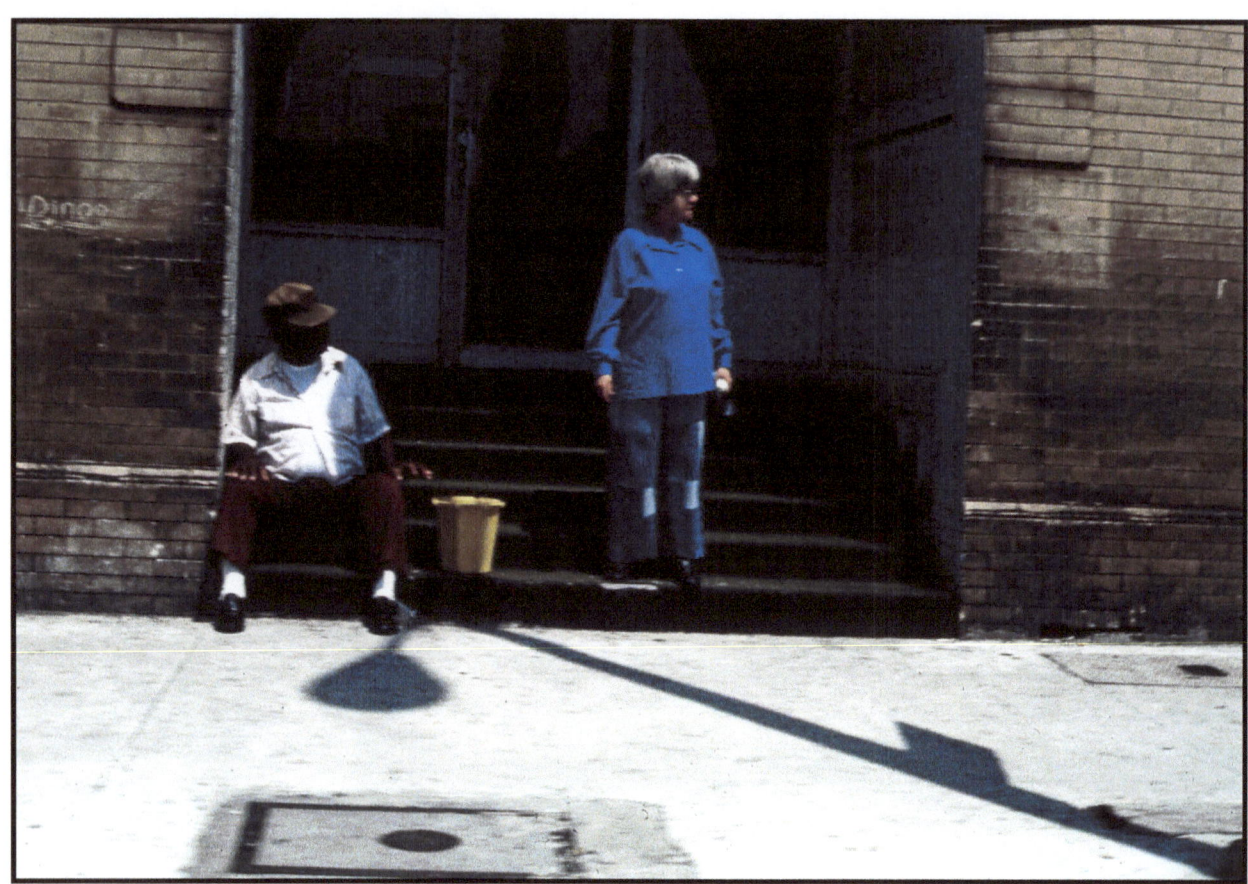

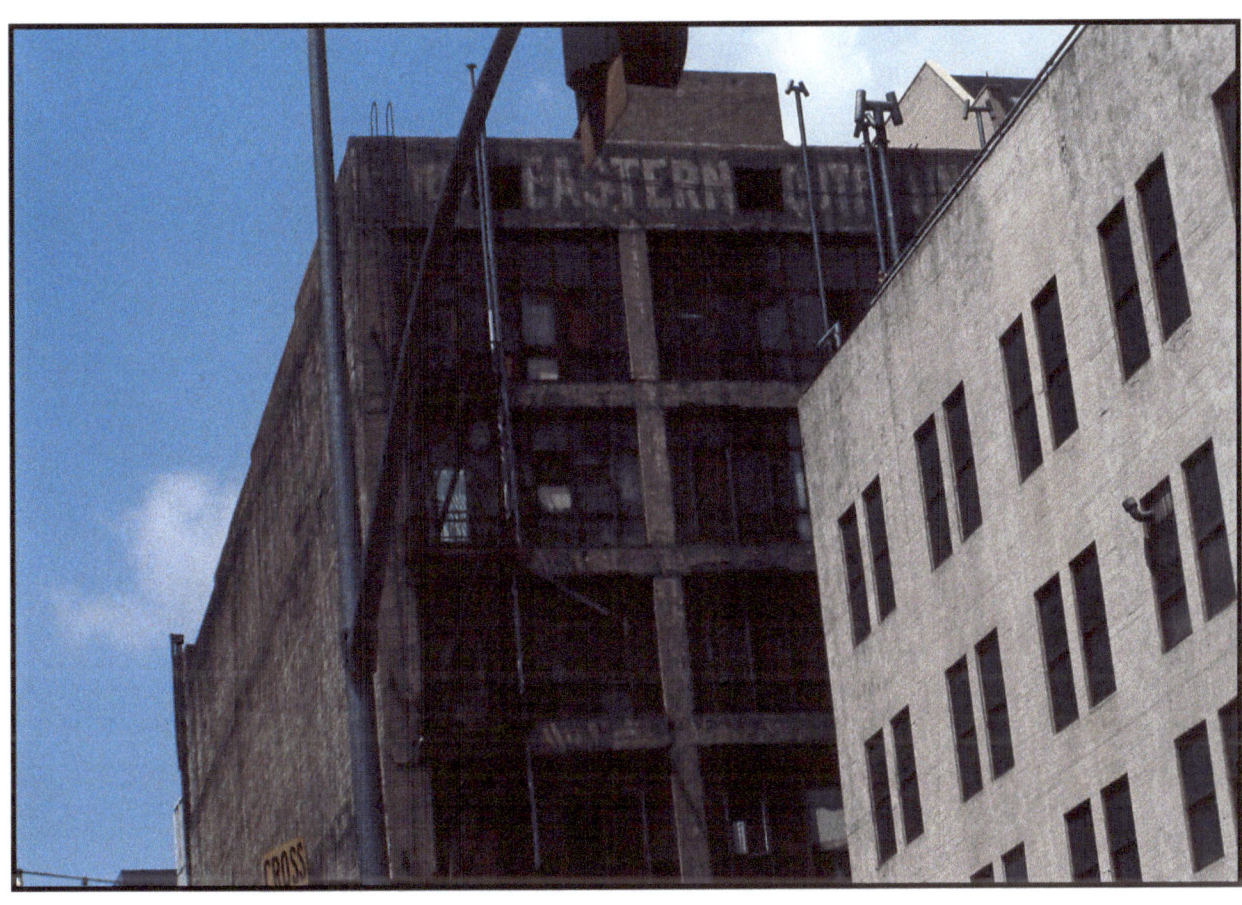

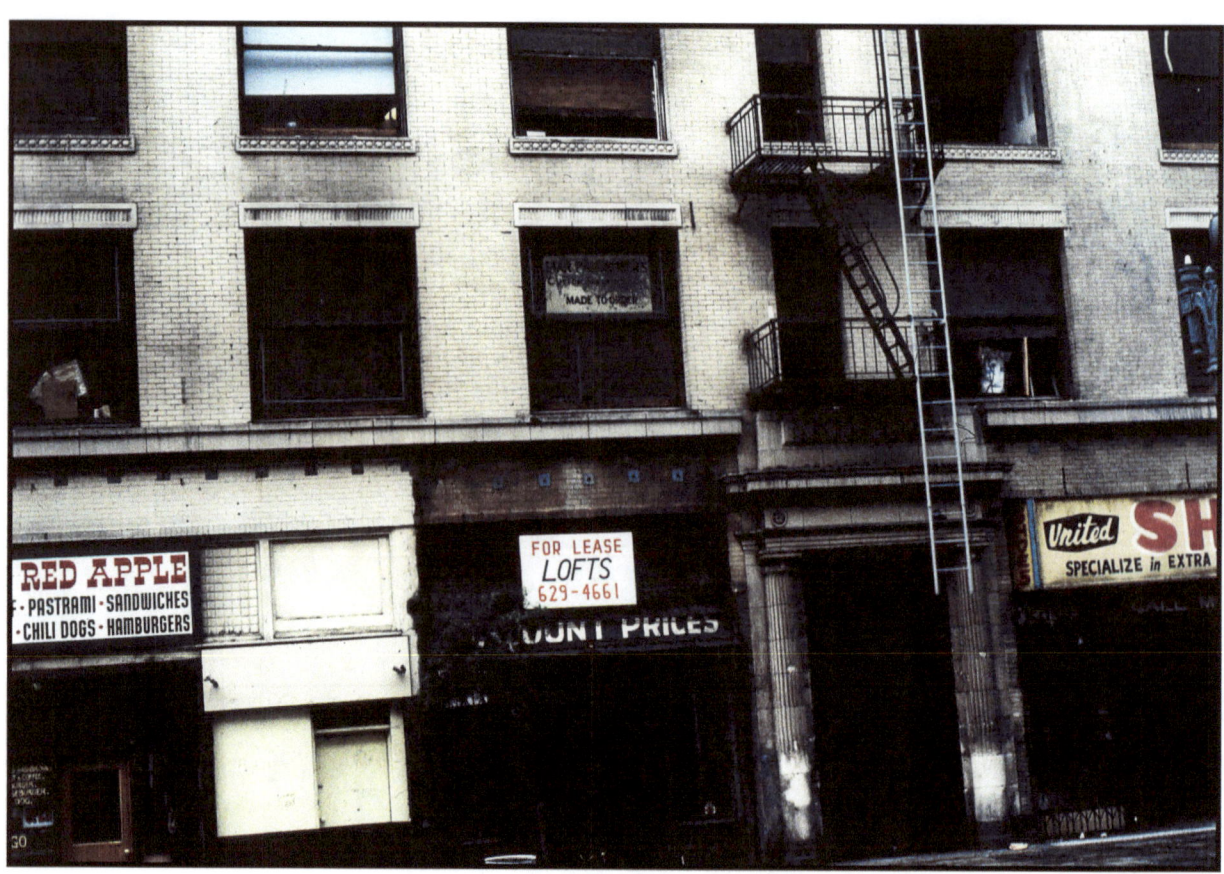

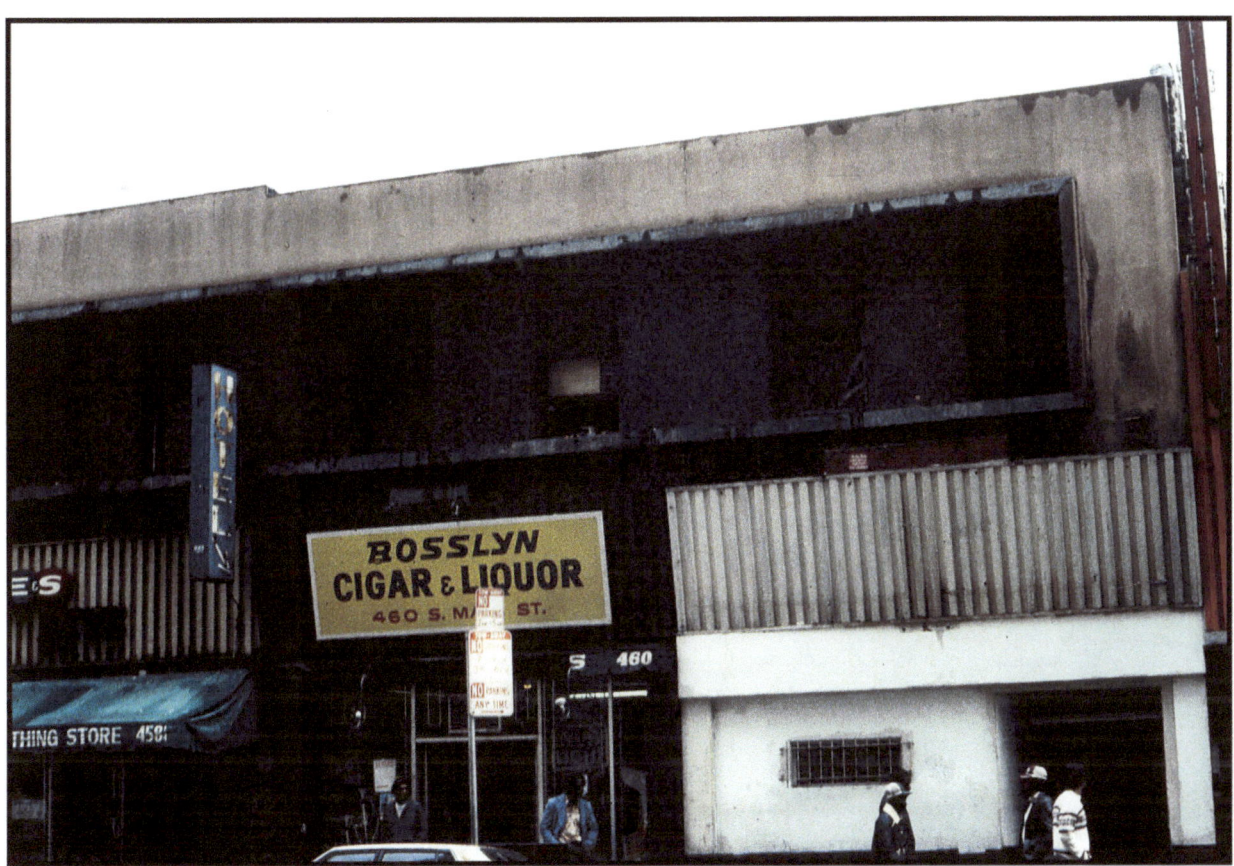

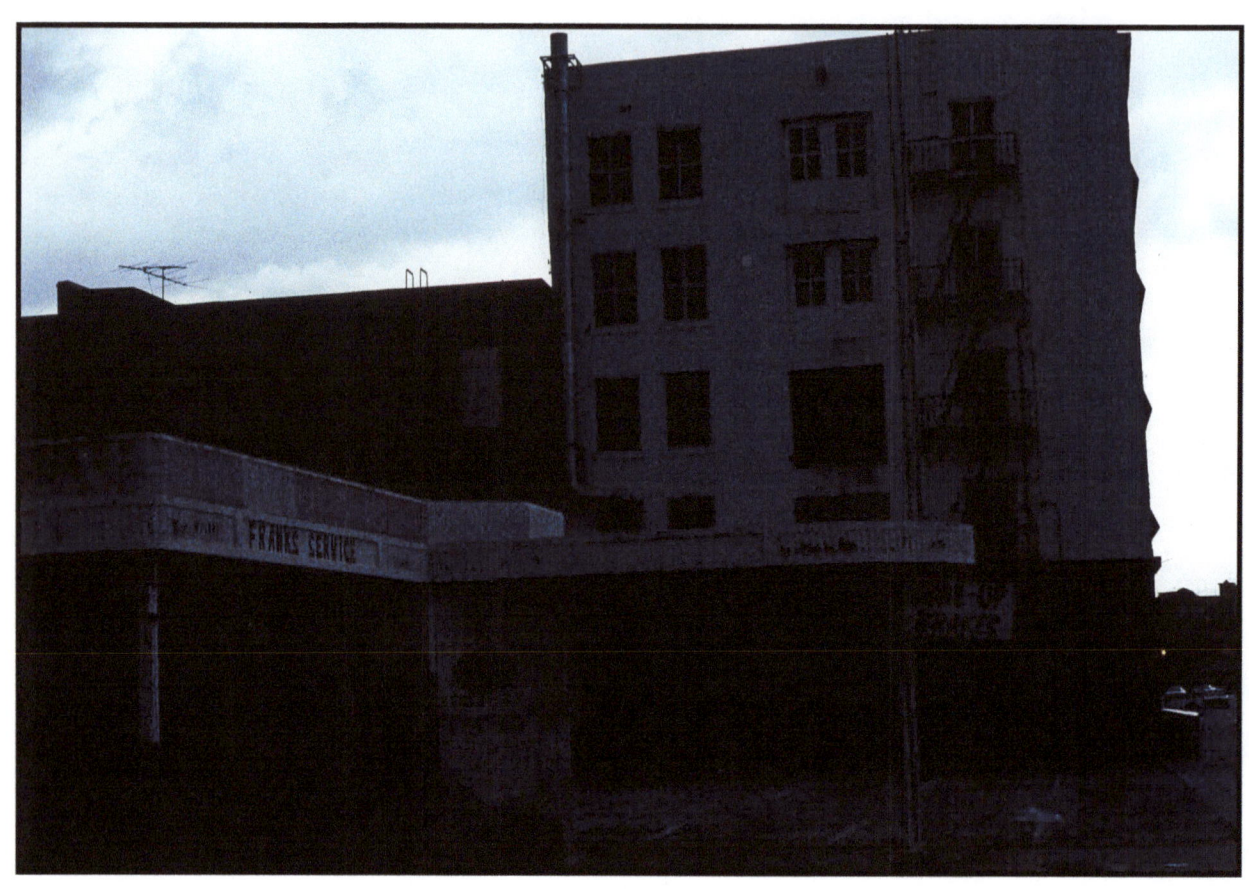

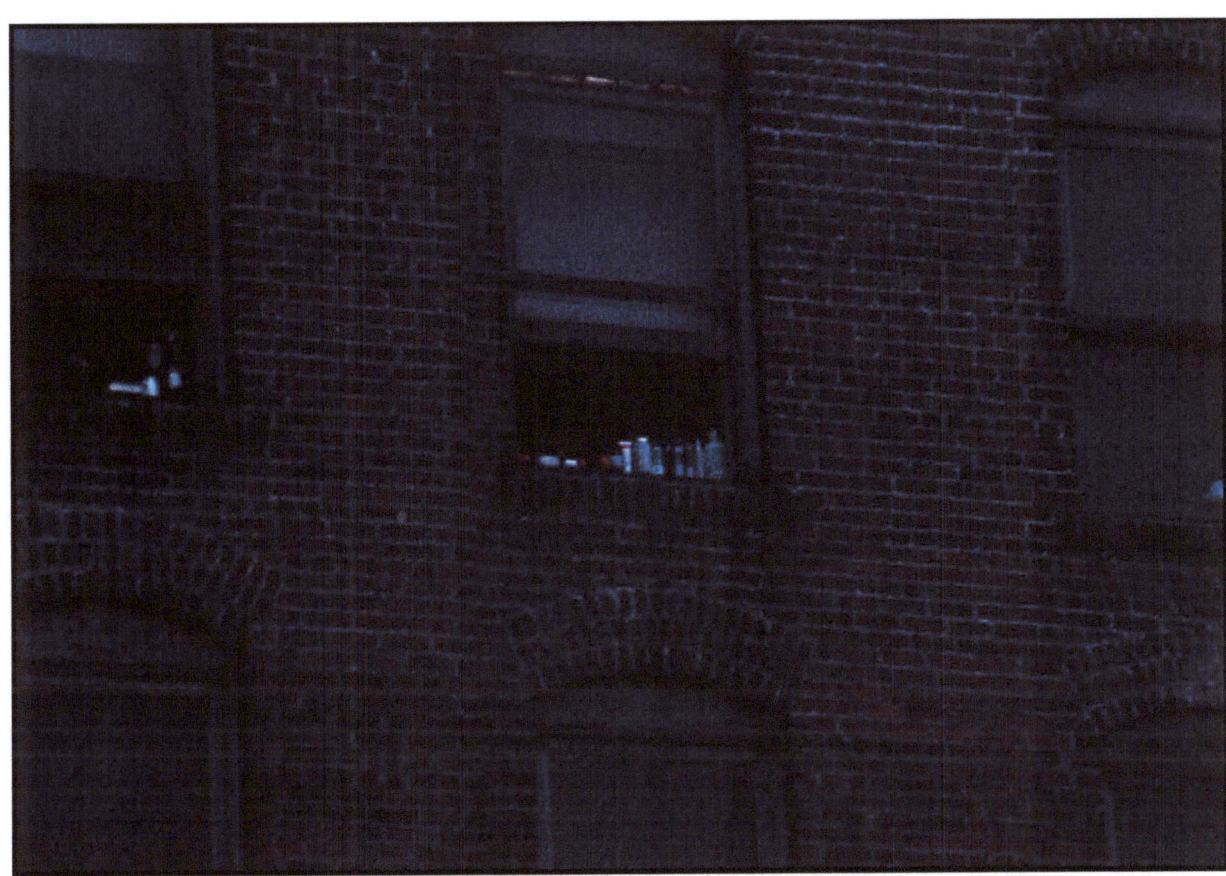

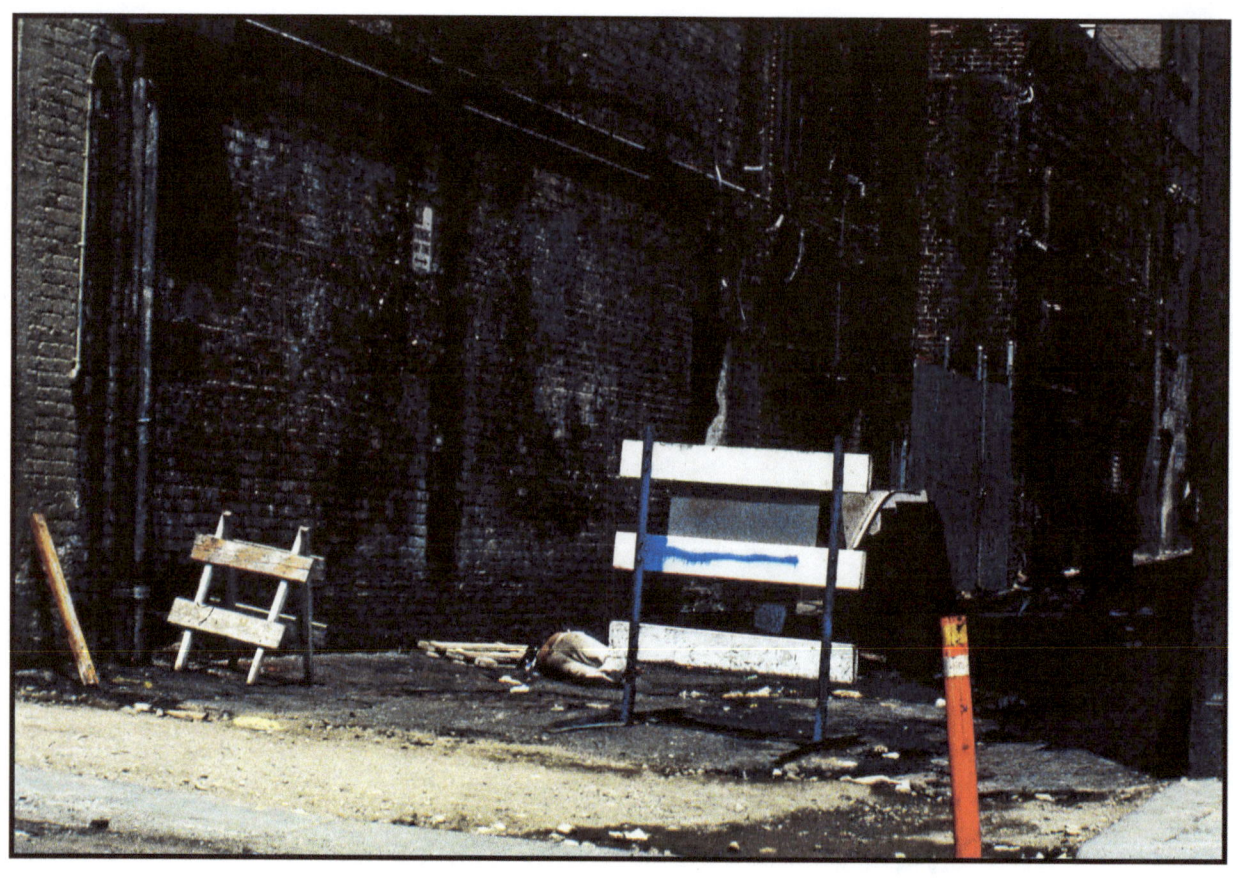

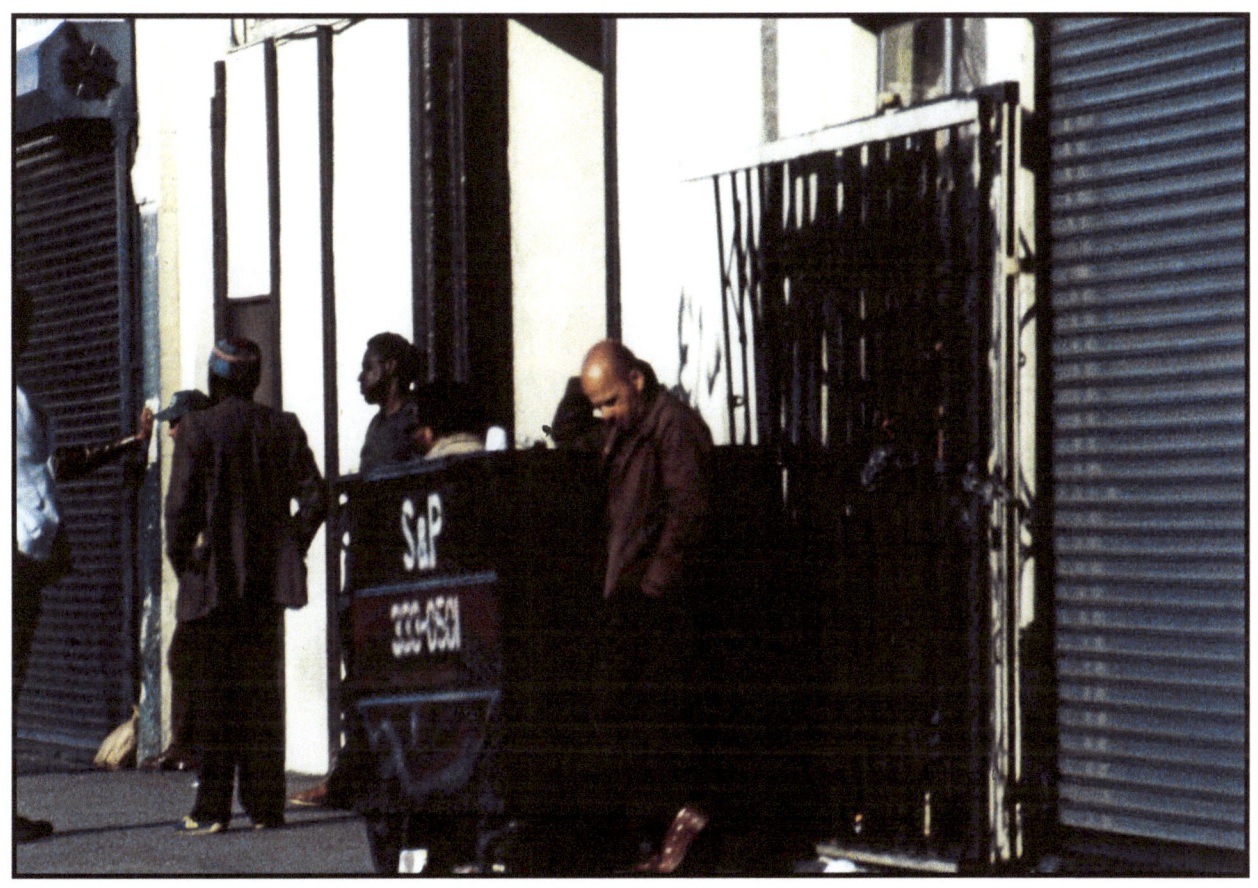

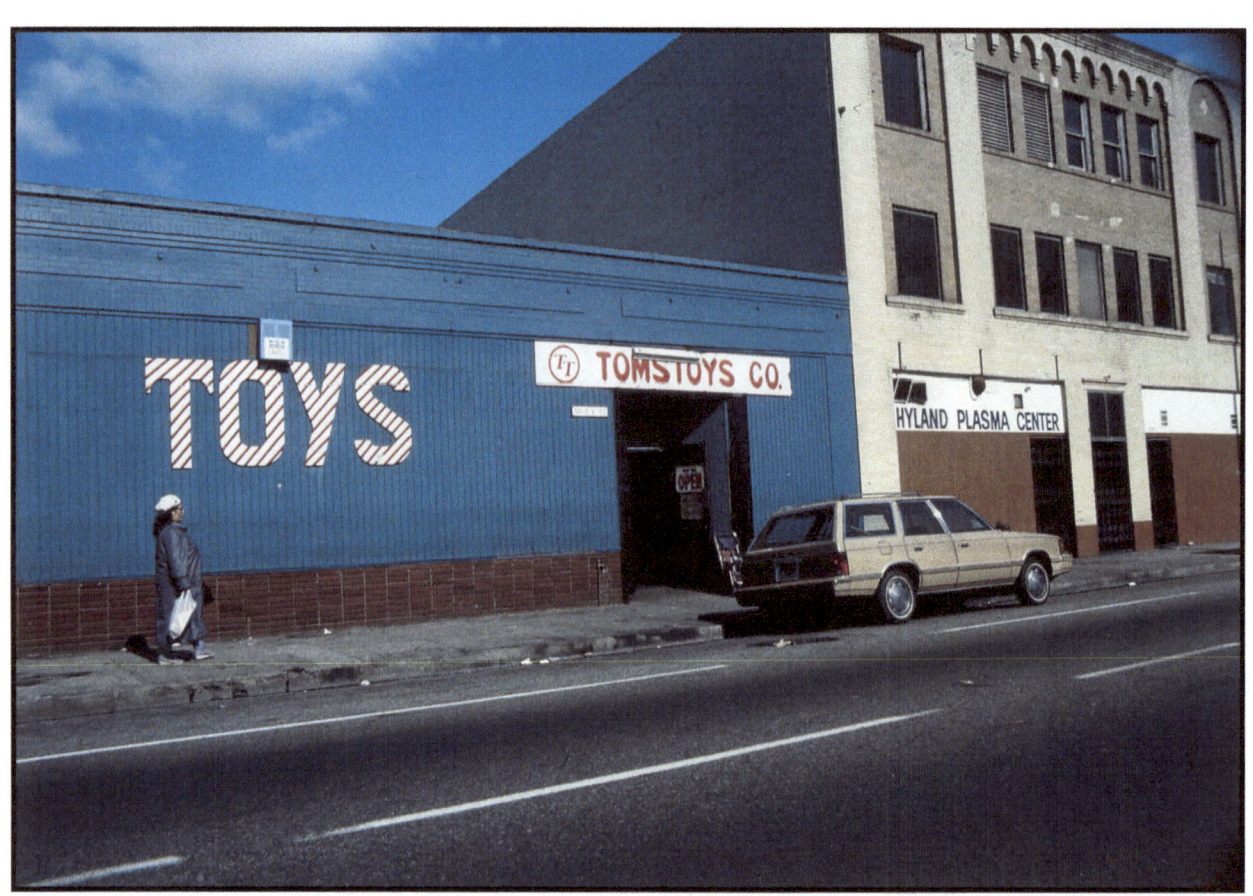

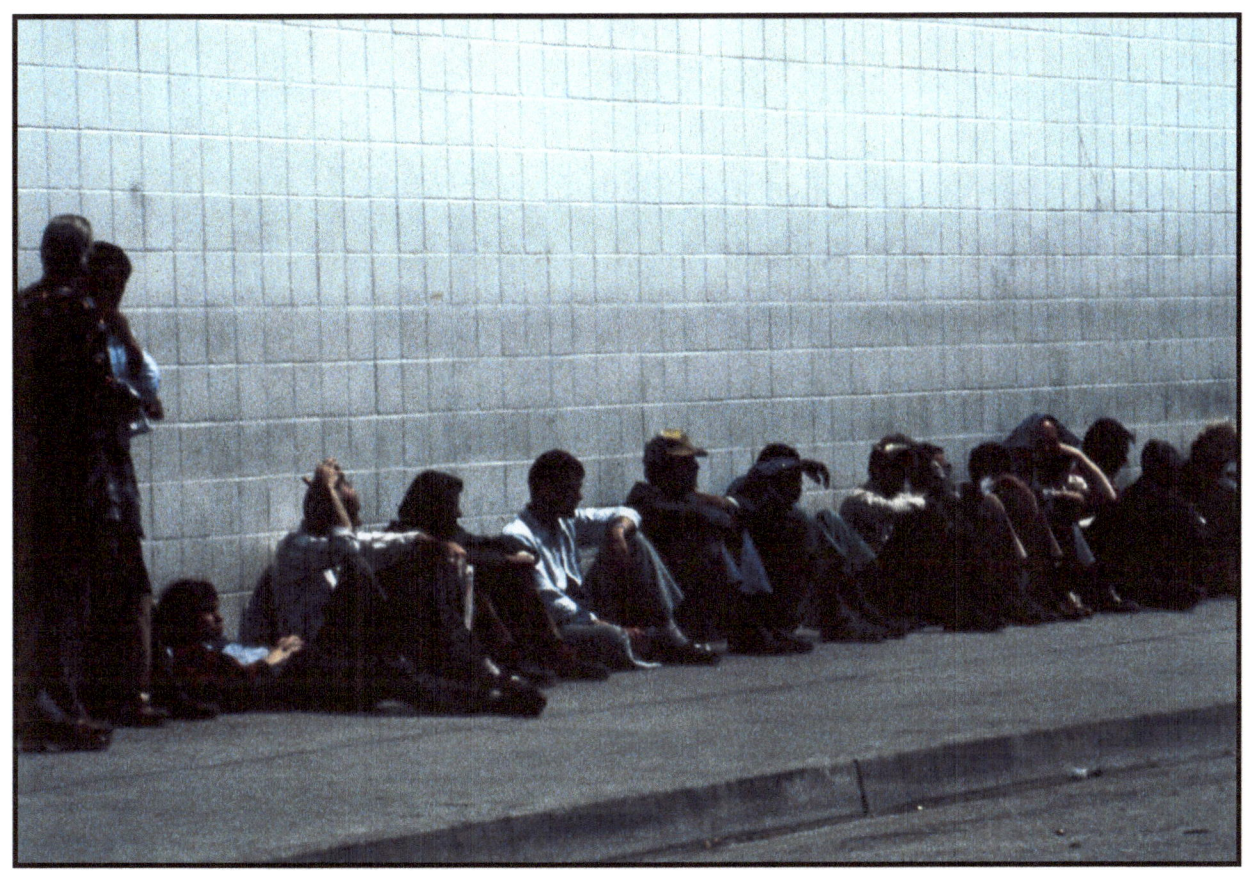

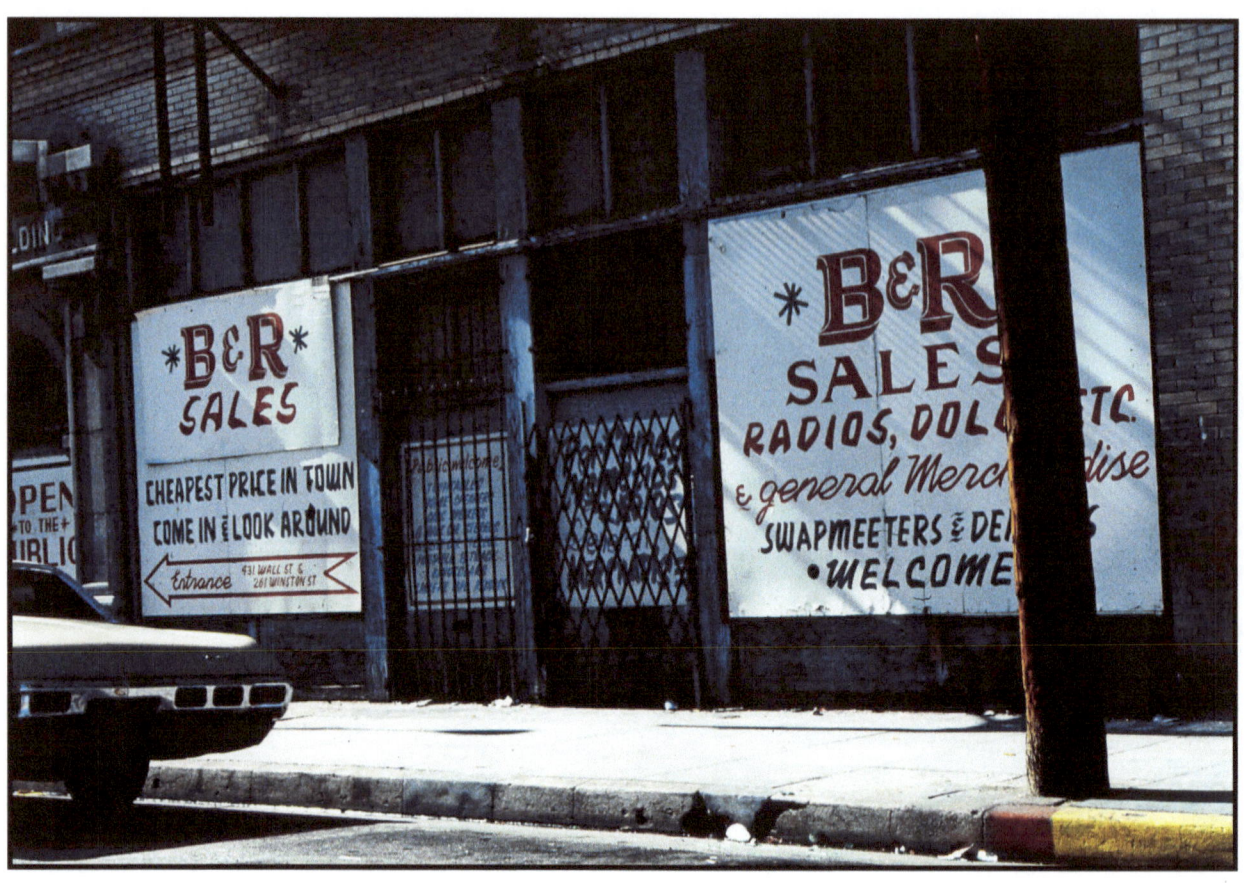

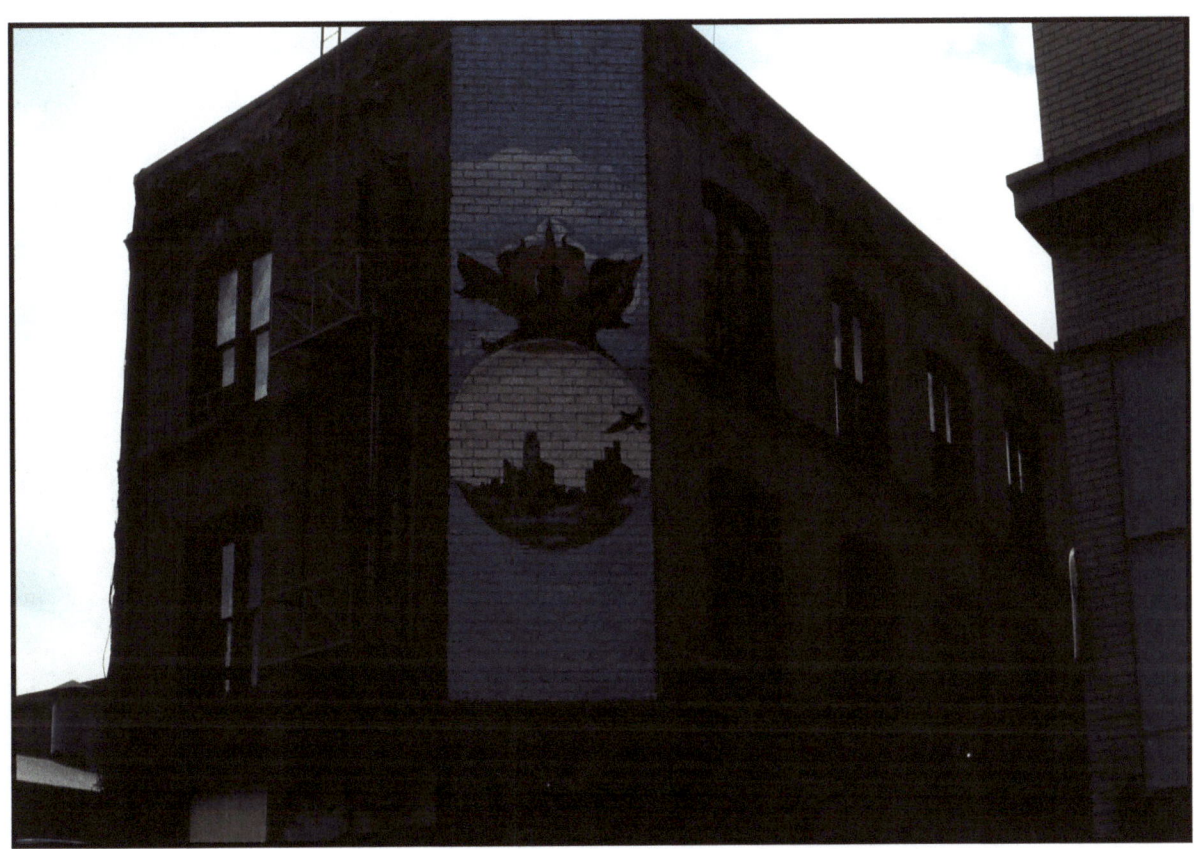

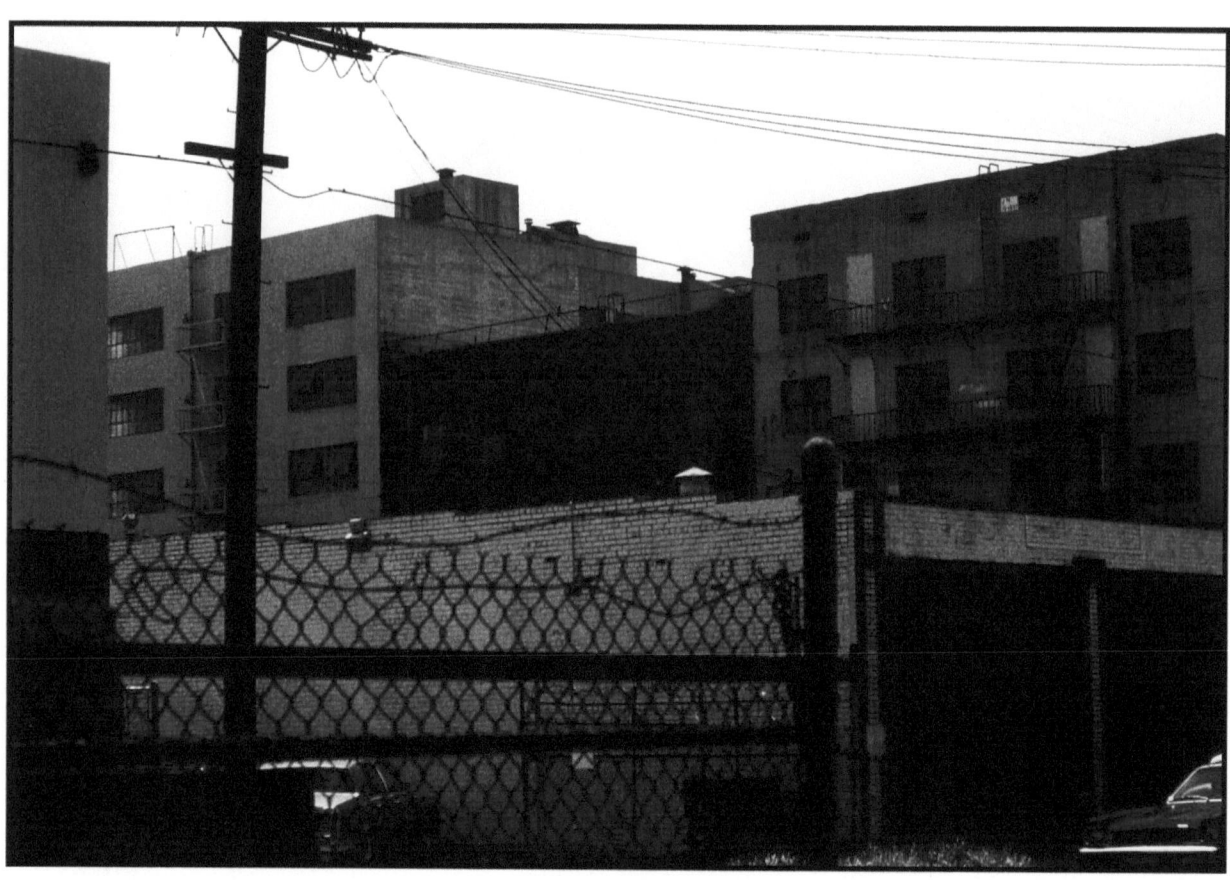

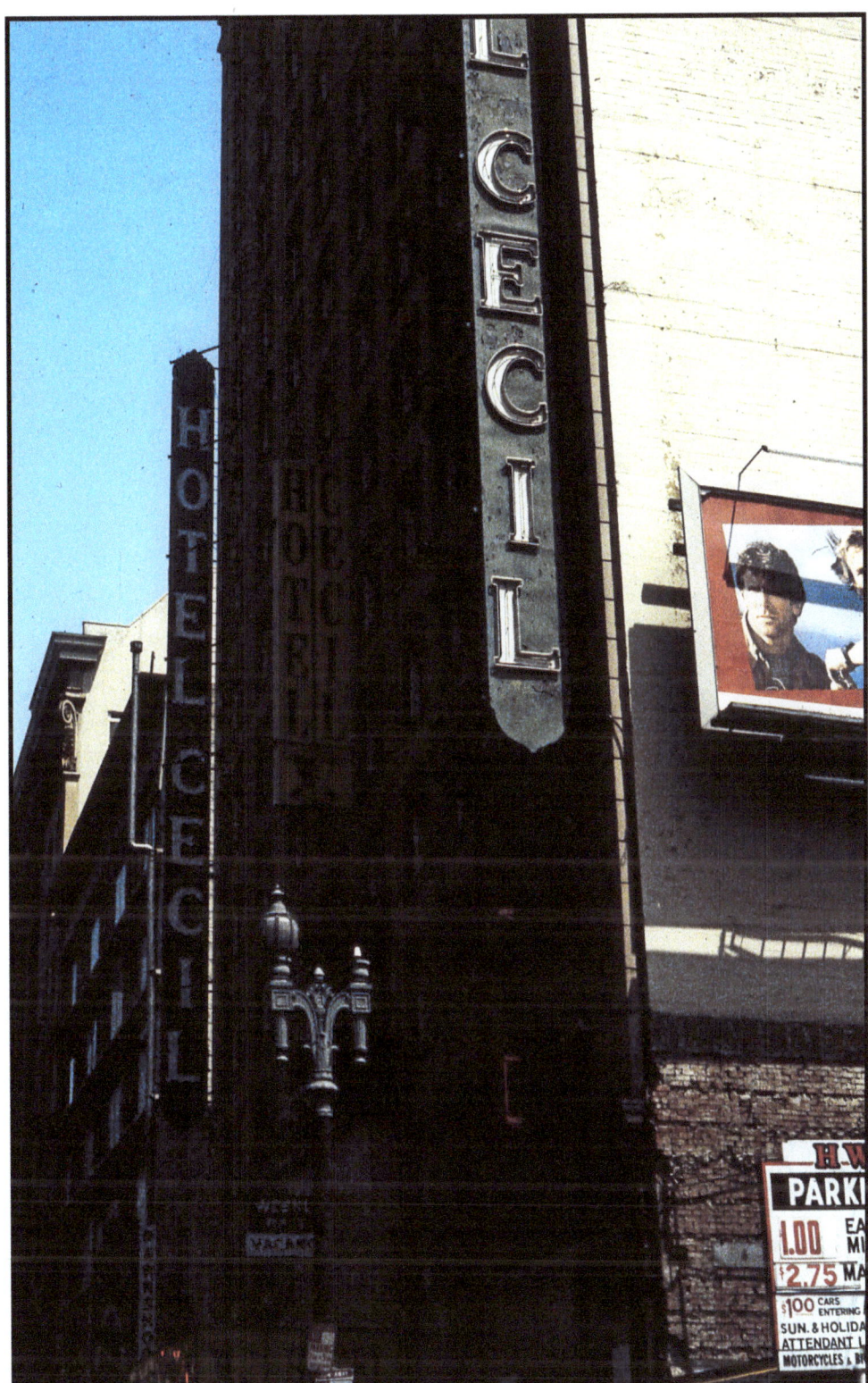

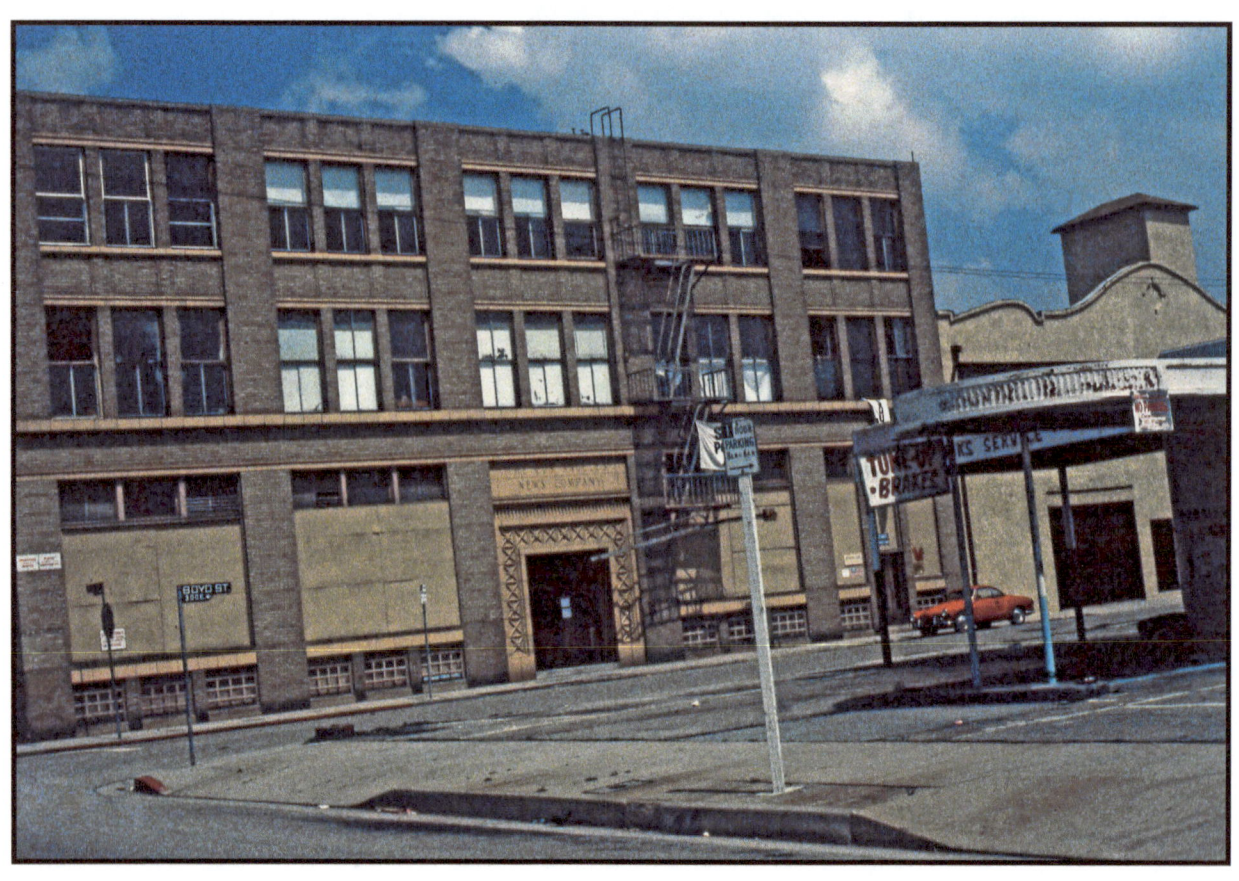

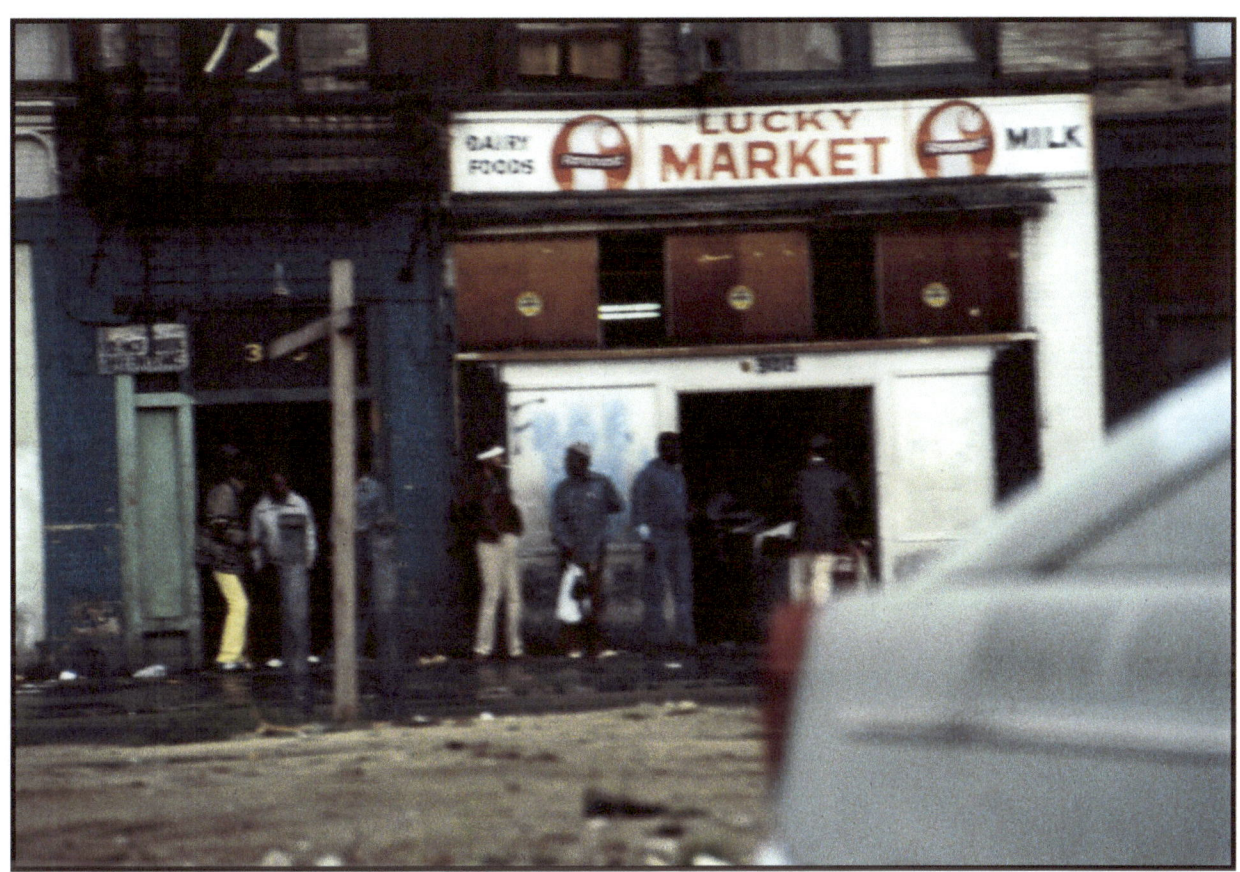

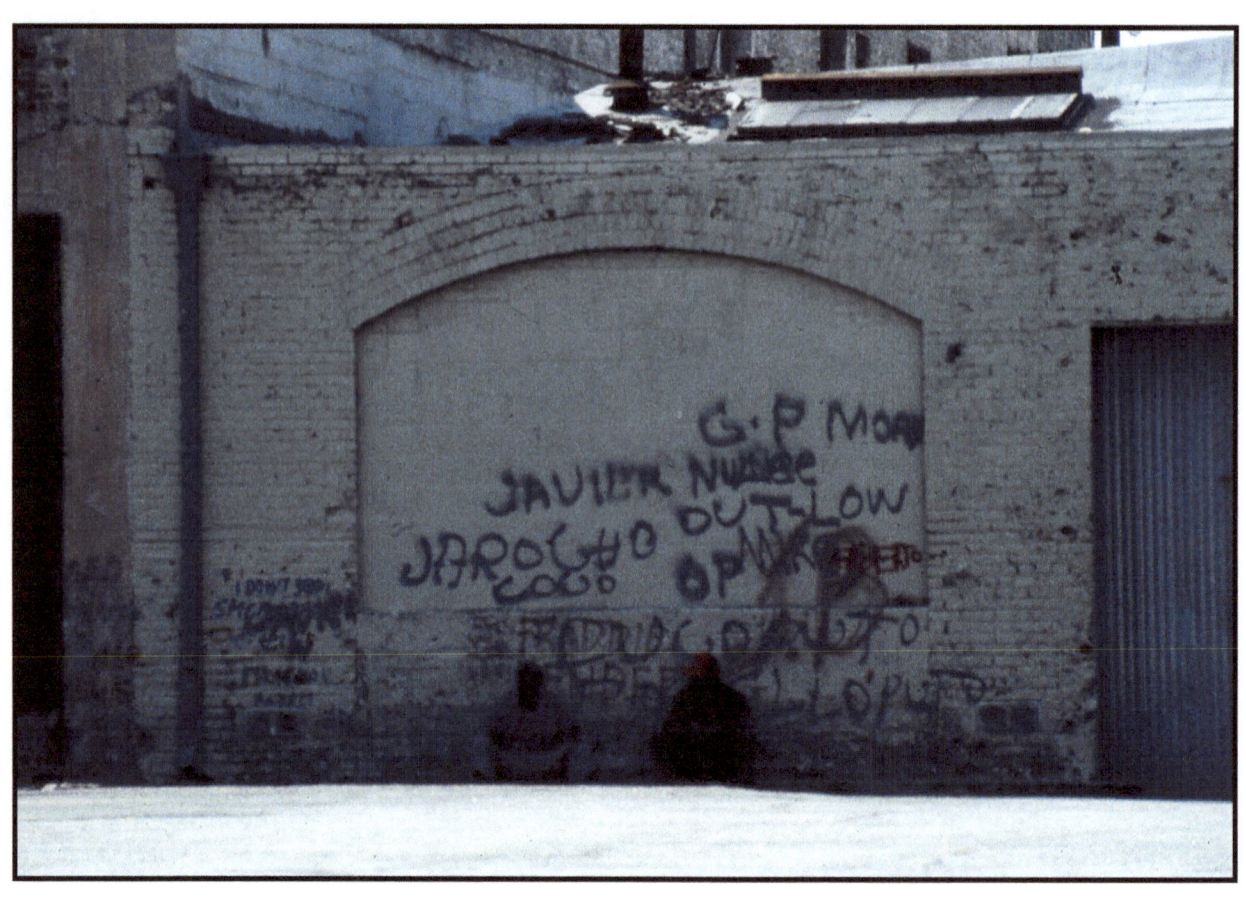

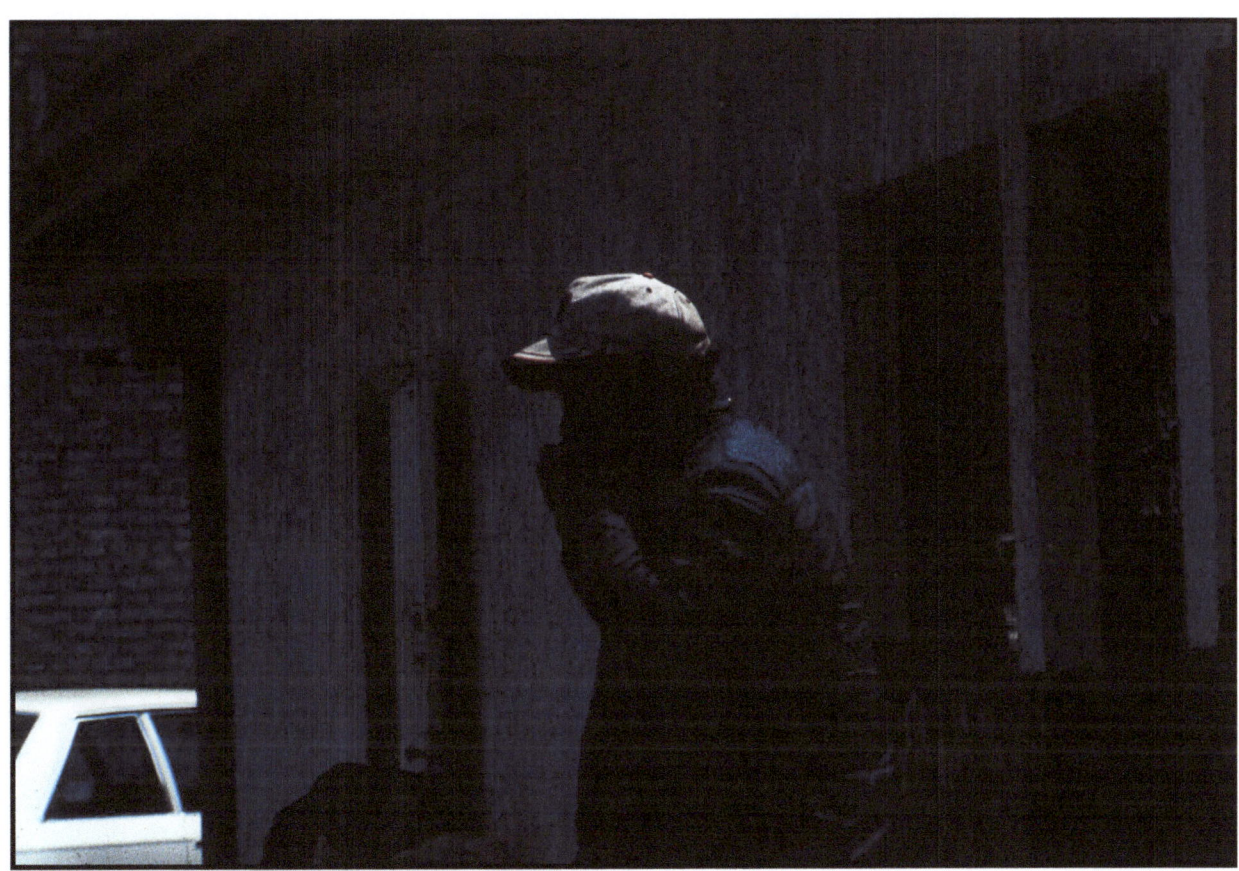

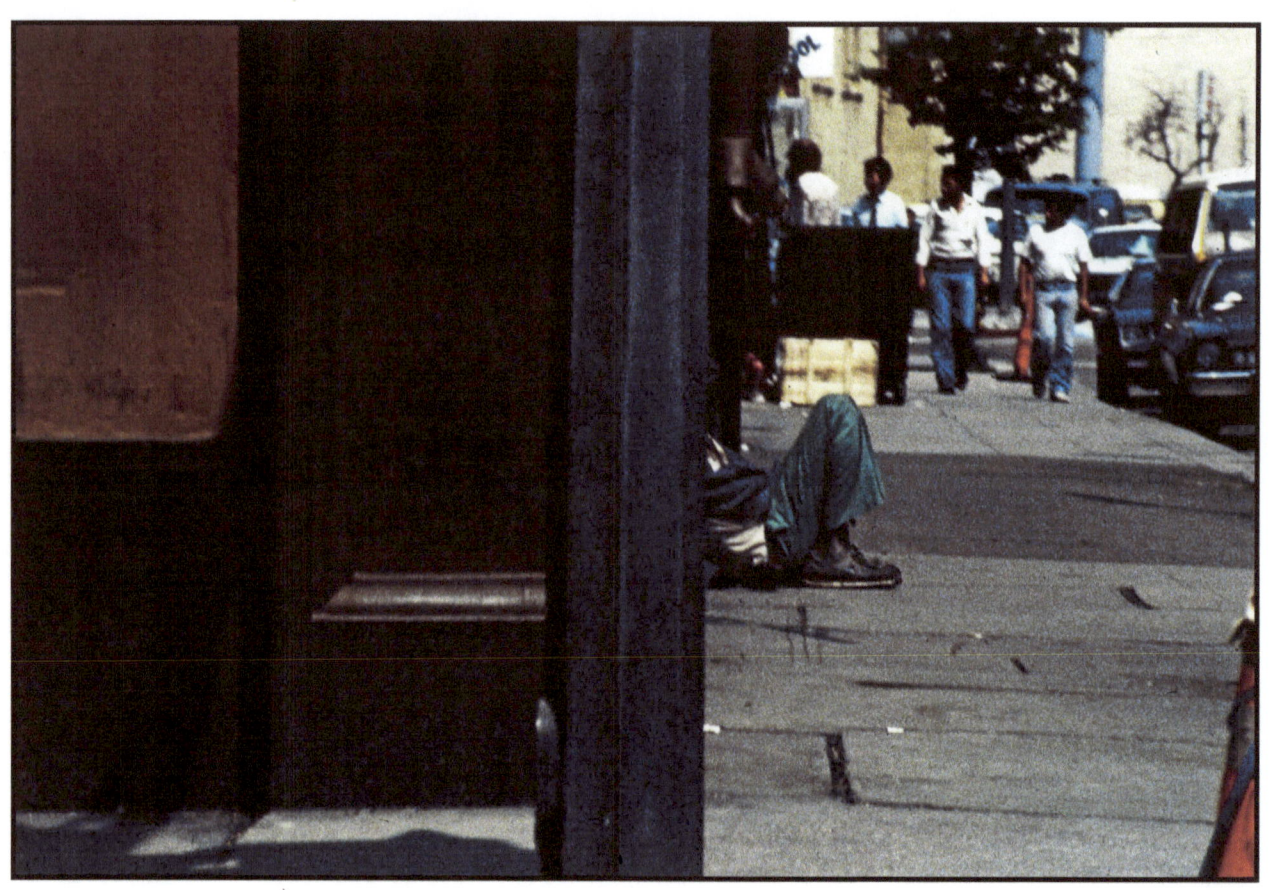

www.ingramcontent.com/pod-product-compliance
Lightning Source LLC
Chambersburg PA
CBHW051147220526
45473CB00003B/685